Food, Faith and Gender in South Asia

Also available from Bloomsbury:

The Emergence of National Food, Atsuko Ichijo, Venetia Johannes, and Ronald Ranta
Food and Identity in the Caribbean, edited by Hanna Garth
Taste, Politics, and Identities in Mexican Food, edited by Steffan Igor Ayora Diaz

Food, Faith and Gender in South Asia

The Cultural Politics of Women's Food Practices

Edited by
Usha Sanyal and Nita Kumar

BLOOMSBURY ACADEMIC
LONDON • NEW YORK • OXFORD • NEW DELHI • SYDNEY

BLOOMSBURY ACADEMIC
Bloomsbury Publishing Plc
50 Bedford Square, London, WC1B 3DP, UK
1385 Broadway, New York, NY 10018, USA
29 Earlsfort Terrace, Dublin 2, Ireland

BLOOMSBURY, BLOOMSBURY ACADEMIC and the Diana logo
are trademarks of Bloomsbury Publishing Plc

First published in Great Britain 2020
Paperback edition first published 2021

Cover design: Ben Anslow
Cover Image © Sumbul Farah

A catalogue record for this book is available from the British Library.

A catalog record for this book is available from the Library of Congress.

ISBN: HB: 978-1-3501-3706-6
PB: 978-1-3502-7803-5
ePDF: 978-1-3501-3707-3
eBook: 978-1-3501-3708-0

Typeset by Newgen KnowledgeWorks Pvt. Ltd., Chennai, India

To find out more about our authors and books visit
www.bloomsbury.com and sign up for our newsletters.

Contents

Contributors

Deepra Dandekar is a researcher at the Center for the History of Emotions, Max Planck Institute for Human Development, Berlin. Her research interests lie in the field of nineteenth-century history, modern Indian religion, gender and politics. Having published on women's rituals, Sufi shrines and religious conversion in Maharashtra, she now researches on partition, migration and the importance of emotions within modern Indian nationhood.

Pascale F. Engelmajer is Associate Professor of Religious Studies at Carroll University in Wisconsin. She wrote *Women in Pali Buddhism: Walking the Spiritual Path in Mutual Dependence*, a book that examines women's spiritual agency; and *Buddhism*, an introduction that provides an understanding of how doctrine informs practice in the contemporary Buddhist world.

Sumbul Farah is Assistant Professor of Sociology at Jamia Millia Islamia, New Delhi. She received her doctoral degree from the Department of Sociology, University of Delhi. Her dissertation examines the Barelwi school of thought within Islam and analyses the ways in which belief circumscribes people's attempts to live ethically in the everyday. She is presently engaged in exploring the idea of *adab* within Barelwi thought and the manner in which modern technology necessitates constant re-evaluation of the idea. Her publications include an exploration of the modalities of being Barelwi and the study of food practices metonymically associated with Barelwis.

Darakhshan Khan completed her PhD from the Department of South Asia Studies at the University of Pennsylvania in 2016. Her doctoral research examines the public construction of personal piety in colonial north India, situating the emergence of Islamic reform movements such as the Tablighi Jama'at against the backdrop of the shifting class dynamics and the unravelling of traditional households. She pays attention to the changes in the understanding of a woman's rights and responsibilities as a member of the family and as a member of the *qaum* and *ummah*. She is also interested in questions about the public sphere in colonial South Asia and the emergence of the gendered reading public. Currently, she is a postdoctoral fellow at the International Institute of Islamic Thought in Washington, DC.

Nita Kumar is Brown Family Professor of South Asian History at Claremont McKenna College, California. She is the author of *The Artisans of Banaras* (1988), *Friends, Brothers and Informants* (1992), *Lessons from Schools* (2001) and *The Politics of Gender, Community and Modernity* (2007); editor of *Women as Subjects* (1994); translator of *Mai* (2000) and has published assorted essays, blogs and plays and also scripted the movie *Shankar's Fairies*. She runs the organization NIRMAN that works for children, families, education and the arts, and the school Vidyashram the Southpoint, in Varanasi, India.

Usha Sanyal is Visiting Assistant Professor at Wingate University, North Carolina, and her prior research has focused on the history of the Barelwi or Ahl-i Sunnat wa Jamaʿat movement in British India. Her book *Devotional Islam: Ahmad Riza Khan Barelwi and His Movement* is in its third edition (2010). Her new book, *Scholars of Faith: South Asian Muslim Women and the Embodiment of Religious Knowledge*, about South Asian Muslim women's and girls' religious education, is forthcoming from Oxford University Press (2020).

Sucharita Sarkar is Associate Professor of English at D.T.S.S. College of Commerce, Mumbai. Her PhD, from the University of Mumbai, deals with mothering narratives in contemporary India. Interested in gender, diaspora, culture and food studies, her recent published works include chapters in *Farm to Fingers: Culture and Politics of Food in Contemporary India* (2018), *Mothers, Mothering and Globalization* (2017), *Maternità e politeismi – Motherhood(s) and Polytheisms* (2017), *Critical Posthumanism and Planetary Futures* (2016); and *We Need to Talk about Family: Essays on Neoliberalism, the Family and Popular Culture* (2016).

Parna Sengupta is Senior Associate Director at Stanford Introductory Studies. Her first book, *Pedagogy for Religion: Missionary Education and the Fashioning of Hindus and Muslims in Bengal* (2011), challenges a widespread myth of modernity – that Western schooling has had a secularizing effect on the non-West – by looking at the centrality of missionaries in the expansion of modern education in India. Her present work, centred on the writing of Rokeya Hossain, looks at how the category of reform in colonial history has become a way to explain away, rather than illuminate, the work of women as thinkers and writers.

Laurel Steele received her doctorate from the University of Chicago, specializing in Urdu literature, and did her undergraduate work at the University of California, Berkeley. A Fulbright grant recipient, she taught at the University of Chicago and the University of California, Davis. She is now a retired foreign service officer who served in the Middle East, South Asia and China, where her work focused on economic analyses. Among her recent publications is 'New Indian Stories @ the Digital Frontline: Women Work, America and Sex', in *Asia Pacific Studies* (2014).

Pnina Werbner is Professor Emerita of Social Anthropology, Keele University. She is the author of 'The Manchester Migration Trilogy' – *The Migration Process* (1990/2002), *Imagined Diasporas* (2002) and *Pilgrims of Love* (2003) – on South Asians in Britain and Pakistan. She has edited several theoretical collections on hybridity, cosmopolitanism, multiculturalism, migration and citizenship, including *Anthropology and the New Cosmopolitanism* (2008) and *The Political Aesthetics of Global Protest: Beyond the Arab Spring* (2014). She currently holds a Leverhulme Emeritus fellowship on 'The Changing *kgotla*: The Transformation of Customary Courts in Village Botswana' and has published *The Making of an African Working Class: Politics, Law and Cultural Protest in the Manual Workers' Union of Botswana* (2014).

Introduction

The politics and culture of food: South Asian women and their agency

Nita Kumar and Usha Sanyal

A young, middle-class Indian woman – let us call her Priya – with everything modern about her, from her education to her career, fell in love with a young man and excitedly accepted his proposal of marriage. The image that flashed through Priya's mind of a happy future was of her cooking in the kitchen and bringing out a tray of tea and snacks to the friends he was entertaining in the living room. Why? We, the subject and the scholars, struggled to understand as she recounted this memory. She had no experience of the kitchen and no interest in a wok of hot oil in which to fry snacks. She knew nothing about ginger and garlic. 'It was pure fancy. Just a nice thought. The tea, by the way, was in little glasses. And so hot that I served it by holding the glasses with the edge of my sari.' Her range of lifestyle practices included neither the sari (especially not using its edge) nor the little glasses of tea. Priya had created a fiction for herself, and since she admits to it happily, we are left to wonder – *why through food?*

There are several possible approaches to this question, four of which we wish to explore in this volume, while addressing, in the Conclusion, some important ones we do not explore. The four approaches that concern us here are: the overall subordination of women and the nature of resistance; boundary-making and the construction of identity and community; everyday life, power and agency; and research methodologies. The first three approaches are addressed in separate sections and the last, namely, methodologies, is discussed in the Conclusion. Together, the four overlap in intricate ways and often ask further questions of each other.

But first, a few words about us, the editors.

We take inspiration from the conundrum of domesticity, the multivocality of eating and fasting, and the way the smallest, remotest corner inhabited by women presents a choice. Caroline Walker Bynum's *Holy Feast and Holy Fast* (1987) shows that for medieval Christian women, fasting was a means of sharing in God's suffering – a means not of fleeing, but of embracing women's physicality – while sharing food with the poor and needy was a means of uniting with and expressing love for the community. For both men and women, food assumed religious meaning primarily through the Eucharist. Imbibing the Eucharist united the community with God – though this ritual act was denied to medieval women – in one metaphysical body. But at a deeper level Christ's physical wounds and torn body themselves signified a kind of spiritual food, an offering to and means of redemption for suffering humanity. For the female mystics Bynum writes about, religion was also a means of escaping the limitations of the enforced domesticity which was the lot of women in thirteenth- and fourteenth-century Europe (224–7). Arranged marriage at 15–17, frequent child-bearing with its attendant pain and danger of early death, and a lifetime 'exposed to the drudgery of household tasks' (226) made some women rebel against family expectations and embrace a life of religious seclusion and asceticism. That such considerations also play an important role in contemporary Catholic women's decisions to enter the religious life is evident from Lester's (2005) study of Mexican novitiates embarking on lives as nuns.

The irony that lies at the heart of the gender dichotomy is that in practice a nun could be assigned to the kitchen, cooking all day long, her hands chafing from the labour, as we see Sister Fenella do through the eyes of the child protagonist in Philip Pullman's *The Book of Dust: La Belle Sauvage* (2017). For her, gruelling housework at home was replaced by precisely the same work at her religious site. As Gutschow (2002, 2005) shows for the Buddhist nuns she studies, the work of a woman does not change markedly after she assumes the habit from what it was before. The model of service remains inviolate.

Food certainly holds an array of multivocal meanings for women. Food equals largesse to be shared. Food is suffering when it comes from one's own body. The lack of food is pain, but it is also noble if associated with a higher, transcendent cause. The preparation of food is a chain that binds. The willing preparation of food is a link that liberates. Religious women, the subjects of many of our chapters, teach us about the conundrums of domesticity and the way these conundrums play out against larger social and discursive structures. In almost every instance, the way they play out also signals the agency of the woman concerned. If agency is not always discernible, we would like to articulate as our position, in every absence of voice and archive, in every apparent failure of revolt or expression, the need to work at constructing a methodology. The desire to posit the 'subject-hood' of women (Kumar 1992; Trouillot 1995: 48–9) is accompanied by a continuous challenge to research and interpretation.

We are interested in a feminist ethnography – or simply an ethnography, as the editors would prefer to say – that uses women's voices, but constantly sees these voices not as 'raw' but as 'processed' data, that is, not as sacrosanct but as the product of larger ideologies and politics (Abu-Lughod 1993). Women often enforce and reinforce men's power over women, and they often exercise power resembling that of men over their own sex. Equally, they protest in small, unrecognized ways. Much of the time, they keep secrets and live private lives parallel to but separate from those of men. The larger issue lies in an overview of history that treats the public, outer world as vastly more important than the private, inner world; men inhabiting the former and women the latter (Strathern 1984, 1988). How do we avoid replicating this constructed and fabricated, that is, false, dichotomy in our scholarship?

We decided that a focus on food would give us the space to bring together women, agency, politics and culture, and ask the important questions upon which we have been working. Food is our lens, but it is not our end. However, neither as feminists – a self-identifier employed by Kumar rather than by Sanyal – nor as social scientists can we say, to rephrase Lévi-Strauss, that food is simply 'good to think with'. Women actively relate to food for the better and the worse, and food contributes in innumerable ways to their power and victimhood, their happiness and suffering.

The subordination of women and the nature of resistance

Anthropologists have taken great interest in the functions and meanings of food. Claude Lévi-Strauss's structuralist studies in the 1940s through the 1960s on the role of food in different 'primitive' societies sought to uncover underlying social patterns through linguistic analysis. Though the 'raw' and the 'cooked' provide a fecund metaphor with which to think of social relations, the South Asian anthropologist R. S. Khare (1976) critiques Lévi-Strauss on an important point: the universalization of the dichotomy. This is part of the larger discussion of how indigenous concepts have their own logic and veracity, best seen in the work of McKim Marriott (1976, 1990). Khare (1976) points out that Hindu discourses have a different hierarchy of food, as the 'raw' occupies a higher rung in the ladder than the 'cooked'. Hindus use a more inclusive understanding of the 'cooked', and in Hindu discourse the 'raw' is not the same as the 'uncooked' (1–2, in Thieme and Raja 2007: xix).

Women are the original planters and harvesters of grain, the farmers of history. Moreover, being the bearers of humans, carrying the seed/field as well as the nourishment for reproduction, they furnish the best metaphors for the earth's fertility. Religion, patriarchal ideology and food are 'entangled' (Pernau 2013) with each other from the very outset, as the power of nature comes to be ascribed to the 'supernatural', and the power of women to reproduce and nurture is integrated to the supernatural in various ways. Humans need food. Either nature/the gods provide it or woman does, and sometimes both do so in succession, together or in competition with one another. Either or both can deny food too. Either or both have to be controlled. But of course, 'humans' includes women. Hence the complication that typically one set of discourses comprises 'religion' for humans, while another set, more practical in orientation, makes up the religion of women (see Doniger (1980), among others).

It is not women as producers of raw food that concern us in this volume, but women as producers of *cooked* food. Lévi-Strauss's insight into the raw and the cooked notwithstanding, historically a discourse allowing women to claim to be culturally the most evolved as they had been given the responsibility, if not the monopoly, of producing the artefact that is cooked food, was absent. In Sherry Ortner's (1974) excellent formulation, women remained historically closer to 'nature' than to 'culture'. Her thesis merits revisiting. It is that

> woman is being identified with – or, if you will, seems to be a symbol of – something that every culture devalues, something that every culture defines as being of a lower order of existence than itself. Now it seems that there is only one thing that would fit that description, and that is 'nature' in the most generalized sense. Every culture, or, generically, 'culture', is engaged in the process of generating and sustaining systems of meaningful forms (symbols, artifacts, etc.) by means of which humanity transcends the givens of natural existence, bends them to its purposes, controls them in its interest. We may thus broadly equate culture with the notion of human consciousness, or with the products of human consciousness (i.e., systems of thought and technology), by means of which humanity attempts to assert control over nature. (72)

Ortner compares children's socialization to cooking:

> Or again, take cooking. In the overwhelming majority of societies cooking is the woman's work. No doubt this stems from practical considerations – since the woman has to stay home with the baby, it is convenient for her to perform the

> chores centered in the home. But if it is true, as Lévi-Strauss has argued (1969b), that transforming the raw into the cooked may represent, in many systems of thought, the transition from nature to culture, then here we have woman aligned with this important culturalizing process, which could easily place her in the category of culture, triumphing over nature. Yet it is also interesting to note that when a culture (e.g. France or China) develops a tradition of haute cuisine – 'real' cooking, as opposed to trivial ordinary domestic cooking – the high chefs are almost always men. Thus the pattern replicates that in the area of socialization – women perform lower-level conversions from nature to culture, but when the culture distinguishes a higher level of the same functions, the higher level is restricted to men. (80)

We have a social fact before us: women are the primary producers and suppliers of 'food' because of their bodies' overdetermined iconicity with fields which yield food. But more accurately, women are in a grey area between nature and culture. As the chapters by Khan and Sengupta in this volume bear out, women are, potentially at least, a little above nature and can aspire to culture, even if in the given moment they are a little short of culture. Reform movements such as the Tablighi Jama'at and intellectual reformers such as Rokeya Hossain wish to raise the moral stature of women, even bring them on a par with men. For everyone, both reformers and conservatives, and for the men and women who are the targets of reform or repression, the social equality of men and women seems to be a separate issue from their moral equality. Women potentially have, and can aspire to, the latter, but they do not have the former.

Many anthropologists have explored how women have found escape from a mundane domestic world to a richer, more empowering, beautifully imagined world through religion. Manisha Roy (1972) evocatively describes the world of middle-class Bengali women in which a young girl in high school goes on to a life as matriarch, nurtured by a diet (pun intended) of stories of Radha and Krishna, Savitri and Parvati, and other mythological women whose rich sensual and sexual lives are suggestively portrayed by writers and performers. As opposed to medieval European nuns, these young Bengali women innocently await a married life resembling that of the fictitious beings with whom they share their imagined lives. Food symbolized nurture and hospitality for Priya, our modern South Asian woman at the beginning of this Introduction. Through nurture and hospitality, it symbolized ideal love, which in turn was part of an ideal conjugal partnership. Thus, given her cultural repertoire, she could see herself as a Radha to her husband-Krishna, or a Savitri or Parvati to their respective partners. She imagined all this in an archetypal, unstated, underrepresented way.

We see thus that religion is not only a model of and for action, but also a complex discourse that continues to offer agents a variety of choices. The virtue of a discourse lies partly in its interpretability. Lindsey Harlan's (1991) Rajput women claim that they are the most 'cultured' people they know because they follow the values of honour and sacrifice to family and land into which they are socialized, including the supreme one of self-sacrifice. These Rajput women include Mira, who dances publicly on the street but who is stubbornly revered by the otherwise domesticated women proud of their domestication. A 'modern' woman may love the performance of subservience and a 'traditional' one the game of public display.

Women's work, therefore, can be assessed partly as performance. Equally, the structures of control that govern their situations can be seen as plural and discursive. Women's 'resistance' is also, accordingly, plural and discursive. It is not predetermined and easily categorized or even recognized. It can consist of feasting or fasting, celebration or abstinence, largesse or frugality. It is not the handling of food at any stage, or the raw or cooked nature of food that clues us in on either subordination or resistance by women. Food has too many resonances to play such a simple role. We have to assess in every single case what the relationships surrounding food are. There *is* no 'enemy', and in each chapter in this volume, women's resistance is directed against a differently formulated problem.

Boundary-making and the construction of identity and community

Food is a particularly pliable and potent means of symbol construction. In *Purity and Danger* (1966 [2013]), Mary Douglas wrote about the role of food taboos in the Old Testament, arguing that they were a means by which Jews distinguished themselves from their neighbours, set boundaries and created social order (Douglass 1966 [2013]; Lévi-Strauss 2013). In the chapter by Sumbul Farah we see how Muslims who call themselves Barelwis use rituals related to food to set off their identity against that of other Muslims.

Within a woman's own community, the subject of interest is rarely her individual subjectivity – rather, as in this volume, the conversation is about relationships: between wives and husbands, women and their in-laws, mothers and daughters, mothers dealing with sick children in the absence of husbands, female students whose absence from home at boarding school deprives their mothers of much-needed household help and women teachers negotiating family relationships and thus family politics. What seems at the outset to be no more than a family network invariably leads us to the wider communities of which it is a part. Food gives us a particular lens into these relationships and how they are constituted. Or rather, we should say that the relationships between food and people tell us something about the relationships between people and people.

As Sarah White writes in *Arguing with the Crocodile* (1992), relationships are what bestow power or powerlessness, not the work itself. Husking the grain, for instance, has different meanings if done by a householder woman to feed her own family; by a working woman for a daily wage; by a male sharecropper under contract for the household income; or by a researcher (she also adds) as participant-observer. In our case, to cook an elaborate meal and serve it with aplomb has different meanings depending, in White's terms, on the relationships involved.

Other meanings and identities are equally context-dependent. Women are regarded as a self-evidently defined community, as, for instance, when Thanvi refers to them as a *qaum* and addresses their particular dispositions and needs in a separate volume designed specifically for them. But as research attests, including all the chapters in this volume, women are not one. At the simplest, there are the 'more' domesticated and the 'less' so; those more religious and those less so; the reformed and the unreformed; and more dramatically, the women with children and those who are childless, and beyond them, the women with surviving children and those who have lost a child. In each case, one side harangues the other and may develop a whole world of myth and ritual, as Dandekar shows us in her chapter, to explain the distance between women in different socially defined categories.

While we have evidence for differences between women, we also have a curious bridging of distance to forge a common womanhood. In her chapter, Sarkar uses the term 'motherlines' to describe the bridge between older generations of the less educated and less well travelled and younger generations of the globalized. This bridge is constructed through food and the memory of recipes and their contexts. Kumar shows that keeping certain fasts creates a common culture between illiterate staff members and educated teachers, two groups of women kept apart in daily life in numerous ways. So women actively use food – and fasting – to consolidate the communities they wish to have, and they use food just as actively to differentiate their community from that of others they wish to exclude through the construction of barriers.

Everyday life, power and agency

Michel de Certeau, the great spokesman for the ordinary man in everyday life, would have considered women's food customs to be part of the non-institutionalized, 'primitive' practices that are in turn part of the tactics of resistance. In an article in *Social Text*, de Certeau (1980: 13–14) argues that what is *not* panoptically controlled, à la Foucault, is obviously multivalent and contested.

The current recognition of the social significance of food has its main historical source in the study of daily life. The Annales school in France, as exemplified especially by Fernand Braudel (1902–1985), was interested in the study of modes of thought – mentalités – and social mores and thus took a keen interest in everyday life, including food. The interest in everyday life, or prospography (history from below), comes together for us with two other historiographical approaches: the emphasis on an anthropological as opposed to a textual study of Islam, and to a smaller degree of Hinduism and Buddhism; and the feminist approach that wrests useful historical mileage from everyday life.

The study of everyday life has given rise to a lively scholarly debate, particularly – but certainly not only – in the field of Islamic studies. As Nadia Fadil and Mayanthi Fernando (2015: 66) write:

> Ranging from [E]rving Goffman's seminal *Presentation of the self in everyday life* (1959), which examines the different frames individuals use to locate and construct themselves as social subjects, to Henri Lefebvre's *Critique de la vie quotidienne* (1958), which calls for a de-familiarization of the everyday, the everyday has been understood as a space of contradictions that help us unravel the ways in which social structures or systems are materialized or contested (or both). A structural tension therefore animates the analytical focus on micropractices: while the concept of the everyday seeks to understand the operation of power, it does so by accounting for its mutability through daily iterations.

In this book, we want to explore through women's food practices the 'operation of power' in their lives and the 'mutability [thereof] through daily iterations'. This debate between the power of the text and the normative structure versus the quotidian life of the individual or the community has been conducted at several levels in the study of both Hinduism and Islam. In the case of Hindus and Hindu women, there are evocative collections attesting to the voices and power of individuals and groups on the ground (Tharu and Lalita 1991; Mines and Lamb 2010 [2002]).

For South Asian Islam, we have a veritable feast of scholarship to draw on. From the Paul Brass and Veena Das (1984) exchange on 'Islam as text' or 'Islam as ethnographic reality' through the painstaking recovery of the individual self by Ayesha Jalal (2001), to the revelation of rich worlds of practice by Barbara Metcalf (2004, 2009), Imtiaz Ahmad (1981) and Mushirul Hasan and Asim Roy (2005), we have incontrovertible evidence that Islamic practices can be understood only by being sensitive to the practitioner. This scholarship should be brought into conversation with recent studies on Muslims in the wider Islamic world, including Saba Mahmood's (2005: 206) important contribution in *Politics of Piety*, in which she argues that the scholarly bias towards feminism should not lead us to assume that women universally desire 'to be free from relations of subordination … from structures of male domination', as such a reading may be contrary to the intentions and aspirations of the women being observed. This argument converges with our recognition of the need to be sensitive to the practitioner and is explored in different ways by Steele, Farah, Sanyal and Khan in this volume.

Many feminist historians have provided innovative scholarship on the constitution of the colonial state as masculine (Sinha 1995; Burton 1999, 2003b) and on women as the site of backwardness or reform (Chatterjee 1990; Mani 1998). For various reasons, woman's agency is silenced. Agency, of course, is a multifaceted concept that permits the subject to find spaces and discourses enabling her to act, but it also creates the illusion that what is available to her or what she is doing is voluntary and not simply a product of a trained sensibility. Subjecthood, as the critique of that subject, including the *Subaltern Studies* volumes, has shown, is always partly an illusion, part of the myth of the Subject who would be free and powerful, acting upon others but disowning the power of others on him/her (Apffel-Marglin 1995; O'Hanlon 2000; Fruzzetti and Tenhunen 2006).

If women's fasting is an act of agency, it is one that is radically different from men's, including Gandhi's, which is associated with the retention of semen (see Roy 2002: 76–8). Unlike normative men who are squarely inside culture (remembering the nature–culture dichotomy), but like women who are in the grey area between the two, Gandhi placed himself in an intermediate, hence powerful, state. As Roy says, his adventures with vegetarianism, starting in London, were not those of a crank, but rather they foretold an unusual political subtlety that used food as theatre (Roy 2002). We see that women's subsidiary roles should be assessed partly as the roles of *performers*, because they all indulge in the political to different degrees. Gandhi, after all, learned of the power of eating or abstaining from food from his mother. *That* is a woman we need to know more about. Gandhi's practice of fasting, moreover, derived moral force from a combination of economic factors and a sincere experimentation with the nature of the body (74–5). This provides a useful comparison with the chapter by Werbner in this volume on the distribution of food to the poor and the observation by her subjects that there are no poor in Manchester, England.

A different scholarly perspective judges women's place in society and consciousness along one of two axes: that of the body, the gendered body, and the process of utilizing the body as fact or as metaphor; and that of space, gendered space, and spatialization. Whereas the body suffers or flourishes according to the availability of food and may accordingly be used to make almost any kind of argument about power and volition, space is interesting because it is less obvious. The gendering of space may be understood first as separable into public and private; then, within the latter, into inner and outer.

Experiences of the *andar mahal* (inner domestic living quarters) are described by many contemporaneous women mentioned by Sonia Nishat Amin in her *World of Muslim Women in Colonial Bengal* (1996). Interestingly, what made it a domain of power was partly the fact that it was autonomous. Abul Fazal (1903–1983) regretted that because he was largely ignorant of women's spaces he had incomplete knowledge of his own society: 'So we would accost our mothers, aunts, sisters or cousins for glimpses of the *unknown* Muslim Antahpur' (quoted in Amin 1996: 43; emphasis added). As Amin says, the education given to women in 'the material aspect of womanhood (such as cooking, sewing, cleaning, account-keeping) as well as its nonmaterial aspect (such as care of husband, tending him, pleasing him)' (53) – what has been called the *grihastini* discourse (Kumar 1991) – was simply unknown to men.

The chapters

We group the chapters in this book in a loosely thematic way, overlapping as most of them are. We start with the smallest, most intimate space, the kitchen, whether it be a dark and smoky kitchen, or a light, airy one, or one that seeks to transition from the former to the latter. Two of the chapters that deal with the female domestic space of the kitchen most directly, those by Laurel Steele and Parna Sengupta, focus on early nineteenth-century texts by Muslims about Muslims, in the context of British colonialism in South Asia. Remarkably, the texts were written at approximately the same time, in the early 1900s, and the second remained largely unknown to its reading public. Although the two texts are grounded in very different realities, geographically speaking – the small town Deoband, in the western United Provinces (today Uttar Pradesh, or UP), in Steele's case, and metropolitan Calcutta, capital of the British Indian Empire at the time and of West Bengal today, in Sengupta's – they share a number of overlapping concerns. Chief among these is that the authors of both texts were religious reformers who wanted Muslim women to be educated so they could lead lives of greater piety.

The subordination of women and the nature of resistance

In 'Curing the Body and Soul: Health, Food and Herbal Medicines for Nineteenth-Century South Asian Muslim Women', Laurel Steele examines a chapter (Book Nine) dealing with medical home remedies omitted from most printed versions of Maulana Ashraf Ali Thanvi's well-known advice manual for women, *Bihishti Zewar* ('The jewellery of paradise'), whose sheer length, at 250 pages, could have made it a book in itself. Instead, for reasons that Steele explains, it largely disappeared from public view. Sengupta looks at a fictional work by the well-known Bengali female writer Rokeya Hossain, in which she offered a pointed critique of contemporary Muslim food practices during the month of Ramadan. By putting these two colonial-era writings and the analyses therein in conversation with each other at the very beginning of this volume, we hope to open up analytical space for the chapters and discussions that follow.

Steele's chapter not only brings to light the missing Book Nine of the *Bihishti Zewar*, but it does so by actually *visualizing* a female reader and devoted follower of Maulana Ashraf Ali Thanvi, the author of the work. The imaginary reader refers to and *uses* the chapter in the course of her daily life in the zenana or female household quarters. This strategy produces a powerful, almost shocking, result. It shifts our focus from Ashraf Ali Thanvi, the author and renowned Deobandi scholar about whom much has been written, to the anonymous user of his book. It is reminiscent of the methodology adopted by Ruby Lal (2005, and especially 2015) in her work where she pursues with some relentlessness voices that other scholars had given up as non-existent, and an essay by Kumar (1992) in which she constructs alternative narratives of what must have happened, given that there are no extant narratives. Steele brings her imagined woman to life by describing her reading the chapter and administering the relevant herbal remedies in it to members of her family in response to real-life illnesses in the zenana. The following is an example of a day in the life of Steele's imagined reader and the zenana over which she presides:

> ***Back in one of the larger rooms, one of her sisters-in-law, her husband's younger brother's wife, complains of a backache. She consults the* Jewelry of Paradise *and finds that sometimes pain in the lower back begins because, she reads, a child was born in winter and the woman did not get proper food. It was true. Her younger sister-in-law's baby was born in winter and she had not eaten much after the birth. So she decides to give instructions for a meat soup to be made. Maybe that will help her sister-in-law. She reads that in cases like this[,] meat soup cooked with warm spices and eggs will help a backache. If the eggs are eaten with Solomon's salt, they are even more beneficial. So she tells her sister-in-law to ask her husband for some money so they may send one of the servants to the bazaar to buy some Solomon's salt.***

Steele imagines a joint family composed of three married brothers and their wives and children. The reader of the *Bihishti Zewar* is the eldest daughter-in-law. She instructs the household servants in the proper foods to be prepared for her younger sister-in-law whose backache she diagnoses after reading the relevant passages in *Bihishti Zewar*'s Book Nine. Later, when another sister-in-law (the youngest of the three) loses her newborn son soon after childbirth despite our imagined protagonist's solicitous care during the pregnancy, she also knows how to offer sound religious counsel to the grieving mother of her bereaved sister-in-law. In this and many other ways, the protagonist plays the role of the wise female head of the zenana, reminding us of the famous Asghari in Nazir Ahmad's *Mir'at al-'Urus* (Naim 1984). In the course of Steele's chapter, we are treated to a rich and vivid picture of the different sections of the zenana and its inhabitants, whether female family members and their small children or servants in the kitchen, which occupies a separate part of the building. The hierarchical relationships between the residents and the distant (and absent) male authority figures, including the author of the *Bihishti Zewar*, also come into full view. To build such imaginary narratives, based on the conventional data we do have, and extending it in unconventional ways, could be an exemplary feminist approach.

Parna Sengupta examines women's relationship to food and religiosity while paying particular attention to domestic space, especially the kitchen. In 'The

Worship of Taste: Rokeya Hossain and the Politics of Ritual Fasting', Sengupta looks at the work of Rokeya Sakhawat Hossain (1880–1932), a Bengali Muslim woman writer whose analysis of food practices allowed her to bring together domains conventionally kept apart: the work of women, religious ritual and the logic of nourishment and nutrition. Rokeya analyses the cooking and eating of – as well as practices of refraining from – food as both the cause and symptom of social and religious pathologies. A recurring image in Rokeya's writing is the dark and smoky kitchen in which women are asked to cook – these descriptions echo her discussions of the *antahpur* or inner quarters in which upper-class Muslim (and upper-caste Hindu) women were expected to remain, a description often given by Rabindranath Tagore of elite Hindu households. Suddenly, redesigning the conventional Bengali kitchen becomes a political question, not merely one of aesthetics or hygiene. It matches the attempt to bring women out into the world. Or, in describing the sumptuous meals prepared for iftar, the breaking of the fast after sunset during Ramadan, she asks: What is the true purpose of the fast – to contemplate God or to worship one's palate? A potentially light-hearted critique of excess during Ramadan becomes in Rokeya's hands a caustic critique of iftar as an example of her fellow Muslims' idolatry rather than piety. The very extremism of the critique sends our minds racing to the examples we have of ordinary women exercising agency in other smoky kitchens such as these (see, for instance, Debi 1993).

Sengupta explicitly compares Rokeya's reformist message for Muslim women with that of Thanvi in *Bihishti Zewar* (referring here to the text as a whole, not to Book Nine). Like Rokeya, Thanvi also disparaged local customary behaviour, including the cooking of elaborate iftar meals, and advocated greater simplicity of practice as being in line with the sharia. The Ramadan fast should be a time of heightened spirituality and self-reflection rather than what it had become, they both wrote. We see the powerful echoes of this argument in Darakhshan Khan's chapter on women in the Tablighi Jama'at: 'powerful' not because the argument is about austerity: idolatory:: man: woman, but rather because it is an internal debate *between* women themselves.

But Rokeya's critique went further, Sengupta argues, because she addressed herself to women's unseen labour in the kitchen. To quote Sengupta, 'In contrast, Rokeya Hossain's criticism of the excess of Ramadan is informed by an explicitly feminist critique of the problem of women's unpaid labour – a labour that ensures their unequal access to spiritual and pious reflection and guidance.' Sengupta laments the fact that academic scholarship on Hossain has not recognized the religious underpinnings of her reformist writings.

The use of irony in Rokeya's writings is underscored by her intentional use of Hindu terminology throughout. Thus she refers to the 'worship' of taste as 'rashana puja' – a term of reproach to Muslim women. But at other times she uses Hindu terminology in order to be inclusive, as when she points out that all religions practice fasting (*upabosh*) in order to encourage piety and self-restraint. This usage shows that Rokeya was addressing multiple audiences, unlike Thanvi.

The third chapter in this first section, Sucharita Sarkar's 'Religious Recipes: Culinary Motherlines of Feasts and Fasts in India', takes us in a seemingly different direction. In India, domestic cooking associated with religious rituals is primarily the domain of women, and it is also a site where women can express their creativity and agency. In the past, religious festivals and fasts were familial and community-based occasions during which women laboured together, sharing recipes and stories. These domestic and ritualistic recipes became part of the culinary and cultural legacy passed on by mothers to their daughters, often through gradual initiation rites involving participation in both the religious rituals of fasting and praying, and the preparing and eating of sanctioned foods.

However, with increasing numbers of women working outside the home, the rites of passage of religious recipes from mothers to daughters have been changing. These changes are significant in the context of increasing urban and transnational migration and the consequent globalization and modernization of culinary tastes and cultural practices. In these changed sociocultural contexts, we are witnessing the emergence of culinary narratives in which daughters are retrieving, documenting and disseminating the religious food practices and recipes of their mothers, in print and on the web. They are also engaging with these recipes from different standpoints and transforming their purposes, processes, outcome and significance.

The motherline is a concept in feminist psychoanalysis first proposed by Naomi Ruth Lowinsky (2009 [1992]) to trace women's journeys to their personal, cultural and female roots. Sarkar undertakes a close reading of selected recipes and recollections of religious occasions from contemporary cookbooks and memoirs by female Indian authors, both in the subcontinent and in the diaspora. She traces the formation and significance of the motherlines of religious recipes among mothers, foremothers and daughters in India's patriarchal, patrilineal society. She looks at the maternal legacies of recipes specifically intended for religious rituals and occasions, and at how daughters have received, recorded, refashioned and often recontextualized their culinary inheritance as part of a larger process of negotiating their personal and social identities and differences both in relation to their mothers and to their own, often displaced, daughters. Sarkar also unpacks the question of whether such ritualistic culinary motherlines are empowering or oppressive to women in the context of their changing roles in the private and public spheres, and of the changing role of religion in their lives.

Boundary-making, the construction of identity and commensality

Moving outside the kitchen, we see that a second theme in this book is that of gifting and self-sacrifice. A number of essays address the idea of women's self-sacrifice through acts of food piety, expressed sometimes through the act of cooking for others in their households or the wider community on designated occasions, and sometimes through the conscious refusal to eat, by fasting for a specified length of time. While they perform these acts of piety, what they are also doing is constructing and reinforcing lines of difference. This theme specifically underlies the chapters by Farah, Werbner and Engelmajer, though it appears in several of the other chapters as well, such as those by Sanyal, Khan and Steele.

In 'Transcendental Transactions: Food Practices among Barelwi Muslims', Sumbul Farah examines the practices of *niyaz* and *nazar*, traditions related to the ritual offering of food. These practices are central to the Barelwi worldview, being linked to the concept of *isal-e sawab* or transfer of merit. As Farah notes, this in turn is predicated on the belief in an afterlife and the existence of heaven and hell, 'an essential aspect of Islamic eschatology'. The transfer of merit flows in different directions: in *niyaz* rituals, the living offer sanctified food to guests and members of their households in order to transfer merit to the sainted dead. In *fateha* rituals, however, sanctified food is offered to the poor in order to transfer the merit of this deed to recently deceased relatives, thus facilitating the relatives' difficult passage from the grave to heaven. These themes of gifting and self-sacrifice connect Farah's chapter with those of Werbner and Engelmajer, both of whom examine women's roles in ritual food-gifting, Werbner through the practice of langar, the communal kitchen at the annual pilgrimage (*'urs*) to the shrine of a Pakistani sufi saint, and Engelmajer through the daily act of food-gifting (*dana*) to Buddhist monks in Sri Lanka. Moreover, both Farah and Werbner discuss the nature of such gifts of food, arguing that they must not be seen as self-interested, calculated transactions in the religious realm, as many scholars have done, because such acts transcend and go beyond 'calculus and communitas' (Werbner 2002: 115). Farah examines the multiple ways in which the self-conception of Barelwis hinges on such food-gifting practices. In order to do so, she focuses on women in Barelwi households, as they are the ones responsible for handling and cooking food within the domestic space, and therefore the ones directly constructing boundaries.

Farah points out, however, that apart from their instrumental role in the management of community identity, women are also subjects in their own right who articulate their piety, as a strong marker of their personal identity, through the idiom of food. She explores the ways in which women attempt to embody the Barelwi ethic by their attentiveness to an attitude of *adab* (respect) towards food in the everyday, in terms of the handling, storage, preparation, consumption, distribution and disposal of food items. In addition to the everyday management of food, women also keep track of the various *niyaz* and *fateha* that mark the Barelwi ritual calendar. They ensure that the food items traditionally associated with each occasion are prepared, consecrated and distributed among relatives, neighbours and the poor. Many of these practices are attacked by adherents of other schools of thought which claim to be 'reformist'. Barelwis, however, defend them not by citing precedence in tradition alone but by quoting the Qur'an and Hadith, and classifying these acts as neither forbidden nor mandatory under sharia, thereby establishing them as definitively Islamic. These food rituals therefore provide form and expression to the attitude of piety that motivates believers while also establishing unequivocally that they self-identify as Barelwi.

In 'Between *Khatm-e Qur'ans* and *Slametans*: Gender and Class in South Asian and Indonesian Interdomestic Rituals', Pnina Werbner compares two everyday domestic rituals in South and Southeast Asia which have much in common both in terms of ritual and commensality. Using the key analytic concept of the 'interdomestic' realm (on which, see below), Werbner links the *khatm-e qur'an* ritual, as celebrated by Muslims in Pakistan and north India, including their diasporas, with the Indonesian *slametan*. In both rituals, she argues, class and gender intersect in the operation of women's networks, allowing for different configurations of inter-household relations in villages, neighbourhoods and urban contexts.

The *qur'an khani* (or *khatm-e qur'an*) ritual consists of several women reading the entire Qur'an (in the original Arabic) in one sitting, usually in the private home of the convener (though in immigrant South Asian Muslim communities it can also take place in a mosque), as an act of devotion. Although most South Asian Muslim women are not Arabic speakers and cannot therefore understand the individual verses being recited, it is the act of reciting it correctly that matters, as the Qur'an is believed to have magical potency and to be a means of channelling religious merit to the reciters and to those in whose name the reading is taking place, either as an act of expiation or thanksgiving, or to ask for blessing. After the recitation is over, all the women present partake in a meal together. This simple ritual, consisting of a reading from a religious text followed by a shared meal, constitutes what Geertz (1960) called a 'core ritual' and is found, in different forms, all across the Muslim world and among Hindus and Sikhs as well. The Indonesian *slametan* is also a domestic ritual centred on praying over food to ask for divine blessings, and the sharing of the blessed food with family members. Werbner notes that despite the ubiquity of rituals like the *khatm-e qur'an* and the *slametan* in the Muslim world, few scholars have given them the attention they deserve.

Werbner's analysis of the structure of the two rituals highlights the centrality of sacrifice. Fundamental to the *khatm-e qur'an*, she writes, is 'transformation through sacrifice of relations between the gods, the sacrifice and the congregation participating in the ritual'. A related part of the ritual is the act of sharing food with the poor. To quote, 'The gift to the poor completes and seals the act of offering or sacrifice.' The specifics of what is shared and with whom vary, of course, depending on context and the convener's intention (*niyya*). Werbner discusses these with fine-grained attention to detail but without losing sight of the common themes that thread their way through both the *khatm-e qur'an* and the *slametan* despite surface differences. One of these differences relates to the fact that the *slametan* is attended by males, while *khatm-e qur'an*s are usually female-centred rituals. But to focus on the men in the front of the house while ignoring the network of women who make and distribute the food at the rear and without whose labour the *slametan* would not be possible is to see only part of the picture.

In 'Buddhist Women and Alms-Giving', Pascale Engelmajer outlines Buddhist women's religious agency through women's traditional roles, especially the preparing and giving of food in the context of Pali texts, and explores how this plays out in contemporary Theravada countries in South Asia (Sri Lanka in particular) in the morning ritual of giving alms to the monastic community. In Buddhist Pali texts, women's religious roles revolve around their social role and function as wives. In the context of these ancient texts, in which social and religious roles were tightly interwoven, women had very little if any control over their life choices and had to find agency within a limited set of possibilities. (Note that gender *inequality* trumps the egalitarian Buddhist message encapsulated in the four noble truths and the Middle Way, which were presumably open to both men and women.) One way in which Buddhism allowed women to develop soteriological agency in their everyday lives, Engelmajer shows, was through religious giving to the monastic community, *dana*, and in particular by encouraging them to make and give food. A particularly interesting trope in Pali Buddhist texts such as the *Vimanavatthu* is the equation of the giving of maternal milk – which could be said to be the ultimate gift of food by a woman – with the giving of the *dhamma*, the Buddhist teachings. Engelmajer shows how, by fulfilling their social roles as wives and mothers, which manifest primarily as the preparing and giving of food, women find ways to achieve religious agency and, further, to literally embody the highest teachings of Buddhism.

As the above discussion illustrates, when we discuss gifting/self-sacrifice, the question of power and agency are not far behind. The two are often seen as antithetical, in that women who 'sacrifice' themselves, not only in terms of the time and labour they expend on cooking for others but also in terms of their willingness to allow their labour and efforts to remain anonymous while credit is claimed by others (usually the male head of their households), are seen as lacking in agency. This is a hotly debated issue in contemporary academic writing. Some argue that this is a false assumption. In contexts as different as the Egyptian mosque movement (Mahmood 2005), Mexican Catholic convents (Lester 2005) and a girls' madrasa in Delhi, India (Winkelmann 2005), scholars have argued that women who voluntarily discipline their minds and bodies to accept rigorous routines of study, prayer and austere lifestyles in which they submit to male authority figures should not therefore be thought of as lacking in agency. On the contrary, the 'docile agent' (Mahmood 2001) who has assiduously cultivated such a habitus (Bourdieu 1980) has done so by means of considerable exercise of will.

This takes us to the third, final theme explored in this book, namely, the intersection of power and agency in everyday life, and the role of caste, class and gender in women's lives.

Everyday life, power and agency

Deepra Dandekar makes a convincing argument for the importance of understanding women's roles in the context of structures of authority in a given society. Her chapter, 'Women's Ritually Shared Bodies and Food-Penance in Rural Maharashtra', is based on her research on women's food taboos, an important part of both women's childbirth and childlessness rituals. Childless women are considered 'afflicted' in the patriarchal society of rural Maharashtra, India, since child-loss and being unable to conceive a male child (read as childlessness) are viewed as illnesses (this has created a huge biomedical industry in urban sectors of India). These food taboos are significantly associated with goddesses in Dandekar's field area because women abstain from the same foods that they dedicate to goddesses in rituals to prevent child loss. The period of expiation, typically five weeks, is one of great suffering for a woman, for not only is she hungry throughout this time but she is shunned by other high-caste women for the duration, being excluded, for example, from community fertility rituals (*haldi-kunku*). Dandekar makes a significant contribution here in pointing out the politics of reproduction and food sharing between women and goddesses in rural Maharashtra, as the childlessness of women whose natal families are wealthy and/or powerful is interpreted differently from that of women from relatively powerless families. In the former case, the woman's failure to produce a male heir for her marital household is attributed to unintended negligence ('girlhood innocence') while a woman whose family is not so well placed may be accused of witchcraft and expelled from the marital group. Dandekar is also explicit in rejecting notions of female solidarity across caste lines, as the goal of both upper-caste women and the lower-caste ritualists who serve them by absorbing their 'sexual sin' is the preservation of 'upper-caste agrarian clan interests'.

Do such women exercise 'agency'? Dandekar's answer seems to be that yes, they do. She tells the story of Maya, a Matang (low-caste) woman who acted as midwife and postpartum ritualist for a dominant-caste Maratha family in November 2006. Maya had her own conception of the 'rightness' of the ritual performed in the first week after the child's birth, in which she had a central role: she pointed out to Dandekar its structural resemblance with the Satvai temple. The Satvai goddess presided over the agrarian structure of the village and its dharma. The high-caste woman's role was to conceive a male child, while hers was to absorb the pollution of the upper-caste woman's (reproductive) body.

Nita Kumar's chapter, 'Eating and Fasting as a Complex Professional Strategy', illustrates the politics of food piety in a very different way. As she explains, teachers have strict worktimes and do not have the leisure to exercise the kind of control over food that Kumar earlier found among housewives (2006). Kumar herself has a managerial role over a set of teachers in India and first became aware of women's fasts because her teachers were causing two significant kinds of *trouble* by virtue of their food practices. Not only did some teachers retreat from partaking in the midday lunch required of all teachers and staff, but they also submitted an unusual number of applications for leave on days that were fasting days for them, though not school holidays. Kumar found that her preferred anthropological approach of underscoring their agency was thus complicated by her perspective as their employer questioning their professionalism, but then coming back full circle to inspecting their strategy as a form of deliberate manoeuvring. The manoeuvring was a feminist strategy in that the teachers wished to continue to successfully live in the two worlds of the domestic and the professional without giving up either of them as men, arguably, are forced to do. It was also a caste-based strategy in that women replicated existing difference between their upper-caste status and the lower-caste positions of the staff by refusing to share the common meal and to find further excuses for abstinence and distancing.

Usha Sanyal's chapter, 'Fasting, Feasting: Social and Religious Food Practices at a Barelwi Girls' Madrasa', is an examination of voluntary fasting by students at the Jami'a Nur girls' madrasa in the small north Indian town of Shahjahanpur. Although food plays a tangential role in the overall purpose of the madrasa, this examination of voluntary fasting allows Sanyal to shed light on questions of agency which are hard to arrive at more directly. Madrasa students do not have much freedom to exercise choice in the course of the school day, as the daily schedule of prayers, classes and study time is relatively inflexible. The most acceptable means of expressing individuality is through the pursuit of excellence in pious behaviour, this being the goal of the curriculum as well as the overall 'cosmology' of the madrasa (Moosa 2015). The student learns that she must discipline her mind and body and must do this *by* herself *on* herself. Her reward for such behaviour will come from God in the afterlife, but it also bears the promise of immediate reward in the respect it wins from one's peers and superiors (though it must not be done for this purpose).

Fasting, or abstaining from food and water for a length of time, usually from dawn to sundown, is agentive behaviour not only in the sense that it is a 'doing' but also a 'becoming'. By doing something repeatedly, by acquiring a pious habitus, one gradually *becomes* a pious person. This transformative process occurs over time and, when successful, is carried over after a student graduates, into her home and the married life that follows. Thereafter she will become a role model for her children, and society as a whole will benefit from her piety and dedication to sharia norms. Sanyal sheds light on this process through an examination of some madrasa girls' voluntary observance of the fast of Shab-e Barat, commemorating the Prophet's ascension to heaven and meeting with God.

In 'Praying in the Kitchen: The Tablighi Jama'at and Female Piety', Darakhshan Khan draws on her ethnographic fieldwork about the rhythms of cooking and eating during the holy month of Ramadan to analyse how the Tablighi Jama'at's ideals of spiritual equality and patriarchal authority shape women's strategies of piety. The Tablighi Jama'at reform movement was founded by Ilyas Kandhlewi (d. 1944) in colonial north India. The movement uses itinerant preaching as a tool to strengthen the moral core of its adherents and as a strategy to recruit new followers. The itinerant Tablighi male – dressed in loose trousers that expose the ankles, flowing beard and a duffel bag slung over his shoulders – has drawn the attention of scholars, but the women, ensconced in their homes, are rarely seen or heard (but see Metcalf 2000). Khan's chapter highlights how the sermonizers at the Jama'at's female gatherings in Bombay and Delhi never failed to point out that women spent too much time in the kitchen. Male scholars reprimanded women for stirring 'pots in the kitchen all afternoon' and for succumbing to 'the fire in their bellies'. 'But who will save you from the flames of hell?' the preachers asked the women repeatedly. The comparison of the human stomach with hellfire – captured by the Urdu phrase *pet ki aag* (literally, the fire in the belly) – came up frequently in Khan's conversations with the women and acquired a particular urgency during Ramadan when the Islamic injunction to fast from dawn to dusk and the Jama'at's emphasis on austerity combined to create a discourse about hunger and eating in which food was imagined as fuel for hellfire. A committed Jama'at member cultivated an indifferent, though never an ungrateful, approach to food so that she could escape the fire in the belly as well as the flames of hell.

The reconfiguration of household duties to make more time for worship is in line with the Jama'at's call for spiritual equality between men and women. Khan demonstrates that the discourse of everyday piety enables the women to transform their daily routine during Ramadan into a meaningful religious experience and gives them the tools to shape their spiritual universe. Reformist piety values moderation and conformity to established norms. While exceptional piety was the calling of a few mavericks in prereformist South Asia, the ideology of reform maintains that every Muslim woman and man is capable of cultivating piety. Khan's chapter demonstrates that the Tablighi Jama'at, in keeping with this reformist spirit, turns the mundane into the pious. It transforms women's domestic responsibilities into religious duties as long as the intent animating their performance of chores is to please Allah (*Allah ki raza ke liye*). However, Khan argues that in merging the Islamic ritual cycle with the rhythms of daily household chores, reformist movements like the Tablighi Jama'at end up limiting the scope of women's piety. It makes an exceptional success of a handful of women – whose peculiar personal circumstances relieved them of household responsibilities at an early age – into the exception rather than the rule.

Conclusion

There are a few things that this volume does that we would like to see taken further, and in conclusion we wish to mention at least two. If one speaks of food, one has to speak of its lack. Our chapters on Hindu women are about Brahmans and other high castes and the middle classes. The chapters on Muslim women are about shaykhs and the *sharif* and upwardly mobile classes. There is no discussion of the agency of women who have established routines and pathways, which, numerous though they may be, are not limitless given the constraints of a tiny kitchen where most of the time almost nothing is available and the idea of *choice* in food, of doing away with an over-elaboration of cooking, is meaningless. Kumar mentions these poorer women, but only as the people from whom the real subjects of her chapter would like to distance themselves.

Similarly, we have little on – to use Sarah Suleri's phrase in *Meatless Days* (1990) – 'the imaginative extravagance of food and all the transmogrifications of which it is capable' (Thieme and Raja 2007: 339). Maybe, since hers is a diasporic study, it is fitting that the one place our volume touches on food-as-artistry is in Sarkar's chapter on the diaspora. For the rest, we certainly allude to the artistry of food, but the sensual connections between the actual object put in the mouth and the animal or plant it might have come from, together with its images and associations, and more sensual connections with the world around us, of which the food is indeed a part – these do not find a place here.

Food is a fecund source for nostalgia, a subject we address only in Sarkar's chapter on the nostalgia of diaspora. As Suleri's *Meatless Days* explores, growing up is intimately linked with the expansion of taste, with parents and particularly mothers introducing the world to their children through the tongue, as the latter are weaned and explore new foods, loving some, rejecting others. A girl growing to womanhood might look back on her life through the lens of food – and thus reconstruct her subjectivity – in ways worthy of a feminist exploration.

Similarly, we do not look at food and its connection with the discourse of Orientalism: the ironies of history as they yield an Orient that is effeminate, being closer to nature than to a masculine (Western) culture, rich with spices, passions, mysteries, yet dumb, passive and controllable. Colonized women are the subjects and inheritors of this discourse, and as women they find themselves internalizing and reproducing it, even as they reflect on it, resist it and play with it.

We make little mention of food as commerce, one of the most profitable and aesthetic avenues of agency. This is crucially related to women's work in that women often do the behind-the-scenes work for men such as *chatwalla*s (sellers of chat, a spicy snack; Kumar 2006: 64–5). But many women also do the cooking and even the distribution of food for money (59–60) as the quiet, informal enterprise depicted by Roy (1997) as being run by the otherwise detestable Mammachi whose husband ignores her work and whose son goes on to ruin it.

We would like to conclude with the importance of methodology for a subject such as ours: for the politics and culture of food as well as for the agency of women. There are three highlights in our volume that deserve reflection. One is the imaginative reconstruction by Steele of women's experiences in the zenana, based partly on reading the archive against the grain. Similar work has been done by veterans in the *Subaltern Studies* collective (Guha 1988, 1997) and by others who have used as their archive women's narratives and family memories (Burton 2003b; Lal 2005, 2015). Steele approaches her material with an even bigger, more imaginative sweep, however. Her study could be taken even further by making the language of the text into a methodology, showing how easily a statement that gives us the sense of *advice* can be turned into its unstated other: *the stance of the advisee.*

The second clear methodology that profits a feminist anthropology is reflexivity, placing the scholar in the narrative of discovery, of the subjecthood of the women being researched or of the complications within this subjecthood. That the scholar is complicit in any conclusions reached, or even descriptions made in the course of an enquiry, is now widely accepted (see the evocative work of Briggs 1998). In every chapter in this book, the author describes her progress through the thickets created by the inscrutability, indifference, active opposition and/or personal reservations of the subjects of study.

Finally, there is the methodological complication produced by the scholar who is both an insider and an outsider to the religious system under scrutiny and to the processes of modernity carrying everyone on and away. She is also both a supplicant searching for data and a worker in a professional relationship with the subjects being studied. Kumar's chapter is partly about the results of such an approach and proposes certain pathways to action that could be opened up further through research along these lines.

References

Abu-Lughod, Lila. 1993. *Writing Women's Worlds: Bedouin Stories*. Berkeley: University of California Press.

Ahmad, Imtiaz. 1981. *Ritual and Religion among Muslims in India*. New Delhi: Oxford University Press.

Alter, Joseph. 1992. *The Wrestler's Body: Identity and Ideology in North India*. Berkeley: University of California Press.

Amin, Sonia Nishat. 1996. *The World of Muslim Women in Colonial Bengal, 1876–1939*. Leiden: Brill, especially chapter 3.

Apffel-Marglin, Frederique. 1995. 'Gender and the Unitary Self: Looking for the Subaltern in Coastal Orissa'. *South Asia Research* 15 (1): 78–128.

Bourdieu, Pierre. 1980. *The Logic of Practice*. Stanford: Stanford University Press.

Briggs, Jean L. 1998. *Inuit Morality Play: The Emotional Education of a Three-Year-Old*. New Haven: Yale University Press.

Burton, Antoinette (ed.). 1999. *Gender, Sexuality and Colonial Modernities*. London: Routledge.

Burton, Antoinette (ed.). 2003a. *Family History: Janaki Agnes Penelope Majumdar (nee Bonnerjee)*. New Delhi: Oxford University Press.

Burton, Antoinette. 2003b. *Dwelling in the Archive: Women Writing House, Home and History in Late Colonial India*. New York: Oxford University Press.

Bynum, Caroline Walker. 1987. *Holy Fast and Holy Feast: The Religious Significance of Food to Medieval Women*. Berkeley: University of California Press.

Chakravarti, Uma. 1990. 'Whatever Happened to the Vedic Dasi? Orientalism, Nationalism and a Script for the Past'. In K. Sangari and S. Vaid (eds), *Recasting Women: Essays in Indian Colonial History*. Delhi: Kali for Women, 27–87.

Chandra, Sudhir. 1992. *The Oppressive Present: Literature and Social Consciousness in Colonial India*. Delhi: Oxford University Press.

Chatterjee, Partha. 1990. 'The Nationalist Resolution of the Women's Question'. In Kumkum Sangari and Sudesh Vaid, eds, *Recasting Women: Essays in Indian Colonial History*. New Brunswick, NJ: Rutgers University Press.

Das, Veena. 1984. 'For a Folk-Theology and an Anthropology of Islam'. *Contributions to Indian Sociology* 18(2) (November): 293–300.

de Certeau, Michel. 1980. 'On the Oppositional Practices of Everyday Life'. *Social Text* no. 3 (Autumn): 3–43.

Debi, Rashsundari. 1993. *Amar Jiban*. Translated by Tanika Sarkar. Delhi: Kali for Women.

Derrida, Jacques. 1991. '"Eating Well", or the Calculation of the Subject'. In Eduardo Cadava, Peter Connor and Jean-Luc Nancy (eds), *Who Comes after the Subject?* New York: Routledge, 96–119, 114, 115, quoted in Parama Roy, *Journal of American Studies* 48 (1) (2014), Review of Kyla Wazana Tompkins, *Racial Indigestion: Eating Bodies in the 19th Century*. New York: New York University Press, 2012, 328–9.

Doniger, Wendy O'Flaherty. 1980. *Women, Androgynes, and Other Mythical Beasts*. Chicago: University of Chicago Press.

Douglas, Mary. 2013 [1966]. *Purity and Danger*. In Carole Counihan and Penny Van Esterik (eds), *Food and Culture: A Reader*. 3rd edition. New York: Routledge.

Dumont, Louis. 1980. *Homo Hierarchicus: The Caste System and Its Implications.* Chicago: University of Chicago Press.

Fadil, Nadia, and Mayanthi Fernando. 2015. 'Rediscovering the "Everyday" Muslim: Notes on an Anthropological Divide'. *HAU: Journal of Ethnographic Theory* 5 (2): 59–88.

Foucault, Michel. 1984. *The History of Sexuality: An Introduction.* New York: Peregrine Books.

Freeman, James. 2000. 'The Ladies of Lord Krishna: Rituals of Middle-Aged Women in Eastern India'. In Nancy Falk and Rita Gross (eds), *Unspoken Worlds.* Boston: Cengage Learning, 110–26.

Fruzzetti, Lina, and Surpa Tenhunen (eds). 2006. *Culture, Power and Agency: Gender in Indian Ethnography.* Calcutta: Stree Publisher.

Geertz, Clifford. 1960. *The Religion of Java.* Glencoe: Free Press.

Ghosh, Durba. 2004. 'Gender and Colonialism: Expansion or Marginalization?' *The Historical Journal* 47 (3) (September): 737–55.

Guha, Ranajit (ed.). 1988. *Selected Subaltern Studies.* Delhi: Oxford University Press.

Guha, Ranajit. 1997. *Subaltern Studies Reader, 1986–1995.* Minneapolis: University of Minnesota Press.

Gunew, Sneja. 2005. '"Mouthwork": Food and Language as the Corporeal Home for the Unhoused Diasporic Body in South Asian Women's Writing'. *Journal of Commonwealth Literature* 40 (2): 93–103.

Gutschow, Kim. 2002. 'The Delusion of Gender and Renunciation in Buddhist Kashmir'. In Diana P. Mines and Sarah Lamb (eds), *Everyday Life in South Asia.* Bloomington: Indiana University Press.

Gutschow, Kim. 2005. *Being a Buddhist Nun: The Struggle for Enlightenment in the Himalayas.* Cambridge: Harvard University Press

Harlan, Lindsey. 1991. *Religion and Rajput Women: The Ethic of Protection in Contemporary Narratives.* Berkeley: University of California Press.

Hasan, Mushirul, and Asim Roy (eds). 2005. *Living Together Separately: Cultural India in History and Politics.* New Delhi: Oxford University Press.

Hasan, Zoya (ed.). 1994. *Forging Identities: Gender, Communities and the State in India.* Boston: Northeastern University Press.

Hawley, Jack (ed.). 1994. *Sati: The Blessing and the Curse.* New York: Columbia University Press.

Jalal, Ayesha. 2001. *Self and Sovereignty: Individual and Community in South Asian Islam since 1850.* New York: Routledge.

Jefferey, Patricia, and Amrita Basu (eds). 1998. *Appropriating Gender: Women's Activism and Politicized Religion in South Asia.* New York: Routledge.

Khare, R. S. 1976. *Culture and Reality: Essays on the Hindu System of Managing Foods.* Calcutta: Indian Institute of Advanced Study.

Kumar, Nita. 1991. 'Widows, Education and Social Change'. *Economic and Political Weekly* 26 (17) (27 April): 19–25.

Kumar, Nita (ed.). 1992. *Women as Subjects: South Asian Histories*. Charlottesville: University of Virginia Press.
Kumar, Nita. 2006. 'The [No] Work and [No] Leisure Worlds of Artisan Women in Banaras'. In Lina Fruzzetti and Surpa Tenhunen (eds), *Culture, Power and Agency: Gender in Indian Ethnography*. Calcutta: Stree Publishers, 52–89.
Lal, Ruby. 2005. *Domesticity and Power in the Early Mughal World*. Cambridge: Cambridge University Press.
Lal, Ruby. 2015. *Coming of Age in Nineteenth Century India: The Girl-Child and the Art of Playfulness*. Cambridge: Cambridge University Press.
Leslie, Julia (ed.). 1991. *Roles and Rituals for Hindu Women*. London: Pinter Publishers.
Lester, Rebecca J. 2005. *Jesus in Our Wombs: Embodying Modernity in a Mexican Convent*. Berkeley: University of California Press.
Lévi-Strauss, Claude. 1964. *The Raw and the Cooked*. London: Jonathan Cape.
Lévi-Strauss, Claude. 1969. *The Elementary Forms of Kinship*. Boston: Beacon Press.
Lévi-Strauss, Claude. 2013. 'The Culinary Triangle'. In Carole Counihan and Penny Van Esterik, *Food and Culture: A Reader*, 3rd edn. New York: Routledge.
Lowinsky, Naomi Ruth. 2009 [1992]. *The Motherline: Every Woman's Journey to Find Her Female Roots*. Cheyenne: Fisher King Press.
Mahmood, Saba. 2001. 'Feminist Theory, Embodiment, and the Docile Agent: Some Reflections on the Egyptian Islamic Revival'. *Cultural Anthropology* 16 (2): 202–36.
Mahmood, Saba. 2005. *Politics of Piety: The Islamic Revival and the Feminist Subject*. Princeton, NJ: Princeton University Press.
Mani, Lata. 1998. *Contentious Traditions: The Debate on Sati in Colonial India*. Berkeley: University of California Press.
Marriott, McKim. 1976. 'Hindu Transactions: Diversity without Dualism'. In Bruce Kapferer (ed.), *Transaction and Meaning: Directions in the Anthropology of Exchange and Symbolic Behavior*. Philadelphia: Institute for the Study of Human Issues.
Marriott, McKim (ed.). 1990. *India through Hindu Categories*. New Delhi: Sage Publications.
Metcalf, Barbara D. 2000. 'Tablighi Jamaʻat and Women'. In Muhammad Khalid Masud (ed.), *Travellers in Faith: Studies of the Tablighi Jamaʻat as a Transnational Islamic Movement for Faith Renewal*. Leiden: Brill.
Metcalf, Barbara D. 2004. *Islamic Contestations: Essays on Muslims in India and Pakistan*. New York: Oxford University Press.
Metcalf, Barbara D. (ed.). 2009. *Islam in South Asia in Practice*. Princeton, NJ: Princeton University Press.
Mines, Diana P., and Sarah Lamb (eds). 2010 [2002]. *Everyday Life in South Asia*. Bloomington: Indiana University Press.
Moosa, Ebrahim. 2015. *What Is a Madrasa?* Chapel Hill: Duke University Press.
Naim, C. M. 1984. 'Prize-Winning *Adab*: A Study of Five Urdu Books Written in Response to the Allahabad Government Gazette Notification'. In Barbara Daly

Metcalf (ed.), *Moral Conduct and Authority: The Place of* Adab *in South Asian Islam*. Berkeley: University of California Press.

Nandy, Ashis. 1976. 'Women versus Womanliness in India: An Essay in Social and Political Psychology'. *Psychoanalytic Review* 63(2): 301–15.

Natrajan, Balmurli, and Suraj Jacob. 2018. '"Provincialising" Vegetarianism: Putting Indian Food Habits in Their Place'. *Economic and Political Weekly* LIII (9) (3 March): 54–64.

O'Hanlon, Rosalind. 2000. 'Recovering the Subject: *Subaltern Studies* and Histories of Resistance in Colonial South Asia'. In Vinayak Chaturvedi (ed.), *Mapping Subaltern Studies and the Postcolonial*. London: Verso.

Ortner, Sherry. 1974. 'Is Female to Male as Nature Is to Culture?' In M. Z. Rosaldo and L. Lamphere (eds), *Woman, Culture, and Society*. Stanford: Stanford University Press, 68–87.

Ortner, Sherry. 1996. *Making Gender: The Politics and Erotics of Culture*. Boston: Beacon Press.

Pernau, Margrit. 2013. Ashraf *into Middle Classes: Muslims in Nineteenth-Century Delhi*. Delhi: Oxford University Press.

Pullman, Philip. 2017. *The Book of Dust: Vol. 1. La Belle Sauvage*. New York: Alfred Knopf.

Roy, Arundhati. 1997. *The God of Small Things*. New York: Random House.

Roy, Manisha. 1972. *Bengali Women*. Chicago: University of Chicago Press.

Roy, Parama. 2002. 'Meat-Eating, Masculinity, and Renunciation in India: A Gandhian Grammar of Diet'. *Gender & History* 14 (1) (April): 62–91.

Scindia, Vijaya Raje, with Manohar Malgonkar. 1987. *The Last Maharani of Gwalior: An Autobiography*. Albany: SUNY Press.

Scott, James. 1985. *Weapons of the Weak: Everyday Forms of Peasant Resistance*. New Haven: Yale University Press.

Searle-Chatterjee, Mary, and Ursula Sharma (eds). 1994. *Contextualising Caste*. Oxford: Blackwell.

Shree, Geetanjali. 2001. *Mai*. Translated by Nita Kumar. Delhi: Zubaan.

Sinha, Mrinalini. 1995. *Colonial Masculinity: The 'Manly Englishman' and the 'Effeminate Bengali' in the Late Nineteenth Century*. Manchester: Manchester University Press.

Strathern, Marilyn. 1984. 'Domesticity and the Denigration of Women'. In David O'Brien and S. Tiffany (eds), *Rethinking Women's Roles: Perspectives from the Pacific*. Berkeley: University of California Press, 13–31.

Strathern, Marilyn. 1988. *The Gender of the Gift: Problems with Women and Problems with Society in Melanesia*. Berkeley: University of California Press.

Suleri, Sara. 1990. *Meatless Days*. Chicago: University of Chicago Press.

Tenhunen, Sirpa. 2003. *Secret Freedom in the City: Women's Wage Work and Agency in Calcutta*. Quebec: World Heritage Press.

Tharu, Susie, and K. Lalita (eds). 1991. *Women Writing in India*. Vols 1 and 2. Delhi: Oxford University Press.

Thieme, John, and Ira Raja (eds). 2007. *The Table Is Laid: The Oxford Anthology of South Asian Food Writing*. New Delhi: Oxford University Press.

Trouillot, Michel-Rolph. 1995. *Silencing the Past: Power and the Production of History*. Boston: Beacon Press.

Uberoi, Patricia (ed.). 1997 [1993]. *Family, Kinship and Marriage in India*. Delhi: Oxford University Press.

Werbner, Pnina. 2002. 'Langar: Pilgrimage, Sacred Exchange and Perpetual Sacrifice in a Sufi Saint's Lodge'. In Pnina Werbner and Helene Basu (eds), *Embodying Charisma: Modernity, Locality and the Performance of Emotion in Sufi Cults*. London: Routledge.

White, Sarah C. 1992. *Arguing with the Crocodile: Gender and Class in Bangladesh*. London: Zed Books.

Winkelmann, Mareike Jule. 2005. *'From Behind the Curtain': A Study of a Girls' Madrasa in India*. Amsterdam: ISIM Press.

Part One

The subordination of women and the nature of resistance

1

Curing the body and soul: Health, food and herbal medicines for nineteenth-century South Asian Muslim women

Laurel Steele

I am living back in time. I am imagining the grandeur of my mother's time. How do I narrate? Only by going back in time.

– Lal, *Coming of Age in Nineteenth-Century India*, 9

It is widely understood that colonial interventions in Indian society involved interventions in customs relating to women in the zenana, the space in which women lived secluded from men who were categorized as strangers. Well into the twentieth century, the colonial lens was directed at those (respectable women, both Hindu and Muslim) who were confined by the custom of purdah and who were restricted to the domestic space. The colonial critique extended to the purdah itself, the real and metaphorical veil that constructed women's seclusion, and to the ills produced by that confinement experienced by these women. But who entered the zenana, and how? In narratives of South Asian colonialism, Western women recorded the very first encounters with the zenana. From Mrs. Meer Hassan Ali's (1973) report on her experiences as a wife of a Muslim in India in the 1830s (and her graphic description of curing cholera with rosewater), to the sometimes titillating reminiscences of Victorian ladies invited to "purdah parties," and to the descriptions by women doctors visiting zenanas, the reporting to the colonial authorities was done by women, who invariably remarked upon the health of the inhabitants. And yet, examining colonial writings regarding South Asian women of the nineteenth century does not necessarily reveal the women themselves or any individual woman.[1]

So who was this woman a hundred years ago, so in need of help and of medical interventions? What can we know of what she ate, what she worried about, how she kept healthy or, indeed, any of the details of her quotidian bodily existence as a landed, moneyed South Asian woman in 1904? This chapter imagines that daily existence, through an examination of the relationship of food and medicine to women's health and daily lives in late nineteenth-century South Asia. The women's lives are re-created by means of a close reading of Book Nine of the *Bihishti Zewar*. The overarching goal of this chapter is to add to scholarly discussions regarding representations of nineteenth-century South Asian Muslim women, especially as individuals and in their daily lives.[2]

First published in Urdu in 1904, the *Bihishti Zewar* (the title can be translated as 'Jewellery of paradise' or 'Heavenly ornaments', among other variations) is an elaborate compendium of rules, guidance and stories written specifically for South Asian Muslim women. The work was composed by the Deobandi scholar Maulana Ashraf Ali Thanvi (1863–1943) during the great wave of late nineteenth-century Muslim reformist activity.[3] It has proven to be enduringly popular.[4] It is now widely available on the internet and can easily be downloaded to cell phones, in various versions. Farah Deeba Chowdhury (2017: 20), a scholar who writes about popular books like the *Bihishti Zewar*, states, 'In my teen years [it used] to be very helpful in learning prayers and understanding basic principles of Islam.'

Originally, the published Urdu versions of Book Nine of the *Bihishti Zewar* consisted of about thirty pages of general comments on health, and then about a hundred pages of recipes for various remedies, interspersed with more advice about healthy living. There is a long section specifically on pregnancy. The *Bihishti Zewar* in its entirety in the oldest published version is over seven hundred pages long, so Book Nine initially made up a significant part of the work.[5] Current-day readers of the *Bihishti Zewar*, whether searching for information and guidance in Urdu or using an academic English translation for scholarly motives, do not see this section on food and health in any detail, if at all. The consequences of that erasure, that is, the disappearance of the women addressed, their discussions about health and nutrition and their everyday lives, demand our attention.[6]

Book Nine was also omitted in Barbara Metcalf's scholarly English translation, *Perfecting Women: Maulana Ashraf 'Ali Thanawi's Bihishti Zewar, A Partial Translation with Commentary* (1990).[7] Metcalf's unpublished manuscript translation of Book Nine, the material that was omitted, is over 250 pages long, excluding her own glossary on herbs and other ingredients, and it is her translation that I use in this chapter.[8]

Along with my reading of Book Nine in this chapter, with its intent of gleaning the texture of the 'lived life' of women and their bodily health a hundred years ago, I will look at Metcalf's remarks on Book Nine in her Introduction to her translation, and then at two other scholars' discussions of this material, Anna Vanzan and Usamah Ansari. Other current scholarship centring on issues that arise from this kind of reading of Book Nine will be used to see how the details of day-to-day existence captured in it overlays with this reading.[9] Finally, this chapter will also engage with scholarship elsewhere in this book that addresses the push-and-pull of the 'patriarchal domestic family structure where female ritual and culinary activity are situated' (Chapter 3, p. 77), as well as the 'reformist spirit [that turned] the mundane into the pious … [by] … merging the Islamic ritual cycle with the rhythms of daily household chores' (Introduction, p. 21).

The impetus for this approach – the goal of extracting a 'lived life' – comes from my own engagement with Barbara Metcalf's project of translating the *Bihishti Zewar*. My approach takes its inspiration from and owes a general debt to the writings of Michel de Certeau, Pierre Bourdieu and other thinkers, as well as from a movement in Germany, the Alltagsgeschichte historians, who have emphasized the importance of the practices of everyday life and what is considered commonplace, and to historians pursuing 'history from below'. While this school of history is less in vogue now than when it emerged in the 1970s and 1980s, the very lack of discussion about the 'lived life' of nineteenth-century South Asian women would certainly justify this style of analysis. In this particular reading, using the detail in the text, I imagine the 'lived life' of a woman as she confronts matters of health in the zenana, women's quarters, at the time of the *Bihishti Zewar*'s initial publication, now over a hundred years ago. The goal is to 'see' the woman to whom the work is addressed and to whom the advice is directed and to 'see' her by means of that advice. By looking through the minutiae of experience that is portrayed in Book Nine as if through clear glass, without theory, or history, or any particular opinion, our understanding of the daily life of that woman will deepen. The task will be to look at the material from the inside and move outward: moving from the specific, for example, from a recipe for a cure for a cough, to a whole, thinking about that long-ago woman, worrying about that cough.

In her second book, Ruby Lal introduces scholar Azra Kidwai as the interlocutor between Lal's 'investigation of respectable, modern Indian womanhood and of feminine cultures' in the nineteenth and twentieth centuries and Azra's own narration of lived memories – 'living back in time' – as a girl-child and woman navigating a twentieth century in a northern India still heavily informed and guided by nineteenth-century writing and thinking. In parsing Azra's recollections of explorations of texts and socio-familial structures, her 'imagining the grandeur' of the previous generation, Lal (2013: Prelude) allows us to see the other, inner life of the girl-child and woman, etched into a palimpsest of South Asian, specifically sharif, families living in the mid-twentieth century.

So it is possible to access the very texture of women's lives as described in Book Nine if one approaches the material as if it were transparent; not focusing on the details of the text itself, but looking through it to imagine these women as they were, free of intervention. It was a loss, though an understandable one, when Metcalf's published manuscript, out of practical necessity, could not contain Book Nine's voluminous material. Not only did the medical instructions disappear, but our ability to 'see' the women to whom they were addressed disappeared as well.

However, if we return to Metcalf's translation, and if we willingly suspend our disbelief, then between the lines of advice, directions and remonstrance offered by Thanvi we can indeed glimpse that long-ago woman, at first dimly, then ever more clearly. The convention throughout this chapter will be to highlight, in bold italic type, the re-creation of the woman that is gleaned directly from the 1904 Urdu text of Book Nine of the *Bihishti Zewar*, translated as 'The jewellery of paradise'. For example, in the unpublished translation of Book Nine, Part One, Thanvi has this to say about water:

> Do not drink water as soon as you get up (nor ought you go directly out into the air). If you are very thirsty, gulp down some water while holding your nose. Then hold your nose for some time and breathe through the mouth. If you have been walking in hot weather, do not drink water right away, especially not if you have been in the *lu* (hot wind). A person who drinks a great deal of water at that point would die. You should not drink water on an empty stomach nor immediately after defecating. (*Bihishti Zewar*, unpublished translation, c. 1982: n.p.)

A woman's outline, her behaviours and choices as referenced by Thanvi, start to take shape within our mind's eye as we read the translation.

> ***She was thirsty, but she knew it would be better to not just drink from the nearest well. The times she did, she tried always to drink water from one that is filled, and not going dry. She knows to not drink water that is salty or hot. Of course, she knows that rain water is best. But as this is the dry season that will not do. She knows how to make the well water more drinkable – by cooking it until only three quarters was left. She will then cool and strain it. She knows to wait to drink water, and that it would be best if the water is filtered through a cloth tied over an earthenware jug, sipped in small quantities at a time. But she***

is alone for the moment at this early hour, and when she finds leftover water in a carafe that belongs to a cousin, she drinks thirstily.

Using Thanvi's observations on 'Movement', we can add to the construction of an individual woman's life. Again, we can see this vision:

She drinks thirstily and contemplates her day. She knows she must get up, be busy about the quarters – and no one will appreciate her just letting others do the work. She reads, 'Too much rest not only upsets the household, but even causes illnesses.' Work was healthy. Movement was healthy. And, if she wanted, she could make her way to the roof. And it was true – her aunt, who was not even that old, lay in bed, and said she was sick, and took medicine. But wouldn't her aunt feel better if she moved around?

As the woman begins to emerge, using this kind of visualizing on our part, we may think further about why there is this general omission of Book Nine from reprints of *Bihishti Zewar*. The most obvious reason is that the material in Book Nine is very long and very specific – it is, after all, an extremely detailed herbal medicine manual within the larger body of the very lengthy *Bihishti Zewar*. Another reason for omitting it could be that Book Nine in its entirety is not now relevant to the reader for practical reasons. While its comments about food and health are of interest, the scores of herbal remedies might currently be of little immediate use. Women nowadays would probably not be responsible for concocting antidotes for snakebites or severe fevers, as is suggested in Book Nine. These remedies have been replaced for some by what is referred to commonly as Western medicine – the current system of medicine as practiced in modern medical schools and hospitals. Others in South Asia, who consult hakims (doctors) and still use the yunani (Graeco-Arab or Graeco-Persian) medical system, upon which the remedies in the *Bihishti Zewar* are based, would most likely not be making medicines up at home.[10]

The yunani medicines could today either be bought at dispensaries, or, even more likely, a serious health crisis would necessitate immediate outside medical intervention. As recent scholarship has suggested, the revival of this medical system in many ways was an invention and reinterpretation of 'tradition'.[11]

Metcalf (1990: 10) notes:

This medicine, *yunani tibb*, was even taught as an ancillary subject at Deoband so that the 'ulama could further serve their followers. Women were enjoined to learn its application, too, and the *Bihishti Zewar* itself, in Book Nine, includes

> a section on *yunani* treatments. Women were now to disdain the interventions of the wise women, who were dismissed as no more than quacks. The reformers sought to include women in what they saw as a higher standard of behavior, but they did so at the cost of areas of family and ritual life that had been women's domain.[12]

Whether or not the contemporary, early reader of the *Bihishti Zewar* was in fact compliant with distancing herself from 'wise women', she was also, clearly, achieving a kind of wisdom herself. It can be argued that the number of recipes and their explicitness empowered women to respond to health and nutrition questions or crises. The work also standardized this health and nutrition information, and by existing as a printed object, as Metcalf observes in her Introduction, allowed this information to be disseminated widely.

Again, we read on in Book Nine. We see a woman drinking water:

> ***Who is she? We know she is older, but is not yet a widow, given her engagement in zenana life, and the jewelry she can still wear to celebrations. She is responsible for the family's health. She is charged with being patient, industrious, and concerned with the well-being of others in her community. She is expected to share both the duties and rewards of being a co-wife, and be invested in her own health, as well as her children's health, while remaining helpful and available to assist in caring for other sick women in the zenana. She is always busy, or at least, has been led to believe that a show of busy-ness showed her in a better light than a display of leisure.***

In order to continue looking for these disappeared women, it is useful to review responses to the *Bihishti Zewar* from South Asian Muslim women themselves. Tahera Aftab described the veneration that her mother, who was born in the early part of the twentieth century, had for the *Bihishti Zewar*, how she would request her daughter to wash her hands before touching the book, such was its place in the older lady's estimation. Aftab went on to study history at Lucknow University, in part because of her mother's recommendation to look to history to discover more about the treatment of women in various cultures and times. Aftab (2008: xxvii) writes, in the Introduction to her annotated bibliography and research guide, that she was in utter disbelief when she realized for the first time that women were absent in historical accounts.[13]

Aftab's (2008: xxxi) questions remain our own; we must ask, as she does, about the absence of South Asian Muslim women: Who were these women? Where were they? What were they doing? Were they forced to remain silent? Did they ever question their silence?

> ***The woman had awakened in the morning early and prayed. She knows also to bundle up in the east wind that blows at dawn. Especially if she has taken some kind of laxative, which could be composed of – well, the one made of figs. It shouldn't become a habit, and so she considers stopping. She will switch to a digestive instead. After dressing for the day, she walks through the sections of the house that she and the children have access to, to make sure it is laid out neatly – the children are not allowed to go to the bathroom just anywhere. The men had complained. She didn't mind it, but having them shout to her to clean it up was upsetting. Now, in fact, there is a separate area with a pot for the children that she has cleaned as often as she can. Sometimes the house smells, so she burns frankincense or camphor. She returns to the zenana, thirsty and thinking about her day. She will have some tea first.***
>
> ***All winter, she has been drinking tea with honey and fennel to keep warm. She will have some today too, on this cool spring day, instead of a cooling drink. She also eats a fresh fig and two dates, hot foods that will help her feel warmer. She wraps a thicker dupatta around her, feeling a slight chill. In the winter, as cold as it got, she knew that she must not sit in a closed room with a stove – people die in rooms with stoves when they shut the doors and windows to try to keep warm. It wasn't just on Thanvi's word. One of her cousins died this way – she had closed all the shutters to keep out the bitter cold, had gone to sleep with the stove burning, and then never woke up. Finishing her fruit, she reminds herself to give instructions for a basket of fruits and flowers to be sent to her maternal aunt, who lives a few streets away, and who is celebrating her day of birth. She has finished her tea, and now considers what instructions to give the zenana cooks for the noon meal.***

We can now look briefly at the concerns of two scholars, Anna Vanzan and Usamah Ansari, in their essays about Book Nine. Neither author's focus is on the daily lived life of the recipient of Thanvi's advice, though both contribute to our understanding of Book Nine (which is, as mentioned, only available in its entirety in Urdu). Vanzan's concentration is on the role of yunani medicine within the Deoband movement. She is interested in Thanvi's medical beliefs and discusses his use of amulets as it relates to his reliance on hakims and a medical system that would discourage such beliefs. Vanzan's (2000: 3–8) exploration is neither of the medical condition nor of the state of health of women addressed in Book Nine.

Ansari's (2010) approach to the material takes a different turn. He looks at a 'self' and the construction of a 'self' as it relates to a Muslim woman at this time, but he is not seeking specifically for the daily existence of that self. He examines the process of what happens when women follow Thanvi's advice. He says:

> I shall argue in this article that the detailed instructions and comments on health, body, and piety in the *Bihishti Zewar* should be understood as a particular 'technology of the self' where the kinds of actions one articulates and perfects are both the means to reaching the status of a pious self and also the effects of being this self. (275–98)

And yet, it is important to recall through this discussion of Book Nine that while most reformists, including Thanvi, sought to bring about a large-scale increase in functional piety and social equality, and while elsewhere in this book one is able to learn how certain women were successful in achieving both social and moral equality (Chapter 10), for the most part Muslim women, even in reformist households, walk a 'tightrope … between accumulating spiritual merit for the afterlife and fulfilling their duties as good wives in this one' (Chapter 10, p. 210). Darakhshan Khan writes: 'Nowhere is this more apparent than in the women's discussions about food – its preparation, serving and consumption – as they catch up with each other before and after the sermons. Stepping out of the mould of scripted conversation, they talk about "returning home to the *chullah-chakki*" (the gas stove and grind mill).' Improving the inner self resonates as a key goal of reformist movements, and yet, with no small irony, such an emphasis on improvement only highlights the unequal expectation placed on the men and women belonging to these movements. As Khan discusses:

> The reconfiguration of household duties to make more time for worship is in line with the Jama'at's call for spiritual equality between men and women. Since every Muslim woman will be accountable for her good and bad deeds in this world, she alone is responsible for living a pious life. However, the push for spiritual equality has consequences, often unintended and unwanted, on household dynamics, especially because Jama'at sermons also maintain that the man is the economic provider for his family. (p. 208)

As Ansari notes, Thanvi does indeed begin Book Nine with an injunction to his women readers, discussing the kind of 'selves' they should be. In fact, Ansari focuses on exactly what it is that Thanvi is trying to enjoin women to do. Here is Thanvi, as he opens the treatise on health with these words: 'This book provides essential methods for securing and maintaining good health. Women who know them can look out for themselves and their children. A woman in good health is joyful at heart. She is drawn to acts of worship and good work. She savors eating and drinking and accordingly gives heartfelt thanks to Almighty God.'[14] He then goes on to say:

> Her body is strong so that she can do her own work and render good service to others. A healthy person can fulfill obligations to those to whom obligations are owed. To provide for one's health in the context of these ends is an act of worship and religion. Women in particular must know these matters because they care for children who themselves know nothing of their own benefit or harm. Not only do children fall ill through the carelessness of uninformed women, but those in a position to study fail to study well. Men, moreover, worry over the illness of children or women because of the expense of medications. In short, illness brings trouble upon trouble. Our Messenger, on whom be the peace and blessings of God, approved of medicine and dietary regimens. For all these reasons a short description of these essential matters is given here.[15]

Beyond the overall conception of a healthy woman who is joyful at heart and then drawn to acts of worship, Thanvi's more practical thesis is that unhealthy women cannot fulfil their obligations and cost money. Thus the advice he gives is particular to the health of the female body and includes recipes for medicines and cures, which are revealing of the reality of day-to-day life. Creating the idealized 'self' that Ansari finds in Book Nine takes numerous practical steps.

As Ansari notes, Thanvi tries to demonstrate that eating correctly is the key to health. So in Book Nine he includes instructions on how to eat properly and about what to eat, and he names and describes dangerous foods. He presents lengthy recipes of remedies for a variety of illnesses and medical emergencies, in which scores of different ingredients are mentioned. Different sicknesses are discussed in detail.

Why should we eat some foods and not others? For example, we could read what Thanvi says about eggplant and simply follow his advice. As unmediated readers of an advice book, as unfiltered recipients of the contents of the large volume we call the *Bihishti Zewar*, we could think that eggplant is hot and dry besides there being a lot of other things about it. The text, as it sets out prescriptive injunctions, by its very detail, specificity and focus helps us to answer numerous health questions. We know what to eat if we are ill.

Again, taking our reading and visualizing a step further, we can see this woman and her eggplants:

> ***She has a basket of eggplants now to cook. The maid bought them from the vegetable seller. Why should she even prepare it? she wonders, crossly. The belly is never fully at peace after a meal of eggplant. In fact, the*** **Jewelry of Paradise** ***has said that 'Eggplant is hot and dry and provides very little nourishment. It is very harmful for a person with hemorrhoids or for those of bilious constitution. Its properties can be somewhat corrected by mixing in a***

> ***substantial quantity of clarified butter and accompanying it with vinegar.' Why even bother? But everyone likes it so much. One cousin makes a roast eggplant dish that everyone in the family demands.***

And to continue to imagine the woman and how she eats, we read on in the book, looking back more than a century:

> ***Unless it is a feast or celebration, the woman always tries to eat less than she needs. But then she reads in the* Jewelry of Paradise *that: 'Consider abstinence more necessary than medicine in sickness, but not in good health. Eat to your heart's delight whatever you wish of seasonal things. Just keep in mind that you should not eat more than your stomach can hold and fast if your stomach feels heavy.'***
>
> ***So she wonders. If she eats things that are seasonal, can she eat her fill? If she does, who will complain? She has been hungry at night again. Her head aches frequently and just that morning she feels like a cold is coming on. She searches through Book Nine and finds a concoction that she can make up. The ingredients are simple – stones from apricots, which she has. She will use the stones of dried apricots. She also needs lettuce seeds and a long-tailed pepper. She makes her way to the middle of the house, where the servants are already busy setting the pots out for preparing the noon meal. She grinds the apricot seed separately, using the heavy grinding stone that she keeps inside the courtyard, and crushing it into water. Then she grinds the lettuce seeds and peppers together and mixes it into the liquid. She applies the mixture on her forehead and around her ears.***
>
> ***With the lettuce seeds, she decides to make up some medicine. There are two new babies in the zenana, and they have cried frequently at night, which is perhaps the cause of her headache. So she takes the lettuce seeds she has on hand for the medicine to soothe her headache, and grinds them together with black and white poppy seeds, purslane and bartang (plantain) seeds.[16] Before taking the medicine, she decides to eat a nourishing egg, which she has learned how to make – the* Jewelry of Paradise *has provided exact instructions on how to boil this healthy food. The men in the household had eaten this for breakfast when they were on tour with the British collector and had asked to eat it in the zenana. She discards the yolk, for Thanvi says it has no nutritional value. And before she takes medicine, she tries to eat properly, and eat the right foods.***

One of Metcalf's (1990) central emphases in her discussion of the *Bihishti Zewar* is Thanvi's belief that men and women are essentially the same: 'This is clear from his emphasis … on the centrality of knowledge and the ability of women to adhere to the standard being set for all, if only they are adequately informed.

There can never be a prima facie case that women are morally inferior to men.' So the woman we see does not rely on men for her motivation, or even for instruction. She has a book and her own moral authority (8).

Such an emphasis was echoed by the South Asian reformist schools like Deobandi or the Tablighi Jama'at and was espoused by Thanvi; however, as Sanyal and Kumar point out in the Introduction, 'for everyone, both reformers and conservatives, and for the men and women who are the targets of reform or repression, the social equality of men and women seems to be a separate issue from their moral equality. Women potentially have, and can aspire to, the latter, but they do not have the former' (Introduction, p. 5).

When Thanvi addresses his audience, women, he does not say that they are 'weak' or will have trouble understanding issues. He accuses them of laziness (in not calling hakims when they should) and of not acting soon enough in certain situations; however, these are not omissions of intellect, but instead are framed as moral failings. The close reading of Book Nine shows that those addressed are required to know a lot about the people, produce and environment accessible to those within the zenana, to assume a lot of responsibility and to have access to a lot of materials – meats, vegetables, herbs and minerals, as well as the ways and means to create, as needed, the recipes described within Book Nine.

> ***Back in one of the larger rooms, one of her sisters-in-law, her husband's younger brother's wife, complains of a backache. She consults the* Jewelry of Paradise *and finds that sometimes pain in the lower back begins because, she reads, a child was born in winter and the woman did not get proper food. It was true. Her younger sister-in-law's baby was born in winter and she had not eaten much after the birth. So she decides to give instructions for a meat soup to be made. Maybe that will help her sister-in-law. She reads that in cases like this, meat soup cooked with warm spices and eggs will help a backache. If the eggs are eaten with Solomon's salt, they are even more beneficial. So she tells her sister-in-law to ask her husband for some money so they may send one of the servants to the bazaar to buy some Solomon's salt.***[17]

There are several instances within Book Nine that point to women cooperating with each other in order to gather all the ingredients necessary for a recipe, or to develop a course of action for a zenana member who has suddenly fallen ill. Both early observers, such as Khursheed Bai, and contemporary academics, such as Gail Minault, argue that the women within zenanas developed and nurtured strong networks of communication and cooperation within their fields of access, and that within the zenanas women had vibrant personalities and varying levels of power depending on their position within the family hierarchy.[18]

Continuing to visualize this interior space of cooperation and power, we see the woman trying to make up a recipe:

> ***The servant returns from the bazaar and the message arrives in the zenana that the spice seller has no Solomon's salt made up. So she looks again at the* Jewelry of Paradise *for the process. She will need rock salt, and table salt, sal ammoniac, called noshadar, celery seeds, black pepper, white pepper, asafetida, spikenard, cinnamon, ginger – so many ingredients! Wait, who has dodder? It used to grow in the yard, and she had not realized that the vine had medicinal use. Better to borrow some from the ladies in the next lane. The grandmother there has a good supply of medicine. She reads more about Solomon's salt; it is a good digestive and very beneficial. It stops stomachache. If you take 16 grains every day on an empty stomach, it makes your eyesight keen. It has been proven effective if rubbed into a wasp's bite whether dry or mixed with rose water. Well, if she has pain in the hands and feet, one can smooth honey on the area and then sprinkle it on. It is supposed to be very beneficial.***
>
> ***Everyone had fallen ill this past winter, which is probably why winter is a time to eat nourishing food, the woman thinks. She prefers the hot weather, because she seldom has headaches then. Hot weather is a time of special foods. When it is summer, she eats flummery, mixing up milk and some plums and letting it cool. The fresh rice that has been brought in from the village she avoids. And she doesn't use the newly harvested wheat either.***
>
> ***The woman made her way toward the courtyard again, to make the Solomon's salt so the zenana cooks could prepare the meat soup and eggs. There are other foods to avoid when ill, and to otherwise eat only in moderation – the list is in the book: Eggplant, white radish, beef and duck; carrots; dried meat; the lobiya bean; the pulse masur; oil; unrefined sugar; sour foods. Yet so many medicines contain sour ingredients! A poison one day could save your life the next, she muttered. There seem to be so many foods that she needed to be careful about – why then does the* Jewelry of Paradise *recommend eating beef for some women, especially those who are pregnant or are looking after babies? Beef, she thought, was delicious. Especially in yakhni.***

Academics who focus on South Asia and think about culinary histories can help us structure what we are reading. According to Angma Dey Jhala (2011), who writes about dining within a royal zenana, 'eating and the process of dining demonstrated the delicate balance of power within the *zenana* not only in relation to the paramount power but also in the hierarchies between women and various factions of the royal court'. While we are not re-creating a woman within a courtly zenana, we can see parallels with the woman we are re-creating (75).

Jhala indicates the complexities of these hierarchies when pointing out that the women of the zenana 'were invariably the producers, patrons, or transmitters of food in the royal household' as they travelled due to marriage. The author adds that zenana women 'were also crucial in creating new ideas of fusion cooking during the colonial period'. Jhala's essay is, obviously, not a cookbook for zenanas, nor are the day-to-day issues of a zenana kitchen discussed with any reference to health, as in the *Bihishti Zewar*. But Jhala quite rightly notes how little academic literature has delved into the culinary traditions of the princely states. It is true, and we could add how little academic literature has explored women's spaces, cooking and culinary traditions with any specificity. Rather, as Jhala points out, cookbooks have done this. In our reading of the *Bihishti Zewar*, it is Book Nine with its instructions on health and making up medicines that is illuminating women's spaces (Ansari 2012: 65).

> ***Well, in the hot weather, she will eat cucumber and squash, because they are cold foods. While preparing the Solomon's salt, she also prepares medicine for colds, in case she or others will need it in the days to come. All the mothers and children can benefit from the concoction she makes of water lily juice or jujube fruit. Even munching on seeds of the sweet basil is good for a cold. She does try to avoid hot and dry foods like arhar dal and potatoes in hot and dry weather, but potatoes would be good to eat now, when the weather still carried a chill in the mornings and nights.***

From the close reading we have just done, we can see that while the medical system Thanvi is using for his text is indeed yunani, he, at the same time, does use herbs (which are part of the medications, and part of yunani remedies) and even resorts to amulets and spells. In fact, he sees some types of spells and such treatments as efficacious. As for removing the medical sphere from midwives, he does not do this exactly. He advocates consulting hakims in cases of seriousness or when things are in question. He also says that the current midwives are not as good as those before. Nevertheless, 'herbs and amulets' are not in the control of some outside agent, even a 'wise woman', but available to the women of the household.

> ***The two new babies in the zenana, older now, have begun to cry at night again. They are in the bed with their mothers, and wake everyone. Perhaps they are too hot. Or it could be teething, because they have diarrhea too, and she knows what to do for that. The bael tree in the courtyard is ripe – so she has bael fruit brought to her and she grinds up the pulp with purslane seeds, some gum mastic and sugar and mixes in some juice from a pomegranate. The babies suck it off their mother's finger.***

Both the babies have wet nurses, and she has given these servants a handful of poppy seeds and a rice pilau with fresh cow's buttermilk in the evening. This is supposed to calm the babies' stomachs. But the diarrhea has continued, and the advice from the* Jewelry of Paradise *is to call a hakim. The last time a hakim was summoned, it was difficult to convey the symptoms of the children to him, for of course no one in the zenana could talk directly to him, and the men seem to have garbled the information. Well, she knew that whatever happened was fated to happen.

On the one hand, the environment that Thanvi describes is a self-contained space of women, health and food, under the distant authority of the males and the elders in the household. When in doubt, consult a hakim – otherwise life and illness and the rhythms of the seasons are contained in the rooms in which the women live. On the other hand, as we know, while Thanvi was writing the *Bihishti Zewar*, the zenana had become the fierce focus of the colonizer's gaze and of Western medical missionaries. Book Nine's concerns are so clearly expressed and so detailed that the content goes far beyond just addressing the problems of superstition or ignorant customs, as Thanvi sees them. The content is a presentation of an alternate universe to colonial stereotypes of the zenana; in Book Nine exists a healthy environment, infused with knowledge, administered by intelligent and deeply engaged women. As Usamah Ansari (2012: 65) writes:

> What is articulated is a sophisticated terminology and method of advice on how to be healthy and how to keep one's family healthy at a moment when anxieties over the well-being of the Muslim community abound.

Now, the woman needs to think about the youngest sister-in-law, the one who married into the family just last year. She is one of her husband's second cousins, on her mother-in-law's side. She has married her husband's younger brother and is his first wife. The girl's menstrual cycles are irregular, and when she bleeds, there is very little blood. Her sister-in-law seems weak, too. The girl has not yet become pregnant. Why not? She consults the* Jewelry of Paradise. *The Maulana has written about 'Illnesses of the Womb'. But there is nothing about becoming pregnant, although there is a lot of information on how to treat pregnant women. She notes that he says: 'In women's bodies, there are three organs to be distinguished below the navel. The highest is the bladder; under it is the compressed womb in which the baby lives; and lowest are the compressed intestines. When you are to apply any medication to the womb, apply it below the navel. If you wish to be protected from illnesses of the womb, always take these points into account:

1. Immediately seek a cure for any excess or deficiency of menstruation.
2. Midwives nowadays are completely ignorant.
Therefore do not simply take their advice on treatment.
Inquire of a physician.
3. For ordinary illnesses, avoid medicines placed inside the body but rather make use of oral medications and ointments.'

She sees that there is a medication for a deficiency of menstrual blood. It looks simple to mix up, and she reads through the ingredients. Melon seed, cucumber seeds, caltrops [water chestnuts], chicory, and maidenhair fern – they are soaked in a little water. She sees that there is another way to bring on menstruation. She can have her sister-in-law eat a preparation of carrots or sit over a smoky coal fire upon which she has sprinkled some carrot seeds.

But the problem is she is not pregnant. Why not? Her sister-in-law looks wearied often. Is she unhappy for some reason, or has she received bad news or a terrible shock? No rumors had gone around yet, but maybe she should talk to the younger woman, and make sure that her sister-in-law is not cherishing some grief or thinking too hard upon some misfortune. It seems like this might be another case for consulting a hakim. Before this, though, she will try these two remedies. They cost very little and might work.

Both Ansari and Vanzan comment in particular on the simple language of the *Bihishti Zewar*. Language alone claims its audience. They can see the audience. Both see the work as an explication of what the role of women might be or could be in the continuing dialogue with colonial authorities, the ulema and reformists. Ansari (2010), a young scholar who focused his attention on the *Bihishti Zewar* prior to his untimely death, wrote two posthumously published essays, the content of which is a presentation of an alternate universe to colonial stereotypes of the zenana. He notes that

> women's actions are thus the object, and constitute the material through which the desired subject (a pious self) can be cultivated. Women are necessary to actualise his notion of tradition through their actions; they are not merely the ground on which what is authentic tradition and what is not may be worked out. Through training women's actions, educating them along Thanvi's definition of correct behaviour, one may actualise the pious self. (17)

We continue with our woman:

Then, finally her youngest sister-in-law becomes pregnant. It must be about her third month, but it is hard to know, because she never bled regularly. The **Jewelry of Paradise** ***has a lot to say about precautions during pregnancy. There***

> ***are many foods to avoid. It is hard to remember them. Cumin, chickpeas, carrots, radishes – the list of things she shouldn't eat is very long. Apples, plums, mangoes, and for meat, quails and small birds are good to eat when one is pregnant. Of course, it is obvious that one should avoid constipation while pregnant. As they did in her own home, here too, in her husband's house (her mother-in-law is her aunt) the whole family eats soup with lots of fat in it. And if her sister-in-law is still suffering, she can give her myrobalan. There is a mixture with rose water that helps as well. The other day, she saw her pregnant sister-in-law trying to move a heavy trunk. She scolded her, for everyone knows that pregnant women should not lift anything heavy or move about in a quick way. She warned her, for it was her seventh month, to be very careful, and not let her husband come to her. This could hurt the baby. So could coughing. Really, so many things.***

While our reading does indeed show Thanvi recommending that women consult hakims in many cases, the picture presented of the general structure of the household still assumes that most decisions are in the hands of women. We see our female reader assessing situations, consulting texts, buying ingredients and following written instructions. Instead of the wise women, whose recipes would not have not been written down in a retrievable, systematic way, Book Nine of the *Bihishti Zewar* would give any literate reader access to a recipe. In fact, Thanvi depends on the literacy of women. A close reading of Book Nine shows that those addressed are required to know a lot, assume a lot of responsibility and have access to a lot of materials – meats, vegetables, herbs and minerals. Again, while Thanvi accuses women of laziness and of not acting soon enough in certain situations, these are not accusations regarding any lack of intellect or reason. In assuming that women have responsibility, his work gives agency to women, which, ironically, according to Metcalf, at the same time 'offers an example of male intrusion into a heretofore largely female domain'.

We continue to see the woman:

> ***Now, the woman is worried about her sister-in-law's health. It is very clear from the* Jewelry of Paradise *what to do. Her sister-in-law must eat very little. She became hungry, and it was permitted to give her some raisins in water. Then, the woman prepared this medicine for her. She read the recipe:***
>
> ***'sweet melon seeds, 1/4 oz.***
>
> ***small caltrops, 1/4 oz.***
> ***chickory root, 1/5 oz.***
> ***maidenhair fern, 1/5 oz.***

garden rue, 1/5 oz.
mountain mint, 1/5 oz.
Indian laburnum peel, 1/2 oz.
water
"the cooling drink," 1 1/2 oz.
Method: Boil the first seven ingredients in water, strain, and add to "the cooling drink". Take luke-warm.'

This she did, but first she needed to make up 'the cooling drink'. The Maulana has a recipe for that too, in the second part of Book Nine. She turned to that recipe. She needed a lot of ingredients for this. This was the recipe she made up first:

'The Cooling drink' (Sharbat buzuri barid):
'seed of cucumber and kakri, 1 oz.
kernel of the seed of bottle gourd, 1 oz.
kernel of the seed of white gourd melon, 1 oz.
gokhuru, 1 oz.
seed of marshmallow, 1 oz.
common mallow, 1 oz.
kernel of the seed of Indian jalap, 1 oz.
chicory seed, 1 oz.
chicory root, 1 oz.
white sugar
Method: Crush all the ingredients except the sugar, and soak overnight. In the morning, boil and strain. Add 18 to 27 oz. white sugar and make a syrup. Take 1 to 1 1/2 oz. If the white gourd seeds are not available, omit. This is very effective and is available in the market.'

For a while, her sister-in-law had morning sickness. They gave her pomegranate seeds and mint and green grapes. The drink worked and settled her stomach. Then there was eating clay. Pregnant women wanted to eat clay. Her sister-in-law asks for clay. This is so common, she thinks. Does the Maulana approve of it? Is it mentioned in the Jewelry of Paradise? *Yes, and he says the urge will go away. She could instead eat little patties made of grain that would help quell her desire for the clay. But the rose water medication is the best. So soothing, and it even helped when she lost her appetite. Her sister-in-law's feet are swollen, and so she has the servant girl grind up aloes, betel nut, and sandalwood to soothe her sister-in-law's feet.*

But now it looks as if the birth is very soon. One of the wet nurses is older, and has seen many births, and helped with many. She does not trust the midwife

lately, after the neighbor's child was hurt in the delivery. The Maulana agrees with her. He thinks that midwives were better in the past. The labor pains began, but it seems too early. Could it be just the seventh month? She has consulted through her husband with the hakim. His advice is the same as in the book. Have her lie down and tie on a waistcloth. But it doesn't work. The baby is born dead. It was a boy.

Vanzan, in her essay 'Medical Education of Muslim Women in the Turn of the Century India: The 9th Chapter of the *Bihishti Zewar*', looks at how the material in Book Nine related to the education of women. She notes a central contradiction within the presentation of yunani medical practices to women, namely, that it is not clear what level of education is expected of women by religious or secular Muslim leaders. Vanzan (2000) is not looking for the woman inside the text, but notes nevertheless that it is uncertain where the learnedness of women fits. She says of Thanvi's writing style and instructions:

> The tone of the discourse is rather informal, with many Urdu words used instead of Arabic ones. Thanawi's aim was to provide women of the *zananah* with a sort of first aid kit so that they would be able to face problems related to health. However, at the same time he introduced women to some of the basic concepts of *unani* medicine, such as the means of diagnosis, the modes and types of treatment. In doing so, Thanawi reveals his deep knowledge of the *unani* system: he must have had some training as a *hakim*, and as such he tried to free women from the influence of impostors and qua[c]ks. In this respect it is significant that he continuously recommends women to call for the doctor (*hakim*) in case of necessity. 'Women's laziness in summoning a physician is notorious – but only if the doctor is too far or the medicine required too expensive the women should limit themselves to praying to God.' (4)

Vanzan also notes:

> The ulama and the secular reformists' solutions were totally different: the former were willing to give women some notions of medicine to be used in the house while at the same [time] preserving for themselves the world of intermediaries between women and the outside world. The latter began to extend medical education to women to be learned outside their house. (7)

Her sister-in-law's mother arrived two weeks later, having left as soon as she got word. The Begum was reportedly angry that she was not informed earlier about her daughter's health. The woman goes to meet her, knowing the importance of remaining calm, but also the importance of stopping the Begum should she start blaming everyone for her grandchild's death. She

knew to reiterate the omnipotence of God, and the dust of their own endeavors or happiness, as humans. She knew to remind the Begum of the mercy of an Almighty God, and once she was calm, to describe the ways in which her sister-in-law had remained unhealthy, despite everyone's best efforts, and the hakim's advice, as well as that of the Maulana. It was the will of God, she would say, and when the Begum finally became calm, she would tell her respectfully of all the mixtures and dishes she had prepared directly for her sister-in-law. The Begum might know of even more cures, or at least, would know what works best for her daughter. She would have some of the cooling drink brought up to the Begum, perhaps with some fruits and nuts. Patient. She had to be patient, for the Begum to realize it was the will of God that the child had passed away.

As we read Book Nine of the *Bihishti Zewar* today, weaving in and out of academic readings, we have tried repeatedly to sense these shadowy, mirrored images, these women, often ill, or concerned about illness, worrying about a child or an older person. We see this reflection of women of long ago, in a way the author, Thanvi, could not have anticipated. While Thanvi's was practical advice, in his lists of admonitions, ailments, foods and sympathetic counsel, his own readers of a century ago have slowly emerged from the past, for us.

Notes

1 Thus, from the official action in abolishing 'suttee' in Bengal in 1829 to the missionary James Peggs's 1832 publication *India's Cries to British Humanity, Relative to Infanticide, British Connection with Idolatry, Ghau Murders, Suttee, Slavery, and Colonization in India*, and on to Katherine Mayo's 1927 *Mother India*, individual lives are not the point. The point is the improvement of the lives of women as a group.

Scholarly work on the relationship between women studying medicine and the zenana can be found in an unpublished dissertation: Lal (1996). Recently, Narin Hassan's *Diagnosing Empire* (2011) engages with the meaning, and thus the mechanisms, of women studying medicine in colonial India.

Except for Hassan's work, the nexus between entering the zenana by women doctors (both Indian and foreign) and the demand by foreign and some Indian women to study medicine and their entering medical schools in England in the nineteenth century seems to have been largely forgotten as part of the overall colonial narrative. It is a subject that is only now being recovered. Indeed, this focus on South Asian women's health by colonial authorities, while frequently documented on a piecemeal basis, could be better theorized and integrated into an overall general understanding of colonialism. Another scholarly work that touches on some of this material is by Sonia Nishat Amin (1996), which contains descriptions of the medical experience of childbirth in the nineteenth century. There is also a recent discussion of women's medicine, food and health in Hollen (2003). Directly taking up this issue is Sehrawat (2013). For an overall description of the history of the engagement of Western medicine in India, see Arnold (2000).

2 There are many variations in the transcription of the title of this work and of the author's name, in which the representation of vowels changes slightly. I have chosen the two that seem most widely used currently, that is, 'Thanvi' and '*Bihishti Zewar*'. It should also be noted that transcriptions of South Asian place names and proper names vary widely and that the original text is retained in the quotations. I have not made an attempt to regularize quoted transcriptions.

3 The Deoband movement (named after its location), of which Thanvi was a leading thinker and writer, was founded shortly after the events in India in 1857, as were a number of Islamic reform movements, like the Aligarh movement and the Barelwi movement. As scholars note about these movements, the loss of political power by Muslims in India, symbolized by the deposition and exile of the last Mughal ruler of India, Bahadur Shah Zafar, and the horrific retribution wreaked on the community, demanded a response. While the Aligarh movement, led by Sir Sayyid Ahmed Khan, took a more cooperative engagement with the British rulers, the Deoband movement sought to reclaim Muslim power using the traditional function of organized wise men, the 'ulema', in the community. Like the Aligarh and Barelwi movements, the founding of a school was the physical instrument the activists used to propagate their ideas. The Deobandis founded, in Deoband, the Dar al Ulum, based on the teachings of the eighteenth-century thinkers Shah Waliullah and Sayyid Ahmad of Rai Bareli. Barbara Metcalf (1982) explains the response of Islamic religious scholars (ulema) to the colonial dominance of the British and the collapse of Muslim political power. Also see Lapidus ([1988] 2014: 703).

4 Versions of it are still widely available in Urdu, English and other languages, in the form of physical books and increasingly in online formats, with a variety of applications for downloading onto mobile devices.

5 While Thanvi is the author of *Bihishti Zewar*, some editions show that Book Nine was written with the help of Maulvi Hakim Muhammad Mustafa of Bijnor. The latter had at first prepared a very long treatise on health and medicine, which was shortened, and the shorter edition was incorporated into the *Bihishti Zewar* as Book Nine. It seems logical that the lengthy herbal contents of the recipes would come from a hakim (see Vanzan 2000: 3–8).

6 Or only partially printed; I could find none published after 1980 that included the detailed recipes for medicines that comprised a major part of the original version.

7 Available online. http://pdfbooksfree.pk/wp-content/uploads/2013/07/bihishti-zewar-urdu-part-9.pdf, in Urdu, retrieves Book Nine, but stops after the narrative and does not include the recipes for herbal remedies. Another online version, in English, omits the section altogether: http://www.islamicbulletin.org/free_downloads/women/bahishti_1_2_3.pdf. The versions are scanned copies of hard copies of the *Bihishti Zewar.*

8 In the early 1980s I worked as a research assistant on Metcalf's project to translate the *Bihishti Zewar*. When it was ultimately decided not to include Book Nine in the final published translation, we both felt that the material was nonetheless valuable and should be made available in English, though it never was.

9 There are three scholarly essays specifically on Book Nine of the *Bihishti Zewar*: Vanzan (2000: 3–8) and Ansari (2010: 275–98; 2012: 49–76). Ansari's work as a graduate student was edited by his colleagues and published after his tragic death. I thank Barbara Metcalf for directing my attention to his work. For Ansari's essays, see http://www.jstor.org/stable/10.1086/665963. Vanzan is not retrievable on the web, and my thanks go to Rebecca Darby-Williams, reference librarian at the University of California, Berkeley, Doe Library, for her assistance in locating this article.

10 The medical system that Thanvi uses is called 'yunani' or 'unani' (meaning 'Greek'), which is the term for Perso-Arabic traditional medicine as practiced in Mughal India and in Muslim culture in South Asia and modern-day Central Asia.

11 See Arnold (2000), for useful comments on yunani medicine.

12 Also see Metcalf (1986: 299–315).

13 Tahera Aftab is the editor and publisher of the *Pakistan Journal of Women's Studies: Alam-e-Niswan.*

14 Barbara Metcalf, unpublished manuscript, Book Nine, *Bihishti Zewar*.

15 Barbara Metcalf, unpublished manuscript, Book Nine, *Bihishti Zewar*.

16 Bartang (*Plantago major*) is found in the temperate and alpine Himalaya; the seeds of this large herb have the same properties as *Plantago ovata*. The leaves and roots are astringent and are used in fever. *P. ovata* is known as Ispaghul or Spogel seeds. Ispaghul is found in the plains and low hills of Punjab, the seeds of this herb have demulcent, cooling and diuretic properties and are used in inflammatory conditions of the gastrointestinal and genitourinary tracts, chronic dysentery, diarrhea and constipation. From Metcalf's unpublished glossary to Book Nine.

17 Solomon's salt is a mixture of ingredients and is described in the recipe that follows in the text.

18 Khursheed Bai, 'The Purdahnashin Question', *Indian Review*, April 1903, 217–18, MSS. EUR, F. 165.119, 0IOC, in Aftab (2008); and Minault (1994: 108–24). See Jhala (2011: 69–101, 75). A number of scholarly writings on topics that happen to intersect in Book Nine can help us think about women and food. In the decades since Metcalf's translation of the *Bihishti Zewar* was published, fields of inquiry

that were nascent or non-existent have developed – most broadly in culinary anthropology and in feminist studies, as well as more narrowly in studies of women in Islam and women within colonial structures. There are academic works that expand on the specific conversation about nineteenth-century advice to Indian women, for example, Minault (1998); and Walsh (2004).

Publications reflecting these varied areas of interest provide evidence of a growing engagement with food and its culture in South Asian studies. This current volume is but one example. Achaya (1994) presented for the first time a comprehensive historical discussion of food in India. Especially relevant to this chapter are his chapters on 'Food and the Indian Doctors', concerning how Indian systems of humoral medicine travelled worldwide, and on Muslims and food in India in 'The Muslim Bonus'.

An early entrant into the South Asia academic food discussion, and relevant to this chapter, is Appadurai (1988: 1–24), which suggested a line of inquiry that was novel at the time for historians of South Asia. He showed that one could ask questions about food, questions that centred not on food production or on food customs such as eating beef, but on the sociology of the domestic sphere.

References

Unpublished manuscript

Metcalf, Barbara. Book Nine of the *Bihishti Zewar*. Unpublished.

Published sources

Achaya, K. T. 1994. *Indian Food: A Historical Companion to Indian Food*. Delhi: Oxford University Press.

Aftab, Tahera. 2008. *Inscribing South Asian Muslim Women: An Annotated Bibliography & Research Guide* in *Handbook of Oriental Studies: Section 1, The Near and Middle East*; *v. 91*. Leiden: Brill.

Ali, Mrs. Meer Hassan. 1973. *Observations on the Mussalmauns of India: Descriptive of Their Manners, Customs, Habits and Religious Opinions Made During a Twelve Years' Residence in Their Immediate Society*. First published 1832. Edited by W. Crooke. Second edition, 1917. Reprinted by Karachi: Oxford University Press, Karachi. Oxford in Asia Historical Reprints from Pakistan, 1973.

Amin, Sonia Nishat. 1996. *The World of Muslim Women in Colonial Bengal 1876–1939*. Koln: Brill.

Ansari, Usamah Yasin. 2010. 'The Pious Self Is a Jewel in Itself: Agency and Tradition in the Production of "Shariatic" Modernity'. *South Asian Research* 30(3): 275–98.

Ansari, Usamah Yasin. 2012. '"Tandrusti Deen Ka Kaam Hai": Health as a Matter of Religion in Book 9 of Ashraf Ali Thanvi's Bahishti Zewar'. *History of Religions*, University of Chicago Press Journals 52(1) (August): 49–76.

Appadurai, Arjun. 1988. 'How to Make a National Cuisine: Cookbooks in Contemporary India'. *Comparative Studies in Society and History* 30(1) (January): 3–24.

Arnold, David. 2000. *Science, Technology and Medicine in Colonial India*, New Cambridge History of India. Cambridge: Cambridge University Press. This provides an excellent overall description of the history of the engagement of Western medicine in India.

Chowdhury, Farah Deeba. 2017. *Islam and Women's Income: Dowry and Law in Bangladesh*. Oxford: Routledge.

Hassan, Narin. 2011. *Diagnosing Empire: Women, Medical Knowledge, and Colonial Mobility*. Surrey, UK: Ashgate.

Hollen, Cecilia Ban. 2003. *Birth on the Threshold: Childbirth and Modernity in South India*. Berkeley: University of California Press.

Indian Magazine, the (London: National Indian Association in Aid of Social Progress and Education in India). '"Mrs. Childers on Indian Life"' (issues 229–40), no. 239, November 1890.

Jhala, Angma Dey. 2011. 'Trans-regional Chefs, Kitchens and Cookbooks: Food in the Colonial and Postcolonial Zenana'. In *Royal Patronage, Power and Aesthetics in Princely India: Empires in Perspective*. London: Pickering and Chatto.

Lal, Maneesha. 1996. 'Women, Medicine and Colonialism in British India 1869–1925'. Unpublished dissertation, University of Pennsylvania, Philadelphia.

Lal, Ruby. 2013. *Coming of Age in Nineteenth-Century India: The Girl-Child and the Art of Playfulness*. New York: Cambridge University Press.

Lapidus, Ira M. 2014 [1988]. *A History of Islamic Societies*. Cambridge: Cambridge University Press.

Metcalf, Barbara. 1982. *Islamic Revival in British India: Deoband, 1860–1900*. Princeton, NJ: Princeton University Press.

Metcalf, Barbara. 1986. 'Hakim Ajmal Khan: Ra'is of Delhi and Muslim "Leader"'. In Robert Eric Frykenberg (ed.), *Delhi through the Ages*. Delhi: Oxford University Press, 299–315.

Metcalf, Barbara. 1990. *Perfecting Women: Maulana Ashraf 'Ali Thanawi's Bihishti Zewar, A Partial Translation with Commentary*. Berkeley: University of California Press.

Minault, Gail. 1994. 'Other Voices, Other Rooms: The View from the Zenana'. In Nita Kumar (ed.), *Women as Subjects, South Asian Histories*. Charlottesville: University Press of Virginia, 108–24.

Minault, Gail. 1998. *Secluded Scholars: Women's Education and Muslim Social Reform in Colonial India*. Delhi: Oxford University Press.

Sehrawat, Samiksha. 2013. 'Zenana Medical Care: The Dufferin Fund, the Colonial State, and Female Medical Experts'. In *Colonial Medical Care in North India: Gender, State, and Society, c. 1830–1920*. Delhi: Oxford University Press.

Vanzan, Anna. 2000. 'Medical Education of Muslim Women in the Turn of the Century India: The 9th Chapter of the "Bihishti Zewar"'. *Journal of the Pakistan Historical Society* 48(1): 3–8. Vanzan is not retrievable on the web; my thanks go to Rebecca Darby-Williams, reference librarian at the University of California, Berkeley, Doe Library, for her assistance in locating this article.

Walsh, Judith. 2004. *Domesticity in Colonial India: What Women Learned When Men Gave Them Advice*. Lanham: Rowman & Littlefield.

2

The worship of taste: Rokeya Hossain and the politics of ritual fasting

Parna Sengupta

In this chapter, I consider the themes of this book – piety, food and gender – through the lens of ritual. Jan Snoek (2006: 13) defines 'ritual' in the following manner: 'Most ritual behavior takes place at specific places and/or at specific times … is more formally stylized, structured, and standardized …based on a script … purposeful and symbolically meaningful for its participants.

Snoek goes on to suggest that it is important to differentiate between ritual and ritual-like behaviour in the study of religion. The transformative and symbolically meaningful aspect of ritual suggests that this distinction should be fairly easy to make. And yet, the description of 'ritual' has expanded considerably into the fields of performance, gender and so on. Even in the study of religion, distinguishing between ritual and mundane work can be difficult. For instance, in his study of Zen monks, Ian Reader (2005: 87–104) argues that cleaning floors, an activity with a very practical (temporal) end, has ritual meaning in Buddhist meditative practice.

Rituals around food – either the consumption of or abstention from – are an especially generative space to explore the blurring of activities and their ritual significance. 'True' rituals ensure the transformation of ordinary food and everyday practices of consumption (or abstention) into meaningful acts that become spiritually powerful. Yet, there are a myriad of other food practices (often marked as 'ritual') that are regularly censured by those concerned with proper religious action and a fidelity to textual tradition (Severi 2002). Differentiating between ritual and ritual-like practices, as well as between the sublime and the banal (between the offering of ritual food and the mere cooking of food), raise crucial questions about what constitutes religious piety and the actual labour required to perform any rite.

While most rituals are assumed to be textually based, in fact ritual practice is routinely contrasted with doctrinal knowledge, with a presumed hierarchy between the 'knowing' and the 'doing'. The religious hierarchy maps onto other (social) hierarchies, so that rituals, and knowledge of ritual practice, are disproportionately a part of the world of women – passed down generationally through the memory of practice rather than the reading of text. Ritual is shaped by familial traditions and local custom, and thus its status is always already suspect. For many reformers of religion, anything categorized as ritual is seen to be inherently unthinking or rote – a symptom of degraded religious practice.

A feminist analysis of ritual and food might begin, then, with the insistence that ritual food practices are and must be considered a part of religious knowledge and seen as equal to theological knowledge. We should accord the ritual practices of women the same epistemic status as the interpretation of religious texts by (male) scholars (Dalmiya and Alcoff 1993). This might allow for the expansion of what constitutes religious practice, such that the cooking of certain ritual foods (and knowledge of how best to cook them or which ones are customarily prepared) would itself be a form of religious knowledge.

Drawing from a very early essay by the feminist writer and educator Rokeya Sakhawat Hossain (1880–1932), I explore the difficulty of any easy alignment of feminism and the place of ritual practice and knowledge. 'Rashana Puja' ('The worship of taste') extends Rokeya's analysis of oppressively patriarchal (putatively religious) customs into the arena of ritual practice. She suggests that the emphasis of Indian society on food preparation and consumption has effectively led to the religious and spiritual diminution of Muslims – particularly Muslim women. The essay, written in anticipation of Ramadan in 1904, provocatively uses the concept of puja (Hindu religious worship) to skewer the excessive cooking, eating and socializing that Rokeya feels has come to characterize the month. It uses for humorous effect and political critique the blurring of ritual-like behaviour and ritual so that the preparation of elaborate meals during Ramadan becomes a form of puja – an idolatrous devotion to an object.

Food is an especially important place to see the gendered aspects of ritual practice because, as Tanika Sarkar (1999: 253) notes, '[food] signified far more than its immediate meaning: it was love, it was womanliness, it was the metaphor for family life'. Yet, the natural relationship between cooking and feminine goodness allows the proliferation of insidious forms of patriarchal oppression. Rokeya is uninterested in validating women's knowledge of ritual food preparation and sees the devotion (puja) to food as precluding women from ever gaining true religious equality with their male counterparts. The worship of food stands in the way of the worship of God; it is impious.

Rokeya's writing makes visible the labour of mothers, sisters and wives in the preparation of ritual food in ways that are unique in critical commentaries on Ramadan. This may appear paradoxical, considering her own elite social position made it unlikely that she ever prepared any food (ritual or otherwise). But her critique springs from her radical perspective on the ways that men *and* women were complicit in the oppression of women – in this case through their shared devotion to the preparation of elaborate iftar meals (the meal to break the fast of Ramadan). In focusing on the food preparations during Ramadan, Rokeya effectively politicizes the kitchen, a part of the *antahpur* (the women's part of the house), and brings it into a larger discussion of the ways women are included in or excluded from religious piety. As she reminds her readers, the laborious aspects of cooking disproportionately affect women and take place in windowless, smoky rooms in which no religious knowledge is allowed to enter. Women must learn to refuse the time, labour and pride involved in food preparation; food should be about nourishment, not aesthetics, intimacy or femininity. Exalting food as a primary avenue for affective and aesthetic pleasure, literally *rashana* or taste, ensures that women can never claim the time or space to properly read, contemplate or pray during Ramadan. They remain forever unequal as Muslims – trapped in the kitchen preparing meals.

The category of reform, and the description of historical actors as reformers, is ubiquitous in nineteenth- and twentieth-century Indian history (and historiography). While the term 'reform' is used to define a range of movements aimed at cultural transformation, J. Barton Scott (2016: 91) reminds us of its religious origins: '[Reform] draw[s] on the notion of the Reformation (as part of the Enlightenment) as a critical attitude, governed through reason, towards forms of (priestly or transcendental) authority.' While religious and social reform is routinely collapsed by reformers and scholars alike, there is nonetheless a clear distinction between those men who could claim the mantle of religious reform (Keshab Chanda Sen, Dayananda Saraswati and others) and the many women who were seen as working towards 'social' upliftment.

Rokeya is largely seen, like most women, as a social reformer (connected to causes like women's education), and her writing fits into the model offered by Scott: she consistently invokes reason and science and can be downright hostile towards religious authority (referring to authority figures in 'Rashana Puja' as 'this country's Muslims ... crying "dharma, dharma"') (Hossain 1973a: 255). Yet, I would argue that she also offers a religious critique, a practice that she recognizes will elicit the hostility of certain parts of the Muslim community (Sarkar 2017: 33). Rokeya directly addresses the tradition of religious interpretation dominated by men, therefore serving the interests of men. Her essays offer alternate *religious* interpretations aimed at ensuring the religious equality of all Muslims. She persists in repudiating not only contemporary religious practices (and a call for a return to earlier authentic customs, closer to those of the Prophet) but also ones initiated by people who have claimed the mantle of true Islam:

> My sisters, you see for yourself that these religious books are nothing but rules fabricated by men. The ancient sages have said all these things. Had there been a woman sage you might have seen the opposite. Some might say, 'Why bring in religion when talking of social customs?' I would say, 'It is "religion" that has made the chains of our slavery stronger and stronger. Men are lording it over women in the name of "religion". So I have been forced to bring religion in. Let the god-fearing and the pious forgive me. (Hossain 2015a: 30–1)

Rokeya is careful to distinguish between her religious sensibilities (as a Muslim) and the religious ritual practices and interpretation with which she disagrees. Her first published essay, a retelling of the story of Muharram ('Pipasha' or thirst), and a later essay about Eid (Eid Sammelan or 'The Gathering for Eid') explore the universal spirit that animates Muslim rituals of grief and fellowship, even as she denounces the overly celebratory Muharram processions or festivities of Eid.

What distinguished Rokeya's voice from those of other progressives arguing for religious reform was that she connected the problem of 'excess' in religious ritual (excessive zeal, excessive consumption) with the reproduction and reinforcement of gender hierarchy. Such a political critique, for Rokeya, was firmly grounded in the fundamental equality of religious belief promised by Islam to women and men. In 'Rashana Puja', Rokeya brings to bear her feminist religious critique of the ritual fasting for Ramadan. Her interest in returning her fellow Muslims to a more authentic and simpler practice is distinguished by her commitment to redefining ritual in ways that align with notions of what constitutes a just society for women and men. Through a criticism of the excessively lengthy process of preparation and consumption of food, she asks what changes would be required to ensure that Muslim women be given the same opportunities for pious introspection as Muslim men. Moreover, how might that goal require a transformation of ordinary spaces, such as the kitchen, and ordinary practices, such as cooking?

Food for thought

Rokeya published continually throughout her life and alongside writing advocated for and established a school for Muslim girls in Kolkata (the Sakhawat Memorial Girls' School, which continues under the aegis of the West Bengal government). She launched her career by writing for newly established liberal Bengali journals which wanted to include more women's voices in their publications. In the journal *Nabanoor* ('New light'), for instance, a call was put out to its women readers 'to participate in our literary activities and contribute to the glow of *Nabanoor*'. This effort, particularly for those women who remained in the *antahpur*, would simply be an extension of their maternal duties – 'They nurture us with their motherly care, sisterly affection and tender wifely love. Will they not similarly assist us in our literary efforts to lead the nation to greater development?' (qtd in Azim and Hasan 2014: 35). *Nabanoor* invited not just readers but also new writers to participate in the efflorescence of publishing opportunities in the early twentieth century.[1] Yet, even as one of the most progressive proponents of women's literary production, *Nabanoor* reveals women's writing as necessarily delimited; its purpose was to 'assist' in the cultural development of the nation, through critique or through praise. Deploying a gendered metaphor of writing as a form of familial care, the publishers of *Nabanoor* framed the acceptable ways in which women could (and should) approach writing.

Rokeya, who published a number of pieces in *Nabanoor* (including 'Rashana Puja'), consistently refused the frame of writing as a form of wifely, motherly or sisterly care. She did this by adopting an intentionally ironic voice. The ironic mode depended in part on Rokeya being able to speak to a discursive community which would be able to understand the intended meanings of her essays – a community constituted by the expansion of vernacular language publications. The ironic mode allowed Rokeya to draw attention to hierarchy and, as Nancy Walker has observed, to 'appreciate the socially constructed nature of certain forms of gendered expectations' (Nancy Walker, qtd in Hutcheon 1994: 32).

Although she may have rejected the 'nurturing' model of writing, Rokeya embraced the notion of writing as a means to 'develop' her community and the larger nation. She shared with her contemporaries a certain modernist orientation towards questions of culture and religion, but 'even the progressive men of the time failed to understand the import of her writings' (Akhtar and Bhowmik 1998: 3). So, while she saw the preparation and consumption of food as symptomatic of a more general problem of cultural excess, she pitched her critique in such a way that it demanded the dismantling rather than merely the reform of the *antahpur*. For her, the kitchen (typically located in the 'women's quarters') represented the continued influence of certain feudal (non-modern) pathologies.

For Rokeya, as for many other 'shurafa' Muslims (those employed by the colonial state – Rokeya's husband was a deputy magistrate), the group that best exemplified such pathological excess was the Muslim aristocracy, which had been displaced in the new colonial economy and state but which seemed wholly unaware of its degraded status. For instance, in the first part of 'Rashana Puja', she describes a typical 'kulin' (here referring to an aristocratic rather than a Brahminical) household that lives in a state of impoverishment and yet refuses to give up its (backward) cultural practices – chief among these being the household's aesthetics of food, its *rashana*, which insists on lavish and rich meal preparations. Through the figure of the 'deputy collector', who in this case represents not the colonial state but a particular reformist and modernizing figure, we are given a glimpse into the household – its lack of furnishings, the cobwebs hanging everywhere and finally the *antahpur*.

Because the (male) deputy collector would have no access to the *antahpur*, and therefore no access to the kitchen, the essay writer makes it visible for (all) readers. She guides the reader to a doorway which is 'malodourous' because of the fowl that are kept nearby. In contrast, once inside the kitchen, one is assailed by the fragrance of rose water and vegetables being cut. Such smells are enough to make a Brahmin tear off his sacred thread (Hossain 1973a: 251). Rokeya's critique works through paradox – in this case, the incongruity between the 'malodourous' outside space of the kitchen and the fragrance of the food being prepared inside, whose seduction is so great that it is enough to make a Brahmin 'tear off his sacred thread'.[2]

The initial contrast turns out not to be such a great one after all, as both the filth outside and the (aesthetic) decadence inside are symptoms of a degraded community, one which continues to maintain aristocratic excess (even in the face of increasing poverty) and a disregard for modern hygiene. The modern Muslim family should ensure the hygiene of space and body and be aware of the need for restraint in both the preparation and consumption of food. A part of the self-definition of modern Muslims (many employed by the colonial government or invested in the colonial economy) would be to improve not just the public world of Muslim men but also the private, 'inner' world of women.

Yet, such an analysis does not exhaust how we might understand Rokeya's observations. Specifically, her description of the conditions of the aristocratic kitchen echoes her critique of the politics of the private sphere of women. The kitchen is in the *antahpur* and as such is unseen by outside men (like the deputy collector). This invisibility allows it to remain a space of darkness, ill-health and disease. Rather than seeing it as (potentially) a place of autonomy (where heavenly dishes are being created), Rokeya sees it as a place where 'someone' has to grind, cut and stuff vegetables, grains and other raw food products, while others who inhabit the outside world – the deputy collector, or the head of the household, or even the Brahmin – are allowed to consume the fruit of that labour. For Rokeya, the kitchen (like the rest of the *antahpur*) is a place of darkness, filth and endless labour. Unlike some who might take pride in the practice of cooking and feeding their families (the 'good housewives' or *sugrihinis*), for Rokeya the best thing that could happen to the kitchen is for it to be utterly transformed.

We are given a glimpse of this utopian kitchen in *Sultana's Dream*, Rokeya's best-known text (and because of its inclusion in many feminist anthologies, one of the best-known feminist texts from India). Among the pleasures of Ladyland, a land where women (and science and peace) reign, Sultana notes with wonder the kitchen in which Sister Sara, her guide, takes her. The kitchen remains a part of the *mardana* (the part of the home where men are engaged in cooking, cleaning and so on, the inverse of the *antahpur* and purdah), but it is wholly reconfigured.

> The kitchen was situated in a beautiful vegetable garden … I found no smoke nor was there a chimney in the kitchen – it was clean and bright; the windows were decorated with flower garlands. There was no sign of coal or fire. 'How do you cook?' I asked. 'With solar heat' … And she cooked something then and there to show me the process. (Hossain 1993)

The utopian kitchen is part garden and part laboratory (a recognizably contemporary vision). What Rokeya is most concerned with is the new scientific approach to cooking – not what is cooked. Cooking must be seen as knowledge – it is the knowledge of solar heat and gardening that Rokeya's kitchen celebrates. What is actually cooked is irrelevant – in fact, we are never told what Sultana is given to eat. Here Rokeya transforms cooking, a 'woman's practice', into science, a domain of modern 'masculine' knowledge. Such a move seems to repudiate the sources of women's knowledge (learning to put saffron into the *ketaki* flower), even as it simultaneously liberates them from the darkness and labour of cooking.

In her essay 'Ardhangi' ('The better half'), Rokeya (1973b: 43) notes, 'From what I have written here about cooking and needlework, let no one think that

I am against these two accomplishments.' In fact, such accomplishments are exactly what Rokeya is against – the insidiousness of cooking is not the fact that it is a necessity but that women and men see it as an art, an 'accomplishment'. The gendered relationship of women with food is asymmetrical. A woman's ability to prepare food and thus feed others demonstrates her generosity and care, as well as her creativity and skill. While such feminine virtues are closely aligned with cooking, women are meant generally to eschew the actual consumption of food (which might demonstrate a lack of control or selfishness on their part).

The accomplishment of cooking – of making the *paratha* or *korma* that smells like heaven – is not unlike the ornaments that married women wear, ornaments that are in fact shackles used to imprison them. The notion that cooking is an accomplishment and that therefore one should spend as much time as possible in the kitchen ensures that women remain captive. Rokeya (1973a: 253) goes on to exhort, 'Life should not be limited within the four walls of the kitchen.' Like the jewellery women receive during marriage, this is (paradoxically) a captivity that women embrace and celebrate, rather than reject.

Metaphors of excess and restraint

'Rashana Puja', which appeared in *Nabanoor* in November 1904 (Bengali date: Agrahain, 1311), has an intentionally provocative title. Rokeya employs the metaphor of the puja – the Hindu practice of a devotional offering to god – to reproach her fellow Muslims. Here the word 'puja' denotes both a practice that is idolatrous and a particular kind of excess. That is, Rokeya seems to draw upon the distinctiveness of Islam as non-idolatrous (in contrast to other South Asian religions, including Zoroastrianism and Jainism) as well as referencing the colloquial sense of the word 'puja'; for instance, being a gourmand is mocked as one who does 'a puja for the appetite'.

Ritual fasting during the month of Ramadan is meant to mark the revelation of the Qur'an to the Prophet Muhammad. The rituals of the Ramadan fast are both individual (in terms of obligation) and collective (in actual practice) and are marked by fasting during the daylight hours and a ritual breaking of the fast through the iftar meal. While there are certainly a range of practices among Muslims the world over that relate to Ramadan, the component of fasting and collective eating remains central to all. But it is puja, rather than piety, that Rokeya feels marks the contemporary celebration of Ramadan. Connecting puja to rashana – whose meaning ranges from the physical organ of the tongue to the idea of taste (related to food) or the palate – already indicates the type of degeneracy that Rokeya intends to skewer. The essay is ostensibly about food, but food is merely a symptom of a more general moral and religious decay.

'Rashana Puja' begins by noting that 'in many societies people worship many things, some worship fire, some worship the sun and the moon, some worship inanimate idols, etc. Only devout Muslims do not worship anything except the Supreme God. But Indian Muslim society also does rashana puja. If I called them devotees of rashana, it would not be improper' (Hossain 1973a: 253). Rokeya thus begins by drawing attention to what is distinctive in the ways that Muslims – in contrast to their idolatrous Hindu, Zoroastrian and other neighbours – worship. The essay appears to begin in a fairly standard manner, but we soon learn that 'Indian' (Bharatbharsha) Muslims are in fact also idolatrous – but the object of their (religious) devotion is the palate. The puja of the palate is then compared to other kinds of Indian Muslim practices that similarly bear a resemblance to Hindu practices. In particular, the practice of rashana puja is akin to the regular visits that Muslims make to the dargah (a religious shrine built over a grave) of a pir (religious master or guide) to address specific (mundane) problems. Such visits, Rokeya suggests, are no different than when Hindus do darshan at the mandir (the auspicious sight of the deity in the temple). Visiting a dargah, like doing darshan at a mandir, is fundamentally an act of idolatry whose purpose is immediate and instrumental – curing an illness, fertility and so on. Similarly, the Indian Muslim relationship to food is one of Hindu-like devotion – a wholly impious and un-Islamic practice.

The timing of 'Rashana Puja', in November 1904, just before Ramadan, is not incidental to its meaning and points to one of the less-remarked-upon ways in which new forms of print media (the monthly journal) paralleled the ritual calendar. Essays in Bengali journals such as *Nabanoor* or *Dhumketu* were written to coincide with ritual periods – Muharram, Durga Puja and others. In anticipation of the ritual period, Rokeya points out to her readers the (ritual) paradox at the heart of Ramadan, one that she uses to ironic effect in her essay. While one might assume that the Ramadan fast would be constituted by the absence of food, in fact the month is 'characterized by the great significance attached to the sharing of food' all over the Muslim world (Hellman 2006: 94). Thus, both the fast and the iftar meal are carried out with an elaborate set of customs and traditions in each locality. Just as there are rules about fasting and modes of expected behaviour, Ramadan is also a time when particular kinds of food are served, and families and communities are expected to uphold certain expectations of hospitality and generosity. The paradoxical twinning of fasting and feasting exemplifies what Rokeya diagnoses as a more general problem of piety among her Bengali Muslim compatriots.

In Rokeya's view, Muslims spend an inordinate amount of time during Ramadan focusing on food. In the process they not only subvert the centrality of the fast as a means to piety but seem to actually *worship* food. Rather than 'desisting from household work' and fasting with a 'pure heart', women spend the majority of their time preparing for the iftar meal. The problem thus is not merely one of excess (though that is certainly a problem); it is the symbolic subversion of religious practice and devotion itself. As Rokeya (1973a: 255) notes: 'Our ancestors used to eat a little fruit or roti and vegetable for evening iftar. What they would eat at night would not concern them during the day.' Rokeya contrasts this to contemporary Bengali Muslims who proclaim their religiosity (crying 'dharma, dharma') and yet spend most of Ramadan inviting others to eat and anticipating the meal, ensuring that for them Ramadan is spent forgetting, rather than contemplating God. The intent of *roza* is lost; the paradox, as Rokeya notes, is that 'indirectly, in the name of roza (fasting), we do a magnificent rashana puja' (255).

The cooking behind the eating

Ritual practice is a common object of critique among religious reformers. Rituals are seen as the locus of local customs and 'backward' practices. The rituals around Ramadan are no exception, and across the Muslim world one can still find contemporary commentators echoing the sentiments expressed in 'Rashana Puja'. In her ethnography of the contemporary Egyptian mosque movement, Saba Mahmood (2005: 49) interviews a woman, Fatma, who offers an extended criticism of the excess of festivities during Ramadan:

> Fatma continued: 'So you know what happens during Ramadan in Cairo. You must have heard the popular saying in colloquial Arabic that the first third of Ramadan is cookies ... Where is the worship in this saying? ... The entire society seems to be focused on preparing food all day long and festivities in the evenings, all of which are contrary to the real meaning and spirit of Ramadan.'

The women involved in the mosque movement in Egypt insisted that fasting is not simply the abstention from food, but an opportunity to train oneself in the 'virtues' of piety and restraint. Mahmood further notes that while there may be a long tradition of interpretation that distinguished between customary and religious practices, in part what marks the contemporary (versus the classical) critique is that what was 'once the provenance of male religious scholars [is] now debated by ordinary women' (55).

In the early twentieth century, Rokeya Hossain was at the forefront of the democratizing of religious interpretation (as were some of her very brave contemporaries). Rather than a retreat from religion, the essays being published in the new vernacular press offered women like Rokeya the opportunity to debate religious ritual and practice. Yet, this came at great cost. Rokeya faced public hostility, and her essays were regularly censured, including the essay quoted earlier in which she pointed out the gendered nature of the religious interpretation offered by religious 'sages'.

But even within the larger framework of the democratizing of religious knowledge and interpretation in the twentieth century, Rokeya's perspective remains distinct. Here it is worth comparing 'Rashana Puja' to another text published almost simultaneously, aimed at instructing women in piety: Maulana Ashraf Ali Thanvi's *Bihishti Zewar* (1905). In *Bihishti Zewar*, 'Thanawi and his fellow reformist 'ulama sought to do nothing less than bring women into the high standards of Islamic conformity that had been the purview of educated religious men' (Metcalf 1990: 7). Thanvi was concerned that Muslim women had no real knowledge of shariat norms and were instead prone to various superstitious beliefs, practices and customs. The *Bihishti Zewar* offered women the same religious education that would be expected of Muslim men, but it also included instructions on maintaining a household and appropriately respectable (female) comportment. Thus, while Thanvi acknowledges that it is impious to take pride in preparing special foods on Ramadan – 'to consider as credit something that is not declared a matter of credit by the *shari'at* is a sin in itself. So you must also give this up' (Metcalf 1990: 156) – he has little to say about the actual cooking of the food. Such an orientation towards both the excessive festivities and the virtues of the fast echoes Rokeya's essay in which she reminds us: 'Roza (fasting) teaches us restraint.' She emphasizes this aspect of Ramadan by turning to the place of the fast in other religions: 'The vows of roza (upabosh) teach us restraint … For this reason, it is seen that 'in almost all the world religions, some form of a vow of fasting is kept' (Hossain 1973a: 254). It is worth noting that Rokeya uses both the term *roza*, which refers specifically to a Muslim fast, and *upabosh*, a Bengali word that is also used by Hindus. But unlike the example of the dargah-mandir, the *upabosh* is not used to mock a 'Hinduized' practice but rather to suggest a shared religious framework. The interchangeability reinforces the notion of fasting as an inherently universal practice and value of restraint and humility.

What is largely absent from the criticisms of the 'feasting' (rather than fasting) that characterize Ramadan in Thanvi's work, as well as from the kind of interpretation offered by the women in the Islamist movements, is attention to the labour of cooking that lies behind the excessive consumption. The spiritual and health problems associated with overeating during Ramadan are catalogued in Thanvi's text and by Mahmood's interview subjects. But they are both silent about the specifically gendered problem of the unnecessary time and work involved in cooking the special foods eaten during Ramadan. In contrast, Rokeya Hossain's criticism of the excess of Ramadan is informed by an explicitly feminist critique of the problem of women's unpaid labour – a labour that ensures their unequal access to spiritual and pious reflection and guidance.

Rokeya sees the food practices of Ramadan as a particular problem for women, upon whose shoulders (and in whose kitchens) this burden is disproportionately placed. Blurring the line between 'ritual' activity and ritual-like activity, she notes that the puja (or devotion) to taste then demands an extensive amount of work to prepare the elaborate meals with which families break their fast, the iftar. This work falls disproportionately on women and has a negative impact on their religious practice. 'Women spend all their time preparing for this puja. They have no opportunity to pay attention to anything else. The whole day and half the night is spent worrying about their cooking. Later, in sleep, they dream, "Oh no! The sugar syrup for the murabba has burned!"' (Hossain 1973a: 255). The fact that this is a puja connected to the palate – to food – is in part why Rokeya has decided to single it out among other non-Islamic practices. Rokeya argues that the downfall of Bengali society is necessarily connected to this insistence that women labour in the kitchen in such a way that it is not merely about food preparation but takes on an aspect of devotional practice – a puja whose object is the god of taste/the palate. This type of puja, like other rituals, requires labour, time and attention. Ritualizing the cooking of food traps women in an endless cycle where their waking and dreaming thoughts are about the best ways to prepare food. It transforms the ritual time of Ramadan into a time of cooking rather than a time of contemplation and crowds out the possibility of any other kind of thinking, or any other object of devotion.

Rokeya (1973a: 253) writes:

> We spend our whole lives doing rashana puja. It is no exaggeration to say that we have no spiritual lives. We know nothing of acquiring knowledge, only a little

> needlework and training in cooking is our education. Knowing how to make 500 types of pickles and chutneys, 400 types of murabba are all one needs to know to be considered a good housewife [*sugrihini*]. Women begin their lives in cooking and end it having known only the life of a cook (*baburchi-jiban lila*). Ordinarily the ultimate limit of our lives is to learn to cook delicious food and to wear many kinds of [wedding?] ornaments.

It is important to note the 'we' here – elsewhere in the essay she addresses Bengali Muslims, at times she seems to be addressing Indians at large, but in this section she is addressing Muslim women. The expectation of elaborate dishes at Ramadan is not only a problem because it defiles the spirit and meaning of Ramadan, but it is part of a larger set of patriarchal practices that maintain the inequality of (Muslim) women in society. The laborious work of cooking during Ramadan (at a time when the women themselves are fasting) points to yet another example of women's limited horizons – specifically that they are educated to do little more than cook, sew and wear jewellery. The problem of limited horizons, in this case, has serious implications for women's piety and thus for their spiritual equality.

To fast while one's mind is otherwise occupied by the kinds of chutneys to cook and whether the sugar will burn is not to do roza. It makes fasting 'ritual-like' rather than a ritual which, when correctly performed, offers the possibility of self-transformation. For Rokeya, true fasting involves restraint (from cooking), humility and contemplation (of God). None of this is possible when women are expected to have, and then claim as an accomplishment, the ability to cook elaborate meals of korma, paratha and murabba. If we use as models our Muslim ancestors, suggests Rokeya, we can refashion not just our ritual practice but our everyday lives such that they are more closely aligned with the true virtues taught by Islam. And among those virtues, she argues, is the virtue of seeing both men and women as worthy of having the time, during Ramadan, to read the Qur'an, pray and contemplate God. That is, to eschew the rashana puja, the idolatrous worship of food, that threatens to eclipse the practice of religious piety.

For Rokeya, a celebratory orientation towards the preparation of food reflects women's perpetuation of their own bondage and constrained lives. The kitchen and cooking are places of darkness and degradation where women are kept purposefully separate and submissive. It is worth considering the term she uses: *baburchi-jiban lila*. The sentence begins with the act of cooking (*radhna*), but ends with cooking as an identity – a *baburchi* (a professional cook). But in this case it is not even a professional identity – to emphasize the irony of the situation, Rokeya describes this as a form of *jiban lila* or the creative play of life. The putative creativity of cooking (by knowing how to make five hundred chutneys) is a chimera, an illusion perpetuated by a system that ensures that women remain confined within the four walls of the kitchen. The time and labour spent in preparing food not only leads to overconsumption and a myriad of health problems, but also wastes women's spiritual energy. Rokeya is brutal in her disdain for cooking and eating, for the rashana puja to which Indian Muslim society has become enthralled, and in which she finds nothing but evidence of a degraded spirituality.

The good housewife: the domestication of Rokeya's critique

In 1905, Rokeya Hossain decided to collect and publish as a book a collection of the essays she had written for a number of different Bengali journals, such as *Mahila, Nabanoor* and *Saogat*. She titled this collection *Motichur*.[3] While she left out 'Rashana Puja' from the collection, she included an essay titled 'Sugrihini' ('The good housewife'). As the title suggests, the essay was a relatively conventional argument about the importance of education in helping cultivate 'good' (i.e. modern) housewifely skills. The praise of 'the good housewife' seems quite at odds with much of Rokeya's other writing. She addresses this contradiction early on: 'Anyway, if women do not understand my words about spiritual equality then let us not talk about high ambitions or any elevated things at all. I will ask today: "What is your aim in life?" Probably you will reply in unison: "To be a good housewife"' (Hossain 2015b: 55).

From this point on, she explains why educating girls in subjects such as botany and chemistry are critical in order to develop the skills of cooking, needlework, gardening and so on that any good housewife will eventually need. She has wholly discarded the kinds of arguments about 'spiritual equality' that animated 'Rashana Puja', choosing instead to speak to the (mundane) ambitions of her readers – to be a *sugrihini*.

In many of her writings, Rokeya complained that she was constantly misunderstood – her irony and sarcasm misapprehended. In 'Sugrihini', we sense this frustration. The demand for spiritual equality that undergirds 'Rashana Puja' does not seem to resonate with her readers. Nor does her earlier mockery of the 'good housewife', who knows only how to make murabba and chutney as she prepares for Ramadan. Certain components remain the same between the two essays: the problem of unhygienic kitchens and cooking techniques and the dangers of overeating and unhealthy foods. These earthly concerns require an earthly education: 'People do not entrust their children to inefficient nurses: likewise, is it proper to entrust the cooking of an entire family to an inefficient cook?' (Hossain 2015b: 59). It is efficiency, rather than piety, that undergirds education.

Sonia Amin (1996: 110) has suggested that the contradictions in Rokeya's writing (in this case, mocking women's obsession with cooking on the one hand, and later insisting on modern education as the means to make women better cooks on the other) can be explained by her more pragmatic aspirations such as when she 'campaigned for her school, Rokeya upheld domestic ideology and emphasized the household skills and training'. Moreover, her essay on the good housewife was very much in keeping with the arguments put forward by other Muslim women reformers, like Sultan Nawab Jahan Begum, '[who] sought to professionalize the household tasks that women performed by imbuing them with a scientific aspect that would elevate their prestige' (Lambert-Hurley 2007: 123). In 'Sugrihini', the good Muslim girl goes to school to become a good housewife – her 'ultimate aim'. It is not spiritual (or temporal) equality but the needs of the modern household that justify giving women the time and space for education.

The woman as manager of the household – efficient cook, nursemaid, charming companion for her husband – eclipsed the other possibilities Rokeya had raised in 'Rashana Puja', including being a pious Muslim subject. It is difficult not to read a certain self-censoring in her work. This is also how Rokeya Hossain is read and celebrated: as an advocate for modern girls' education. Rokeya's genuine exploration of questions of ritual and piety and their significance for modern Muslim women and men has been ignored. This impoverishes not only how we apprehend Rokeya Hossain as a thinker but also how we understand the complexity of twentieth-century ideas of Islamic ritual and practice. Even in a recent essay by Firdous Azim and Perween Hasan (2014: 37), the astute analysis the two authors bring to bear on the changing discourse on gender among Bengali Muslim women disappears when they discuss Rokeya's use of religious language: 'The use of terms such as "God-given" or "doors of heaven" keep the religious discourse intact, even when she criticizes the limitations imposed on women.' Their assumption here is that Rokeya's religiosity is a practical choice to ensure that her real criticism (the limitations imposed on women) will be palatable to her readers. In fact, as I have tried to show, it was her demand for religious equality and her efforts at religious interpretation that engendered the most significant hostility towards her. Feminist scholars compound this insult by doing the same, that is, by marginalizing Rokeya as a serious thinker of religion in the twentieth century.

I will end by quoting the poignant questions with which Rokeya (1973a: 257) leaves her readers: 'When will Muslims become human? When will they stop being devoted to the appetite (rashana) and instead devote themselves to God?'

Notes

1 Unlike in Europe, the relatively late development of prose forms of Bengali meant that 'women [in Bengal] did not start writing too long after men had done so' (Sarkar 1999: 7). While there were certainly religious and social prohibitions on women learning to read and write among many Hindus and Muslims, the emergence of new forms of writing coincided with a reformist interest in remodelling a whole range of cultural and social practices – including the place (and role) of women in Bengali society.

2 Itself a humorous observation since a Brahmin would never find himself in the kitchen of a Muslim household and would have to risk his caste status (thus the tearing off of the sacred thread) to eat.

3 'Sugrihini' was originally published in *Nabanoor*, Baishakh 1311 (April 1904).

References

Akhtar, Shaheen, and Moushumi Bhowmik (eds). 1998. *Women in Concert: An Anthology of Bengali Muslim Women's Writings, 1904–1928*. Kolkata: Stree.

Amin, Sonia. 1996. *World of Muslim Women*. Leiden: Brill.

Azim, Firdous, and Perween Hasan. 2014. 'Constructions of Gender in the Late Nineteenth and Early Twentieth Century in Muslim Bengal'. In Leela Fernandes (ed.), *Routledge Handbook of Gender in South Asia*. London: Routledge, 28–40.

Dalmiya, Vrinda, and Linda Alcoff. 1993. 'Are "Old Wives' Tales" Justified?' In Linda Alcoff and Elizabeth Potter (eds), *Feminist Epistemologies*. New York: Routledge, 217–44.

Hellman, Jorgen. 2006. *Ritual Fasting on West Java*. Gotenburg, Sweden: Gotenburg Studies in Social Anthropology.

Hossain, Rokeya. 1973a. 'Rashana Puja'. In Abdul Qadir (ed.), *Rokeya Rachanabali*. Dhaka: Bangla Academy.

Hossain, Rokeya. 1973b. 'Ardhangi'. In Abdul Qadir (ed.), *Rokeya Rachanabali*. Dhaka: Bangla Academy.

Hossain, Rokeya. 1993. *Sultana's Dream*. In Roushan Jahan (trans. and ed.), *Rokeya Sakhawat Hossain: Sultana's Dream, a Feminist Utopia and Selections from the Secluded Ones*. New York: The Feminist Press.

Hossain, Rokeya. 2015a. 'The Degradation of Women'. In Ratri Ray and Prantosh Bandhyopadhyay (trans.), *Motichur: Sultana's Dreams and Other Writings of Rokeya Sakhawat Hossain*. New Delhi: Oxford University Press.

Hossain, Rokeya. 2015b. 'Sugrihini'. In *Motichur: Sultana's Dreams and Other Writings of Rokeya Sakhawat Hossain*, trans. Ratri Ray and Prantosh Bandhyopadhyay. New Delhi: Oxford University Press, 55.

Hutcheon, Linda. 1994. *Irony's Edge: The Theory and Politics of Irony*. New York: Routledge.

Jahan, Roushan (ed.). 1988. *Rokeya Sakhawat Hossain: Sultana's Dream, A Feminist Utopia and Selections from the Secluded Ones*. New York: The Feminist Press.

Kreinath, Jens, Jan Snoek and Michael Strausberg (eds). 2006. *Theorizing Ritual: Issues, Topics, Approaches, Concepts*. Leiden: Brill.

Lambert-Hurley, Siobhan. 2007. *Muslim Women, Reform and Princely Patronage: Nawab Sultan Jahan Begum of Bhopal*. New York: Routledge.

Mahmood, Saba. 2005. *Politics of Piety: The Islamic Revival and the Feminist Subject*. Princeton, NJ: Princeton University Press.

Metcalf, Barbara Daly. 1990. *Perfecting Women: Mawlana Ashraf 'Ali Thanawi's* Bihishti Zewar, *a Partial Translation with Commentary*. Berkeley: University of California Press.

Qadir, Abdul (ed.). 1975. *Rokeya Rachanabali*. Dhaka: Bangla Academy.

Quayum, Mohammad A., and Mahmudul Hasan (eds). 2019. *A Feminist Foremother: Critical Essays on Rokeya Sakhawat Hossain*. Hyderabad: Orient Blackswan.

Reader, Ian. 'Cleaning Floors and Sweeping the Mind: Cleaning as a Ritual Process'. In Graham Harvey (ed.), *Ritual and Religious Belief: A Reader*. New York: Routledge.

Roy, Ratri, and Prantosh Bandhopadhyay (trans.). 2014. *Motichur: Sultana's Dream and Other Writings of Rokeya Sakhawat Hossain*. Delhi: Oxford University Press.

Sarkar, Mahua. 2017. "Rokeya Sakhawat Hossain and the Gender Debate among Muslim Intellectuals in late Colonial Bengal." In Mohammad A. Quayum and Mohammad Md. Mahmudul Hasan (eds), *A Feminist Foremother: Critical Essays on Rokeya Sakhawat Hossain*. Hyderabad: Orient Blackswan.

Sarkar, Tanika. 1999. *Words to Win: The Making of Amar Jiban, a Modern Autobiography*. Kolkata: Kali for Women.

Scott, J. Barton. 2016. *Spiritual Despots: Modern Hinduism and the Genealogies of Self-Rule*. Chicago: Chicago University Press.

Severi, Carlo. 2002. 'Memory, Reflexivity: Reflections on the Ritual Use of Language'. *Social Anthropology* 10(1): 23–40.

Snoek, Jan. 2006. *Theorizing Ritual: Issues, Topics, Approaches, Concepts*. Edited by Jens Kreinath, Jan Snoek and Michael Stausberg. Leiden: Brill.

3

Religious recipes: Culinary Motherlines of feasts and fasts in India

Sucharita Sarkar

Introduction: the kitchen and the prayer room

In Hindu thought, there has always been an essential and intimate connection between food and divinity, as 'the production and consumption of food are part of a single cycle of transactions with the gods' (Appadurai 1981: 496). Within the geography of the traditional Hindu home, this inseparability of food and divinity is often reflected in the positioning of the kitchen and the prayer room close to each other. Food scholar K. T. Achaya (1994: 64) writes: 'The domestic hearth in a Hindu home was considered an area of high purity, even of sanctity. In fact, it was set up adjacent to the area of worship.' The household kitchen has traditionally been the domain of women. By extension, even the prayer room and the practice of domestic worship are primarily under the control of women.

Observing the analogies between the kitchen and the temple – both being spaces of ritual purity where one traditionally enters freshly bathed and barefoot and where menstruating women are disallowed – Pika Ghosh (1995: 21) comments that 'the preparation of food is regarded as an act of worship similar to rituals performed by a priest'. Logically, it may thus be assumed that women within the domestic sphere would have the same kind of authority and responsibility that priests have in the sphere of public worship. Yet, there is no such simple correlation between women's control of the domestic sphere and their position within (and outside) it. The responsibilities of the kitchen and the prayer room are entrusted to women for multiple reasons, one of these being the need 'to keep the family in good favour with the divine powers' (Bose 2010: 137). Although women's roles in the kitchen and the prayer room are connected to, and commensurate with, their position and seniority as wives and mothers in the familial hierarchical structure, these roles are structured upon the patriarchal ideal of the self-sacrificing mother devoted to the physical, cultural and spiritual nurture of her family.

One important assumption of this glorified motherhood is the existence of an intergenerational womanly tradition where mothers/mothers-in-law teach their daughters/daughters-in-law their appropriate roles and responsibilities in the kitchen and the prayer room. This involves training them in the elaborate rituals, taboos and rules of propriety, purity and pollution that mark specific Hindu religious festivals and occasions. Jashodhara Bagchi (1993: 2216) critiques this feminine tradition where women remained 'the main vehicles of the ritual purity of the patrilineal transmission of the brahmanical patriarchy' within the family, where 'little girls were socialised into growing up as model wives'; she identifies the major religious rites and minor 'ritual practices of everyday living' – practices such as the keeping of *vrata*s (religious vows) which intermeshed the kitchen and prayer room – as the 'tools of this socialization'. Samjukta Gombrich Gupta (2000: 96) notes, 'From early girlhood, a woman is encouraged to take up several vows aimed at producing a desirable husband … prosperity of her marital home and family, a good harvest, long life for her husband and children.' The older female relatives performed the role of cultural bearers who encouraged their children, especially their daughters, to learn and practice traditional domestic rituals. Such training would also imply the continued existence of multigenerational households where the traditions of food and worship could be seamlessly – and obediently – passed down from grandmother to mother/mother-in-law to daughter/daughter-in-law, creating a willing and uninterrupted lineage of disciplined and docile female subjects who selflessly served the family but not themselves, inhabiting the kitchen and the prayer room as spaces *by* women but not *for* women.

There are two oppositions to this assumption. The first is that, even in orthodox Hindu homes, women have always been seeking and finding a measure of autonomy and creativity within the confines of their normative roles as the ideal mother/wife/daughter. The other is that a number of social, economic and cultural changes have altered the relational dynamics and the rites related to the passage of religious recipes from mothers to daughters. In this chapter, I will try to unpack the assumption of obedient transmission of rituals of food and piety between generations of women by deploying the concept of the Motherline. As defined by Jungian psychologist Naomi Lowinsky (1992: 1–4), the Motherline is 'a name for that pattern, … for the experience of continuity among women … as a central organizing principle' connecting a woman to her roots through sharing 'stories of female experience: physical, psychological, and historical … stories of the life cycles that link generations of women'. The Motherline – originally culturally located in African American mothering – represents 'ancestral memory' and 'traditional values': it empowers mother figures as 'cultural bearers and tradition keepers' and serves as maps of 'warning or encouragement' for the daughters (O'Reilly 2014: 109). The Motherline is a versatile theoretical concept used by motherhood scholars to theorize the mother–daughter relationship as a potential site for maternal and daughterly creative agency and communication, even within controlling patriarchal and patrilineal family structures. I will borrow and extend the concept of the Motherline to include the sharing of religious recipes and stories, redefining it as a consciously articulated, documented and transmitted culinary and cultural connection between foremothers, mothers and daughters in Indian Hindu families.

Whereas traditionally Motherlines have been orally transmitted, the gradual breakup of the multigenerational 'joint' families into scattered nuclear units; the growing number of women employed outside the home; the rise in urban and transnational migration and subsequent geographical distancing of family members; the changes in communication with the growth of social media; the opening up of markets under neoliberal economic policies; and the consequent globalization and modernization of culinary tastes and cultural practices have all interrupted the oral, local, intimate ways in which recipes and roles were transmitted from mothers to daughters. Under these changed circumstances, culinary narratives have emerged in which the religious food practices and recipes of mothers are retrieved, documented and disseminated by their daughters in print and on the web. The daughters' negotiations of religious recipes are often markedly different from their mothers', transforming their purposes, processes, outcome and significance. This chapter will explore these intergenerational continuities and changes in the transmission and reception of culinary Motherline knowledges.

In the Introduction to the *Oxford Anthology of South Asian Food Writing*, editors Thieme and Raja (2007: xl) comment: 'Conventionally, kitchens have been, and are, encoded as women's spaces, heavily gendered sites, but nevertheless locations that are open to multiple and potentially conflicting interpretations.' The gendered and multigenerational domestic spaces of the kitchen and the prayer room are sites where the politics of food and piety are played out – earlier often covertly and now increasingly overtly – through a complex and contested negotiation of subordination and self-assertion. Refusing to categorize cooking as either 'something imposed on women as a result of patriarchal ideology' or 'the basis for an "authentic" women's culture', Ashley et al. (2004: 138–9) suggest that we need to examine how the 'relationships between gender and cooking are a site of struggle and transformation in specific historical locations and power relations'. In this chapter, I will attempt a close reading of selected recipes and recollections of religious occasions from contemporary cookbooks and memoirs by Indian Hindu female authors, both in the subcontinent and in the diaspora. Hinduism scholars have noted that 'in the world of vrata stories, women seem to join in each other's lives without bothering about caste or class barriers' and have recorded instances of 'vrata stories in which Brahmin and cowherd women are great friends and observe the same vratas' (Gombrich Gupta 2000: 100). However, all the texts studied in this chapter are written by women belonging to privileged intersections of class, education and location, indicating that the opportunity to write and publish texts is, mostly, a classed prerogative, unlike the original, premodern, oral culture of *vrata* performance.

Although this chapter focuses exclusively on culinary transmissions from mothers to daughters, urban domestic culinary legacies are increasingly mediated between fathers and daughters or mothers and sons. In some of the texts studied here, daughters record how they learned to cook with 'intuitive' measures by observing their fathers; or they mention recipes – like 'the rice delicacy biriyani' – inherited from their fathers (Vishal 2016: 28; Basu 2010: 6). However, these paternal culinary legacies usually centre on secular food; popular domestic religious rituals such as *vrata*s, and associated fasts and foods, were almost exclusively the domain of women. Mandakranta Bose (2010: 138) notes that even in scripturally sanctioned religious events, it was the male priests and householders who participated in the 'core of the rituals', while women were relegated to assistants' roles, 'setting out materials, cooking sanctified food, serving priests and cleaning'. Hence, religious culinary Motherlines were – and continue to be – almost exclusively female transferences. The notion of a culinary Motherline is envisioned in Sandeepa Mukherjee Datta's (2013: 168–9) *Bong Mom's Cookbook*: 'In this journey I can also tell [my daughters] who they are, where they came from and where they belong. Through the parade of spices in my kitchen I can talk to them about my dida, their didun, their thammi – and I hope they will talk about me one day in a similar fashion, in their own warm kitchens.' In the following sections, I will attempt to investigate whether such ritualistic culinary Motherlines are empowering or oppressive to women, in the context of the changing roles of women in the private and public spheres and of the changing role of religion in women's lives.

Receiving recipes

Most scholars agree that the patriarchal domestic family structure where female ritual and culinary activities are situated is regulatory and oppressive to women, in spite of the larger role women perform in these activities. Arjun Appadurai (1981: 497–8) contends that women's control of the hearth is actually an indicator of their subordinate status in the family, as evidenced in the priority given to men while serving food even as they are disengaged from the labour of preparing it. Jasodhara Bagchi (1993: 2216) emphasizes that although *vrata*s impart a degree of autonomy to women, 'we must never lose sight of the fact that these rituals operate within the overarching governance of Brahmanism', which is characterized by the subjugation of women. Thus, female culinary and religious labour and agency were not commensurable with male-dominated familial power relations.

To perpetuate this paradoxical and disproportionate relationship between domestic labour and power, it was necessary to hierarchize and socialize women. Leela Dube (1988: 181) suggests that although women are not 'passive, unquestioning victims' of asymmetrically gendered ritual practices, 'Hindu rituals and practices set certain limits in terms of the dispositions they inculcate among women and the different kinship roles with varying status within the family'. Many of the writers studied in this chapter record memories of how, as children, they would observe the women in their families performing religious rituals and preparing specific religious recipes. As a gradual socializing step, they would sometimes be gently persuaded to follow the ritual practices by their elders. In her narration of the recipes related to the 'entirely feminine' and 'quaint' fertility ritual of 'Ritu or Itu Pujo' performed by unmarried women, Chitrita Banerji (1997: 126) writes that 'there were some attempts to induct me into this practice too'. These ritualistic familial occasions were 'major sources of the personality-formation of the girl child', initiating them into practices that perpetuated their own subordination (Bagchi 1993: 2216). Mandakranta Bose (2010: 140) opines that *vrata*s were the vehicle through which 'women are taught from childhood to regard selfless service as a core virtue for women'.

Yet, the disciplinary function of the *vrata*s is contested by other scholars who focus instead on the transformative and creative possibilities of such rituals. Anindita Ghosh (2011: 214) challenges this notion of female docility, and argues that though the kitchen or the puja room might be gendered spaces intended to help men secure and enjoy the privileges of patriarchy, women could 'also subvert and create their own socially specific meanings of that space'. In fact, it is through rituals of religious piety that women acquire 'a very private space' and gain the 'empowering self-perception' that they are – albeit temporarily – 'freed from their quotidian life, in direct and private communion with God' (214–15). Ghosh's theorization also aligns with the concept of the Motherline as an enabling maternal legacy which daughters can valorize and from which they can learn.

The liberating potential of everyday religious rituals is manifested in diasporic culinary writer Chitrita Banerji's memories of her grandmother, from whom she learned her first lessons in the connectedness between food, piety and self-realization. Sitting 'quietly in a corner' and watching her 'grandmother as worshipper', Banerji (2001: 16) would witness the 'seamless sequence [that] bound us firmly through the pleasure of partaking – offerings were made, the gods supposedly accepted them, and the sanctified food, *proshad*, was then consumed by the worshipper to bridge the gap between mortality and divinity'. Lowinsky (2009: 115) writes of how grandmothers are often 'the first to tell her granddaughter the stories from her Motherline'. Banerji's (2001: 18) grandmother prioritized her identity as the devotee/cook, and she offered her service directly to the divine without any mention of male intervention or control: 'Remember, *you* are food, because the god who made you is also food. And in order to live, *you* must love him every day with food' (emphasis mine). In her explanation, cooking for the gods became indistinguishable from cooking for the self. Therefore, Banerji realized that in her grandmother's 'notion of religiosity', the prayer room 'was the space to be enjoyed exclusively, territorially, as her own … In this one room, she was still absolute mistress and unquestioning worshipper' (19). Although not as 'unquestioning', Banerji acknowledges and valorizes this creative and self-fulfilling agency of her foremothers, which is realized within the patriarchal domestic matrix of food and worship.

In a different way, Tutun Mukherjee (2006: 84) appreciates how her mother utilized the creative and empowering potential of the enclosed kitchen-space: 'For my mother, the kitchen was a microcosm, a place of power in a patriarchal household, where the woman's control remained uncontested.' Her mother found creative satisfaction in cooking and feeding others: 'Festivals provided the occasions for serving *dahi-chuda* at *Paus Sankranti*; *khichdi-chokha* at *Saraswathi Puja*; *malpua and chholey* at *Holi*; varieties of sweets at *Bijoya Dashami*, for all who came by' (85). Here, the purpose of the cooking was not just to please the gods or the self, but the satisfaction gained by pleasing others and receiving appreciation in return.

C. S. Lakshmi (2006: 50–1), writing of her mother Alamelu's engagement with festive and seasonal foods, notes how the latter 'turned food into a mode of communication, assertion and adventure', how she unfailingly produced food for her family even in the most difficult of circumstances. This kind of devotion to feeding members of the immediate and extended family can be read as another expression of piety, taking us back to the original Latin sense of the word *pietas*, which means fulfilling one's responsibilities to gods, parents and kin. Performing piety through cooking for others was a source of pride and satisfaction for the writers' grandmothers and mothers, and the *vrata*s and other religious festivals provided a platform for such culinary performances. Bose (2010: 140, 147) terms this the 'paradox of authority gained through servitude' and locates the source of this authority in the fact that women are the 'most active actors' within the family, 'even when they are not its first citizens'.

However, the pride associated with serving others through food and piety is almost never overt or self-promoting. Tutun Mukherjee (2006: 85) recollects her mother's extreme self-effacement, how she 'never considered what she did as significant' and how she always insisted that 'she worked merely to pass time'. The religious self-realizations and culinary achievements of such women have usually been hidden from public view, circulating in private family lineages through orally narrated stories or sometimes in handwritten notebooks. By deciding to recuperate and publish the often-neglected recipes, rituals and stories of their female ancestors, the cookbook writers and memoirists have relocated them from the private to the public domain, expanding and perpetuating their reach.

Recording recipes

All the writers studied here acknowledge their debt to their mothers and grandmothers for the recipes they have received. Sometimes, their own works germinated in their foremothers' handwritten recipe books. Tara Deshpande Tennebaum's (2013) cookbook originated in the 'precious, tattered manuscript' of her great-grandmother's recipes. She decided to 'translate and contemporize' it and expand it into a culinary auto-ethnography of the Gour Saraswat Brahmins – while sitting on a bench in the United States, far away from her Indian origins (ix). With diasporic writers, it is usually the awareness of geocultural distances that spurs the desire to reconnect with and retrieve the culinary Motherline. It was the 'pent up nostalgia' for the food and festivities of Durga Puja that made Chitrita Banerji (2001: 5) write to her mother 'asking for recipes and directions' and embark on 'an experimental period of long-distance cooking lessons'. Sandeepa Mukherjee Datta (2013: 3) emphasizes the legacy of her foremothers in creating her culinary Motherline: 'I gather their recipes from my mothers, my husband's mother, my Kolkata neighbour's mother … in short, all Bong motherhood – and re-create them in my far-off kitchen, along with the stories and memories they bring with them.' Ammini Ramachandran appreciated the 'special' value of her mother's festival laddus only after migrating to the United States. This 'gastro-nostalgia', as Srinivas terms it, impelled her to learn from her mother: 'Mom taught me to cook through recipes she sent every week in her letters' (Srinivas 2006: 191; Ramachandran 2011: 144).

Rosalyn Eves (2005: 282) reads cookbooks as 'memory-texts' that commemorate 'female domestic traditions – such as recipe sharing' – and 'provide a space for vernacular and countercultural memory to flourish'. The documentation and circulation of these received recipes become assertive political acts that validate the womanly labour of domestic cooking and worship as legitimate and meaningful acts of self-actualization. By invoking their foremothers' culinary contributions, the writers '(re)construct a sort of feminine culinary genealogy' (291). By both *recording* the recipe and *reproducing* the dish, cookbook writers honour the creative and productive agency of their foremothers. Chitrita Banerji (1997: 114) calls the mutton recipe her grandmother cooked the 'pious' way on Navami during Durga Puja 'Grandmother's meat without onion and garlic', and she recollects how her mother 'still cooks meat her mother's way'. Banerji (2001: 129) also celebrates the creative fulfilment achieved in the performance of the *vratas*, which imbricated piety and culinary performance with storytelling skills (the *vrata-katha* or narratives) and artistic decoration (the *alpana*). As Pika Ghosh (1995: 25) observes, 'Through these elaborate religious and social rituals, as well as the more modest daily ones of … cooking, … worshipping the gods, singing folk songs, … women create their own identity.'

While recording their memories, many of the writers realize how their mothers and grandmothers had subtly and covertly contested the patriarchal norms that determined their existence; this in turn often helped them to locate and historicize their own identity struggles. Lowinsky (1992: 13) posits that the Motherline enables a woman to 'gain female authority' by providing her with a 'life-cycle perspective': 'As she makes the journey back to her female roots, she will encounter ancestors who struggled with similar difficulties in different historical times.' C. S. Lakshmi (2006: 52), for instance, realized that women like her mother 'were just pretending to comply with the rules of the family and the society, but were simultaneously quietly breaking them'.

Anoothi Vishal (2016: 161), in her culinary auto-ethnography, *Mrs LC's Table* (Mrs LC was her grandmother), critiques fasts like Karva Chauth for married women: 'In patriarchal Hindu society, the burden of the husband's well-being and longevity has always been placed on the woman – and her virtuousness.' Yet she also records how, in her own as well as many other 'Kayasth homes', the 'laissez-faire meal' at the end of the Karva Chauth fast substituted the scripturally mandated 'simple, Sattvic, or "pure", no-onion-no-garlic meal' with 'rich fare, including even non-vegetarian food': this may be read as an act of gustatory resistance and self-indulgence within the mandatory confines of 'the strict ritualistic austerity' and piety of Karva Chauth (163). Chitrita Banerji (2001: 53) documents the 'inexpensive, unpretentious' but very tasty dish of water lily stems in a hot and sour tamarind sauce that women in East Bengal cook and offer to the Goddess Durga: this dish – 'a supreme act of imagination and courage' – is served only to the women, marking their identification 'with the womanly aspect of this most powerful goddess' and subtly undermining the hierarchical priority of the 'males of the household, those mortal gods with immediate power to punish and reward'. As Anindita Ghosh (2011: 221) writes, 'Reclaiming the visibility' of previously marginalized domestic spheres is an act of resistance in 'seemingly normative situations'. The documentation of recipes reveals a layered, *double resistance*: the daughters resist the separation of the private and public spheres that marginalized their mothers' contributions; and there are instances of resistance within the private sphere by their mothers themselves.

It has been argued that 'behind the assiduous documentation and defense of the authentic lies an unarticulated anxiety of losing the subject' (Bendix 1997: 10). This anxiety can be caused by the rupture of the traditional flows of Motherline legacies, a rupture exacerbated by 'increasing industrialization and urbanization' (Patil and Bharadwaj 2002: 113). This anxiety of loss of religious tradition underpins the documentation of recipes that we see in popular multiregional cookbooks, like the *Festival Cookbook* (2002) by Vimla Patil and Monisha Bharadwaj. They have collected over 150 recipes thematically grouped under 'festivals' such as Pongal, Holi, Diwali, Teej, Karva Chauth and others, including non-Hindu festivals such as 'Ramzan Id' and 'Christmas and Easter in Goa' (39, 105). The popularity of such multiethnic, multicultural cookbooks among readers can be indicative both of a loss of familial culinary Motherlines by the readers (which makes them purchase such books as substitute resources) and of an increasingly secular, cosmopolitan desire to experiment with the cuisine of other regions.

Such narratives of anxiety and desire for substitute religious-culinary resources are found not only in postglobalization cookbooks, but even in much earlier community cookbooks like *Rasachandrika* (1943). According to the Saraswat Mahila Samaj of Bombay, the *Rasachandrika* elaborates on 'advice and guidance concerning the observance of Hindu religious days and festivals, the special foods to be prepared … which were traditionally given by the experienced elders in a joint family' (Saraswat 1991: 220). Factors like urban migration were breaking down 'joint families' into smaller nuclear units which, nevertheless, wished 'to preserve our religious culture and traditions' (220). When Mukherjee Datta (2013: 263) confesses, 'I was lax [about continuing the tradition of making special foods on festivals] until I realized how a piece of fried sweetened dough on Sankranti could link my daughter to her roots,' she is reproducing both the anxiety of loss and the desire for preservation.

In the next section, I will explore how this desire for compliance and cultural preservation both conflicts and coexists with the desire for resistance and self-expression.

Refashioning recipes

In spite of her compliant preservation and perpetuation of received homeland culture through food, Mukherjee Dutta (2013: 7) also declares: 'In reality it was supposed to be about *my* food, finding *my* way through the recipes I cooked at home, which worked for *me*' (emphases in original). This duality of tradition and individualism can be explicated through the revisionary capacity of recipes. Susan Leonardi (1989: 344) foregrounds the capacity for revision inherent in the reproducibility of recipes: 'Like a narrative, a recipe is reproducible, and, further, its hearers-readers-receivers are encouraged to reproduce it and, in reproducing it, to revise it and make it their own.' The long-distance letters and digital conversations through which mothers share recipes with their daughters function as sites of intersubjective engagement; a negotiation of identification and difference between mothers and daughters. One recurring point of difference is in the measurement of ingredients. Ramachandran (2011: 144) recalls her mother using 'a lot of "handfuls" and "pinches"' to make 'perfect' festive laddus, whereas she has to rely on the precision of candy thermometers and measuring cups. Instead of 'andaaz – intuition', Sandeepa Mukherjee Datta (2013: 4) binds 'recipes in measures of standard teaspoons and tablespoons', but she encourages her daughters and readers to be guided without being 'constrained' by such fixed measurements. The guidelines are necessary to re-create the tastes of home, but this narrative of authenticity is compromised by factors such as changes of location, daily routine and social roles.

Sometimes, to re-create the tastes associated with piety in the old home, it becomes necessary to 'seek creative strategies to fabricate authenticity' (Mannur 2007: 15). Instead of the traditional jaggery in *narkel narus* (sweet coconut balls), Mallika Basu (2010: 221) uses 'dark muscovado sugar', which is a 'splendid and more readily available substitute'. Chitrita Banerji (2007: 166) reconstructs the *pulipithe* that her mother and grandmother regularly made during the winter festival of Poush Sankranti without the 'vital ingredient is *khejur gur*', substituting white sugar for it because that is the 'only way to make this in the West': 'In the absence of *gur* a vital flavour of Bengal will be missed, but the *pitha* itself will provide an essential Bengali delight.' The 'fabricated authenticity' is made possible by a leap of imagination, a leap where memory substitutes for the lack of the original ingredients.

Sometimes new ingredients and techniques are substituted to make the best use of available resources as well as to save time and labour. The focus on speed and convenience indicates how urban and transnational migration flows, the breakdown of extended family structures and the fact that most of the writers (and presumably, their readers) are working professionals, have interrupted and transformed the traditional rhythms and patterns of religious and culinary practices in Hindu households. Chitrita Banerji (2007: 166) notes how *pulipithe* is 'laborious to make without the extra hands of an extended family, and yet winter could never be complete without it'. Sandeepa Mukherjee Datta (2013: 3) admits: 'I adapt, tweak and adjust to blend those dishes in my busy workday.' She remembers how her mother would thicken and sweeten milk for making *patishapta* (crepes), but she cuts 'the method short with condensed milk' and substitutes maple syrup for 'liquid patali gur' (265). When she makes *narkel naru*, a 'must during Kojagari Lokkhi Pujo', instead of the mounds of coconut freshly hand-grated by her mother and aunts, she uses 'frozen grated coconut that I get here in the US', because the labour of her mother and aunt 'takes away a whole lot of time and joy' (266). These shortcuts and substitutions are necessary because 'the "time crunch" for both urban Indian women and their diasporic counterparts is very real' (Srinivas 2006: 200). They are also aware of the gendered asymmetry of the domestic labour relations within the household. This asymmetry both underpins and is exposed during the frequent religious rituals and the cooking associated with them. Mukherjee Datta (2013: 263) recollects how her grandmother 'celebrated every small and big festival listed in the Bengali almanac in the manner she knew best – through food', but she also remembers how her 'grandfather would beckon to all and sundry to come and have a taste of the wonderful sweets' prepared during these occasions and her 'poor, harried Dida … rush[ing] about grating, grinding, stuffing and frying'. This inequality between male ownership and female labour is typical of Hindu homes, endorsed and perpetuated by religious practices. Thus, shortcuts and substitutions also attempt to address the inequities of domestic labour, although they do not destabilize the primary role of women as culinary and cultural nurturers.

However, I would argue that sometimes the reshaping of recipes and ritual practices that gradually interrupt the connection between food and piety are also acts that challenge the traditional roles and expectations of Hindu womanhood. The compromises with the technique and substitution of the original ingredients with non-traditional ones sometimes subvert the original *purpose* of preparing the food item. Shoba Narayan's (2003: 3) *Monsoon Diary: A Memoir with Recipes* begins with a recollection of her first food, the 'rice and ghee' that is fed to newborns at the 'formal choru-unnal [rice-eating] ceremony at the famous Guruvayur temple in Kerala'. Living in the United States, she re-creates this ghee by using the unorthodox method of melting '2 sticks (1 cup) of unsalted butter' (8). Although Narayan reminisces about the 'copious quantities of ghee' used in the 'prasadam' of the 'many temples' she was 'dragged' to as a child, her personal suggestion is that the 'guilty' pleasures of ghee – 'the vegetarian's caviar: slightly sinful, somewhat excessive, but oh so delicious' – are best enjoyed sparingly, 'as a condiment' (6–8). We see here a transgressive shift from piety to pleasure. Anoothi Vishal (2016: 166) shares the recipe for 'charnamrit' (the elixir from the lord's feet): her grandmother made this holy ritualistic drink with the mandatory addition of a few drops of water from the river Ganga 'as part of every major puja as prasad', but 'it became a gourmet delight for the family' and 'all of us drank several glasses of it'. Here again, there is a shift from the abstemious restraint associated with piety to an excessive indulgence associated with pleasure. However, Vishal is not initiating the transgression (as Narayan was doing) but documenting and participating in a shift that was part of her familial practice. This indicates that such shifts from piety to pleasure were a mode of (often unarticulated) resistance that were practiced by generations of women and passed down the Motherline.

Tara Deshpande Tennebaum's (2013) culinary memoir offers an interesting conflation of the sacred and the profane, the traditional and the modern. While recontextualizing her grandmother's recipe for *sabudana wade* (pearl sago fritters), she informs us how such dishes 'are consumed by Hindus during religious fasts when cereals and grains are not allowed' (132). She then modernizes the recipe by redesignating it as 'vegan, gluten-free fritters'; this is an attempt to give the dish (as Tulasi Srinivas says of cosmopolitan Indian mothers' recipes) 'both nutritive and "cultural" content' (Deshpande Tennebaum 2013: 132; Srinivas 2006: 194). Deshpande Tennebaum (2013: 132) then rewrites the self-abnegating narrative of fasting as a narrative of pleasure: '[The fritters] are soft and crunchy, salty, sweet and nourishing. I like to serve them as appetisers with a glass of limbu pani or a dry, crisp, white wine.' Immediately after rewriting the sacred recipe in profane contexts, she resacralizes the recipe by stating: 'I also serve these during Passover, the Jewish holiday when the observant abstains from grains or leavening agents' (132). Not only does this recontextualization foreground the commonality uniting different religious practices, but it also reveals an agentic playfulness with inherited sacred recipes that is often seen in the writings of personal cookbook daughters. This playfulness permeates Deshpande Tennebaum's culinary memoir, particularly her memories of homeland religious rituals. When she narrates the 'culinary utopia' of the Ganesh Chaturthi festivals in her grandmother's home, she also recounts a 'fun' story of a distant boastful uncle who had had his fill of the 'ladoos and mithais', and had fallen asleep under the Ganesh idol's robes. After being unknowingly immersed along with the clay idol, he was eventually found 'hanging on to Lord Ganesh for dear life as he floated away towards the sea' (84–6).

The significant shifts from piety to pleasure are impelled in part by the changes in culinary discourse post globalization and modernization. The valorization of the local and the authentic (as evidenced in the demand for such family-based recipe collections) coexists with an increasing focus on health and convenience motivating the preparation and consumption of food. The contextual shift from religious to secular also reveals the changed role of religion in the lives of modern, urban, educated women. Unlike their mothers and grandmothers, who were rooted in the kitchen and the prayer room, most of the writers discussed in this chapter are women working outside the home and living diasporically outside their South Asian homeland. Their secular liberal education makes them question what Leela Dube (1988: 181) terms the 'certain givenness' of 'religious rituals and social practices' and contest what their mothers had accepted as 'part of the natural order of things'. There is also the identity-difference tension in mother–daughter relationships, where the primary identification with her mother that teaches a girl her 'adult gender role' is complicated as she grows up, when she is usually 'sufficiently differentiated' to experience herself as a 'separate individual' who questions her mother's acts and positions (Chodorow 1978: 177). However, in her theory of the Motherline Lowinsky (1992: 72) suggests that 'the wrestling of this mother and daughter' can be reconciled through acts of 'a mother's affirmation of her daughter' and/or 'a daughter's affirmation of her mother'.

In the texts studied here, there are instances of the daughters' critiquing or rejecting the piety of their foremothers (and fathers), even as they affirmed and memorialized the stories and recipes connected to piety. Chitrita Banerji (2001: 21) narrates how, after her college education, she 'entered and remained in a terrain of scepticism utterly alien to the self-forgetful joys of loving Krishna and making him offerings': for her, these rituals 'became simply a part of the daily routine ... instead of intersections with another reality', more a practice embedded in quotidian life than a liberation from it. Mallika Basu (2010: 152) recollects, 'It took me 14 years to muster up enough courage to admit [to my parents] that I wasn't sure God existed'; she engages with Durga Puja not as a religious occasion but more as an 'annual reconnect-with-our-Bengali-brethren event'. Basu prefaces her recipe for *narkel narus* (a sweet associated with Bijoya Dashami, the last day of the Durga Puja) with a story of how she often cures a 'raging hangover' after a 'big night out in the highest heels imaginable' with her Bengali girlfriends with 'this celebratory coconut sweet' (221).

The daughters' refashioning and recontextualization of the inherited recipes are not only linked to changing urban and transnational lifestyles but also – as indicated in the first section of this chapter – embedded in intergenerational shifts in the understanding and performing of domestic roles. Critics like Samantha Barbas (2004: 121) have pointed out that the recipe-sharing between mothers and daughters may also be sites of 'intergenerational strife' because 'women's traditionally glorified role as nurturers and food providers has been one of the most visible symbols of female oppression' and 'food, cooking, and the kitchen have become a cultural battleground in the ongoing struggle to redefine gender norms and women's social roles'. In the Indian context, although the texts affirm and preserve continuity rather than overt conflict, there are also, as discussed above, significant differences in the ways in which grandmothers/mothers and daughters engage with food. The daughters' engagement with recipes related to ritual and domestic roles is informed by their changing consciousness of women's roles and rights. Whereas their mothers' generation often found gustatory pleasure in the consumption of pious food (as in Vishal's story of the Charnamrit), the recipes were prepared for specific religious occasions and purposes. The daughters extended this shift from piety to pleasure by substituting a secular context for a religious one (as seen in Deshpande Tennebaum and Basu above, and Mukherjee Datta below). Thus, we see a gradual shift of focus on the function of food from a vehicle of sanctified piety to a medium of sensory pleasure. In the texts studied here, cooking becomes an act of reclaiming and legitimizing the body and its desires. Although the traditional nurturing roles persist, there is a greater focus on self-satisfaction than on self-abnegation. Separating the recipe from its religious context metonymically liberates it from patriarchal control and allows it to be reclaimed as an empowering legacy of the Motherline.

The transgenerational journey of such recipes from their roots in ritualized piety, via the transmission through the Motherline, to a reimagined, secular inheritance can be traced in Mukherjee Datta's (2013: 20) narration of '"Chire Doi Aam" – beaten rice aka poha mixed with yoghurt, sweet mangoes and bananas', a sanctified, uncooked dish eaten to break ritual fasts. She begins by locating the dish in its ritualistic context, explaining how it was regularly prepared by her mother every Tuesday during the summer month of Jaistha, during a 'fast followed by a katha (story) and pujo for the Goddess Mangalchandi' on 'Jai Mangalbar' (20). She documents her childhood memories of initiation into the ritual, how she was unmoved by the religious 'significance' but was tempted by the synesthetic, combined pleasures of the spiritual and the sensual: 'sitting on the pujo room floor with Ma and grandma, the heady smell of incense and flowers making the dish ethereal' (21). She also narrates how her mother would covertly subvert the connection between food and piety by giving her this dish 'normally', as a summer breakfast 'without the "holy" tag' (21). Then, she shares the recipe, emphatically and overtly repositioning the dish as an epicurean consumable: 'Now I make a *fancy version* of this old favourite with honey and in parfait glasses. Tastes *just as good*' (21; my emphasis). Through a conscious decoupling of the gustatory appeal of food from its spiritual context, Mukherjee Datta creatively reimagines the religious recipe to memorialize a maternal legacy that she can transmit to her progeny, thereby resisting her earlier socialization into the obedient acceptance of ritual food and worship. In the next section, I will address the debate between compliance and resistance as expressed through the act of transmitting culinary Motherlines.

Transmitting recipes

Soumya Aravind Sitaraman (2007: n.p.) has written a series of e-books on Indian festival recipes, which she dedicates to 'contemporary families who strive to nurture their culture and reserve their traditions despite time and energy constraints. You make happy memories for your children'. In this dedication we may read the desire – namely, to shape the cultural legacy of future generations – that informs the authors of such cookbooks. Mukherjee Datta (2013: 168) also reiterates 'the need to do it more for my daughters than anyone else'.

There is scholarly debate over whether the transmission of culinary Motherlines not only perpetuates maternally received local, ethnic or familial recipes but also perpetuates normative maternal roles of primary nurturer and devoted caregiver. Tulasi Srinivas (2006: 198) writes that even in cosmopolitan families, 'the image of the good mother is conceptualized as a nurturing relationship between the mother and child', and 'the 'good' mother is one who feeds the child on demand with wholesome homemade complex foods of the particular ethnic and caste based group of the patriliny'. Nancy Chodorow (1978: 208–9) theorizes that the asymmetries in 'women's location and responsibilities in the domestic sphere' are reproduced by the 'reproduction of women's mothering', because 'women mother daughters who, when they become women, mother'. It is true that the shifting context of many of the recipes from a patriarchally imposed piety to a self-assertive pleasure is often unaccompanied by any structural transformation of domestic power and labour asymmetries. While the culinary memoirists and cookbook writers have reclaimed and reshaped the religious recipes they received via their mothers' stories, most of them have neither rejected nor even significantly questioned their approved roles in the patriarchal family structure. In fact, the popular *Festival Cookbook* by Patil and Bharadwaj (2002: 113) appears to endorse the gendered division of labour involved in domestic religious practices:

> No more can the housewife wake up at dawn, have a bath and then ritualistically prepare food for the gods – which later is eaten by the family as prasad or blessed food. No longer can the householder sit over a Pooja or worship for long hours. It is likely that both must rush to work after a quick prayer. On festival days, however, this daily routine changes [back to the old ways].

A radical feminist vision may reject the normative, gendered roles of devoted cook-worshipper by envisioning a rupture of the Motherline, which would potentially lead to freedom from the daily duties of kitchen/prayer-room and cooking/worship. Mukherjee Datta (2013: 7) articulates a maternalist counterpoint to such radical feminist politics, when she locates her agency in a suburban New York kitchen where 'a mother was finding a way to share her roots with her two daughters through a culture of food'. This determination to construct and consolidate culinary Motherlines is aligned with the concerns of maternal feminists like Tutun Mukherjee (2006: 86), who writes: '[I am now] conscious of a tremendous responsibility – to ensure that the legacy of the Motherline that I have inherited passes on to my daughter.' The cookbook writers studied here seem to be more focused on preserving than disrupting, and more interested in passing on to their daughters the cultural memories and joys of cooking than in preventing them from cooking. Yet, as Anindita Ghosh (2011: 221) reminds us, resistance need not mean a 'dramatic rupture between unchanging tradition on the one hand and radical social transformation on the other', because there is 'tremendous potential of hidden domains of conflict in fostering enduring social opinion and struggle'. Refusal and rupture are not the only ways to resolve historical inequities: as Lowinsky (1992: 13) suggests, Motherlines ground women in their 'feminine nature' as they struggle 'with the many options now open to women'. I have argued in this chapter that the acts of recording, refashioning, and transmitting religious recipes are deliberate acts that contest the normative expectations controlling women in the kitchen and the prayer room. Acknowledging the location of this debate in the context of everyday practices in urban and transnational Hindu families, I do not see these texts as a capitulation to oppressive, institutionalized and feminized norms of domestic cooking and worship. Rather, I read them as nuanced, imbricated responses of subversion and subservience to the politics of food and piety, and as enduring testimonies of enabling Motherline relationships and legacies.

References

Primary texts

Banerji, Chitrita. 2006 [2001]. *The Hour of the Goddess: Memories of Women, Food and Ritual in Bengal.* New Delhi: Penguin.

Banerji, Chitrita. 2007 [1997]. *Bengali Cooking: Seasons and Festivals.* London: Serif.

Basu, Mallika. 2010. *Miss Masala: Real Indian Cooking for Busy Living.* London: HarperCollins.

Deshpande Tennebaum, Tara. 2013. *A Sense for Spice: Recipes and Stories from a Konkan Kitchen.* Chennai: Westland.

Lakshmi, C. S. 2006. 'When Alamelu Shrugged'. In Rinki Bhattacharya (ed.), *Janani – Mothers, Daughters, Motherhood.* New Delhi: Sage Publications, 47–56.

Mukherjee Datta, Sandeepa. 2013. *Bong Mom's Cookbook: Stories from a Bengali Mother's Kitchen.* Noida, India: HarperCollins.

Mukherjee, Tutun. 2006. 'My Mother's Gardens'. In Rinki Bhattacharya (ed.), *Janani – Mothers, Daughters, Motherhood*. New Delhi: Sage Publications, 80–6.

Narayan, Shoba. 2003. *Monsoon Diary: A Memoir with Recipes*. New Delhi: Penguin.

Patil, Vimla, and Monisha Bharadwaj. 2002. *Festival Cookbook*. New Delhi: Rupa.

Ramachandran, Ammini. 2011. 'A Dessert, a Graduation, a Wedding: Laddu'. In Linda Murray Berzok (ed.), *Storied Dishes: What Our Family Recipes Tell Us about Who We Are and Where We've Been*. Santa Barbara: Praeger, 143–5.

Saraswat Mahila Samaj, Bombay. 1991 [1943]. *Rasachandrika: Saraswat Cookery Book*. Mumbai: Popular Prakashan.

Sitaraman, Soumya Aravind. 2007. *Let's Celebrate with Festival Food for Deepavali*. Bengaluru: What Is India.

Vishal, Anoothi. 2016. *Mrs LC's Table: Stories about Kayasth Food and Culture*. Gurgaon: Hachette India.

Secondary texts

Achaya, K. T. 1994. *Indian Food: A Historical Companion*. New Delhi: Oxford University Press.

Appadurai, Arjun. 1981. 'Gastro-Politics in Hindu South Asia'. *American Ethnologist* 8(3) Symbolism and Cognition, 494–511. *JSTOR*. Accessed 16 August 2016. http://www.jstor.org/stable/644298.

Ashley, Bob, Joanne Hollows, Steve Jones and Ben Taylor. 2004. *Food and Cultural Studies*. London: Routledge.

Bagchi, Jasodhara. 1993. 'Socialising the Girl Child in Colonial Bengal'. *Economic and Political Weekly* 28(41): 2214–19. *JSTOR*. Accessed 16 August 2016. http://www.jstor.org/stable/4400259.

Barbas, Samantha. 2004. 'Review: A Bite off Mama's Plate: Mothers' and Daughters' Connection through Food'. *Gastronomica* 4(4): 120–1. *JSTOR*. Accessed 16 August 2016. http://www.jstor.org/stable/10.1525/gfc.2004.4.4.120.2.

Bendix, Regina. 1997. *In Search of Authenticity: The Formation of Folklore Studies*. Madison: The University of Wisconsin Press.

Bose, Mandakranta. 2010. *Women in the Hindu Tradition: Rules, Roles and Exceptions*. London: Routledge.

Chodorow, Nancy J. 1999 [1978]. *The Reproduction of Mothering: Psychoanalysis and the Sociology of Gender*. Berkeley: University of California Press.

Dube, Leela. 1988. 'Socialisation of Hindu Girls in Patrilineal India'. In Karuna Chanana (ed.), *Socialisation, Education and Women: Explorations in Gender Identity*. New Delhi: Orient Longman, 166–92.

Eves, Rosalyn Collings. 2005. 'A Recipe for Remembrance: Memory and Identity in African-American Women's Cookbooks'. *Rhetoric Review* 24(3): 280–97. Web. *JSTOR*. Accessed 16 August 2016. http://www.jstor.org/stable/20176662.

Ghosh, Anindita. 2011 [2007]. 'A World of Their Very Own: Religion, Pain and Subversion in Bengali Homes in the Nineteenth Century'. In Anindita Ghosh (ed.), *Behind the Veil: Resistance, Women and the Everyday in Colonial South Asia*. Ranikhet: Permanent Black, 191–222.

Ghosh, Pika. 1995. 'Household Ritual and Women's Domains'. In Michael W. Meister (ed.), *Cooking for the Gods: The Art of Home Ritual in Bengal*. Newark: Newark Museum, 21–6.

Gombrich Gupta, Samjukta. 2000. 'The Goddess, Women and Their Rituals in Hinduism'. In Mandakranta Bose (ed.), *Faces of the Feminine in Ancient, Medieval and Modern India*. New York: Oxford University Press, 87–106.

Leonardi, Susan J. 1989. 'Recipes for Reading: Summer Pasta, Lobster à la Riseholme, and Key Lime Pie'. *PMLA* 104(3): 340–7. *JSTOR*. Accessed 16 August 2016. http://www.jstor.org/stable/462443.

Lowinsky, Naomi Ruth. 2009 [1992]. *The Motherline: Every Woman's Journey to Find Her Female Roots*. Cheyenne: Fisher King Press.

Mannur, Anita. 2007. 'Culinary Nostalgia: Authenticity, Nationalism, and Diaspora'. *MELUS* 32(4), Food in Multi-Ethnic Literatures, 11–31. *JSTOR*. Accessed 16 August 2016. http://www.jstor.org/stable/30029829.

O'Reilly, Andrea. 2014. 'African American Mothering: Home Is Where the Revolution Is'. In Andrea O'Reilly (ed.), *Mothers, Mothering and Motherhood across Cultural Differences: A Reader*. Bradford: Demeter Press, 93–118.

Srinivas, Tulasi. 2006. '"As Mother Made It": The Cosmopolitan Indian Family, "Authentic" Food and the Construction of Cultural Utopia'. *International Journal of Sociology of the Family* 32(2), Globalization and the Family, 191–221. *JSTOR*. Accessed 16 August 2016. http://www.jstor.org/stable/23030195.

Thieme, John, and Ira Raja (eds). 2007. *The Table Is Laid: The Oxford Anthology of South Asian Food Writing*. New Delhi: Oxford University Press.

Part Two

Boundary-making, the construction of identity and commensality

4

Transcendental transactions: Food practices among Barelwi Muslims

Sumbul Farah

Everyday life offers infinite potential to believers to live piously, and the consumption and distribution of food provides significant ways of interacting with the divine. The routine act of consuming food also provides a moral opportunity to the pious subject, as was pointed out to me by a respondent in Bareilly. A devout young girl of about twenty pointed towards the snacks laid out in front of us when I was visiting her at her house and told me that their consumption could be transformed into *ibaadat* (worship/prayer) through the mere utterance of the *Bismillah*[1] before the meal: '*Agar dua se shuru karein toh khaana bhi ibaadat ban jaata hai*' (If we begin a meal with a prayer, the act of eating itself becomes a form of worship). The transformative power of the utterance invests the everyday act of eating with a moral compass. The transformation is arguably even more marked when the utterance is made to consecrate food to earn merit for oneself and for others. The rituals of *niyaz* and *fateha* entail the utterance of Qur'anic verses over food in order to effect a dual transformation. The food gets consecrated and is beneficial to all those who consume it, and religious reward accrues to the praying subject, the consumers, saints, the deceased and all those who have been included in the prayers.

Food and food practices are often central to the process of defining the self vis-à-vis the other.[2] They serve as an effective code that encapsulates and expresses relationships of inclusion and exclusion (Douglas 1972; Ohnuki-Tierney 1993) and thereby allow social and religious boundaries to be policed and identities carved out through its consumption (Counihan 1999; Ulrich 2007). In this chapter, I seek to examine how Barelwi Muslim identity derives from their defence of certain food practices. The legitimacy and significance of these rituals derives primarily from the eschatological beliefs on which they are based. Central to the self-conception of Barelwis, these rituals are predicated on the existence of an eternal world beyond the one which we inhabit. The two worlds occupy distinct spiritual and temporal realms but allow the possibility of transactions across them. Operationalizing the link between the two domains, a range of objects, people, places and texts enable the establishment of transcendental relationships between the human and divine worlds.

Through an analysis of the ethnographic data I had collected for my doctoral dissertation, I attempt to explore the rituals of *niyaz* and *fateha*, which are metonymically associated with Barelwis. The significance of these rituals can be gauged from the fact that adherence to them (or their disregard) serves to mark out the believer's denominational affiliation. I argue that the importance of these rituals derives from their embodiment of the Barelwi worldview, both structurally and ideologically. Specific food practices provide the means of tapping into an inexhaustible source of religious merit and simultaneously serve to express the underlying cosmology that legitimizes them. In order to understand how these practices are linked to the Barelwi imagination of the universe, we need to examine the eschatological principles underpinning them.

The Barelwi interpretation of Islam defends traditional, shrine-based practices and the veneration of saints by citing authoritative Islamic texts. It emerged in nineteenth-century India around the same time as a variety of reform movements, within and outside Islam. Metcalf points out that the ascendance of the British and the loss of central authority for Muslims in eighteenth-century India profited the Islamic religious leadership by allowing both ulema (religious scholars) and Sufi pirs (spiritual guides) to assert their influence in an altered political scenario (Metcalf 1982). In this context, a range of reform movements began within Islam in the subcontinent, such as Deobandi, Firangi Mahalli, Ahl-e-Hadith, Ahmadiyya and Barelwi.[3] Among Barelwis, a nineteenth-century alim (Islamic scholar) named Ahmad Raza Khan Barelwi[4] (1856–1921) is credited with renewing and reviving the faith as it was practiced by the Prophet Muhammad himself. Through his *fatawa* (sing. fatwa, legal ruling in accordance with Islamic law) and writings, Ahmad Raza Khan defended Barelwi practice as being authentically Islamic. Barelwis believe in the principle of intercession, and particularly the intercessory power of saints and relics, believed to be efficacious in accessing Allah and his *barakat* (grace/blessing). They also believe that saints and holy men do not die when their souls leave their corporeal bodies but that they remain alive in their graves and continue to possess the ability to intercede between Allah and believers.[5] Barelwis employ the medium of the saint to pray to Allah in the belief that although the pleas of an ordinary sinful mortal might not be heard, Allah will grant their wishes if they are made through the mediation of a pious and holy man. Such an interpretation of Islam is often criticized by its detractors as being 'unreformed'. Indeed, Barelwis are often castigated as 'grave-worshippers' and followers of un-Islamic rituals. However, I concur with Sanyal's (2010) insistence that they should be viewed as reformist on account of their self-conscious adherence to religious texts and emphasis on individual responsibility in practising religion. In their attempt to live ethically, Barelwi believers continually attempt to follow what they understand to be 'proper' Islamic practice.

In examining Barelwi food practices, we must remember that believers attach a multiplicity of meanings to their acts of piety. Also, it is inevitable that the body of believers will be constituted of people with varying degrees of access to and comprehension of religious texts. Thus, although the practices cited here might not be considered acceptable to all Barelwis, this does not mean that they are not widely practised by others, who are equally Barelwi in terms of the interpretation of Islam that they follow. It is helpful to recall the criticism of symbolism in food studies by Tuzin, who points out that studies that draw on cultural data for the analysis of the symbolic significance of food are often obliged to overlook the individual meanings that people ascribe to food. For practical reasons they assume that the entire population uses and interprets the symbols uniformly (Tuzin 1972). It is, therefore, helpful to remember that what is referred to as Barelwi practice can assume a multiplicity of forms, all of which are accorded varying degrees of legitimacy.

The principle of *Isal-e Sawab* (transfer of religious merit)

The term '*sawab*' refers to reward or religious merit and *isal-e sawab* refers to the transfer of reward to someone else. The reward can be earned through a pious act, and its merit can be granted to anyone. Although it is widely understood that the Barelwi belief in intercession emphasizes the mediational powers of saints and relics, I wish to draw attention also to the ability of ordinary believers to intercede on behalf of others. The principle of *isal-e sawab* enables all believers to pass on the reward of virtuous acts to the intended recipients. In some ways, *isal-e sawab* is an inversion of the living person seeking the intercession of a saint who has departed from the world because here the living intercede on behalf of the dead. Unlike wealth that diminishes through sharing, *sawab* gets multiplied when shared, irrespective of the number of beneficiaries (Naeemi 2008: 289).

The transfer of reward can be effected through material sacrifice (in the form of donations and charity) or bodily forms of devotion (recitation of the Qur'an, offering namaaz, fasting and the like).

The recitation of the Qur'an is, indeed, one of the easiest and most common ways of achieving *isal-e sawab*. *Qur'an khwani* is the recitation of all thirty *juz* or *siparah* (parts) of the Qur'an at community readings. The ritual is usually organized on important occasions by women in their homes, with female relatives and neighbours sitting together and reciting the *juz* of the Qur'an until all thirty have been completed.[6] Male relatives and neighbours also join in the recitation in gender-segregated gatherings. On occasion, madrasa students might be invited to sit together and finish the recitation, following which they are served an elaborate meal. Werbner (Chapter 5) examines this ritual recitation of the Qur'an in greater detail and analyses the elements of prayer, sociability and sacrifice embedded in the ritual. She explores the multiple reasons that might prompt someone to host the ceremony as well as the manner in which it is conducted. I am particularly interested in the use of *Qur'an khwani* for *isal-e sawab* and therefore focus on the ritual performed after a death when it is important to complete as many recitations of the Qur'an as possible and to donate the merit thus earned to the deceased, a process known as *bakhshna* (donation), to ensure that the passage of the departed soul from this world to the next is less traumatic. The period immediately following a person's death is believed to be the most difficult for him/her because the soul is questioned in the grave and the horrors of the grave are revealed. This makes it imperative for members of the family of the deceased and loved ones to donate as much merit as possible to alleviate their suffering. Through the belief in intercession and *isal-e sawab*, a mutually responsive relationship is established between this world and the hereafter, and their respective denizens. Funerary prayers held prior to burial are also intended as *isal-e sawab* for the deceased who is in need of merit but is no longer in a position to earn any.

The term *fateha* derives from Surah Fateha, which is the first chapter of the Qur'an recited for *isal-e sawab*. *Niyaz* specifically refers to the ritual where a saint is the focus of the *isal-e sawab* and always entails the consecration of an item of food in the process, while *fateha* may not always involve food (although it usually does) and is recited in order to transfer merit to either a saint or an ordinary person who is no longer alive.[7] The primary distinction between the two is thus that while *niyaz* is offered to transfer merit to saints (and simultaneously to the offerer), *fateha* is offered for deceased family members and relatives. It is customarily recited after the death of a person on the *teeja* (third day), *daswa* (tenth day) and *chaleeswa* (fortieth day), and then at *shashmahi* after the passage of six months, finally culminating in the annual *barsi*. On these occasions, the Qur'an is recited and food is consecrated and distributed. In order to offer *fateha*, families often ensure that they cook food favoured by the deceased during his/her lifetime. The *fateha* thus also becomes a way of displaying one's affection and respect for the departed and offers a way to 'communicate … with the dead, just as food exchanges regularly do with the living' (Counihan 1999: 17).

While noting the significance of the knife as the symbol and tool of transformation of neutral meat into legitimate and edible food (or otherwise) for Christians and Muslims in Ethiopia, Zellelew (2015: 63–4) compares it to the Christian ritual of transubstantiation that converts bread and wine into the body and blood of Jesus Christ. The knife here serves the purpose of the ritual speech act[8] that consecrates food. That very speech act also serves to establish a relationship between the human and the divine. Indeed, food is instrumental in forging and preserving this link in many cultures (Babb 1970; Ortner 1978; Bynum 1987; Horwitz 2001; Scheid 2011).

Counihan (1999: 15) points out that offering food to the deceased enables the living to maintain a cordial relationship with them. A distinction, however, must be drawn in the case of Barelwis, because food is not offered *to* the deceased but to others in their name. Indeed, the food should be offered to the poor and the needy so that their prayers can benefit the deceased. However that may be, Counihan is correct in contending that 'food offerings connect the living and the dead, humans and their gods, neighbors and kin, and family members' (17). By establishing a relationship that transcends the physical location of the believer, the principle of *isal-e sawab* allows for communication between the two worlds. '*Zindon ke àmàl se murdon ko sawab milta hai aur faayda pahunchta hai*' (The practice of the living conveys religious reward to the dead and benefits them) (Azmi 1999: 313). In this chapter, I will examine the implications of thus transferring/conveying/donating religious merit to others.

Apart from the significance of the choice of food, the pattern of consumption is also aligned with the objective that the *fateha* is supposed to serve. In her discussion of the choice of people who are given specific portions of the *qurbani*, Werbner also notes that the choice is not arbitrary. Whereas the food consecrated through *niyaz* can be consumed by the supplicant and his/her family, the food over which *fateha* has been recited must be given away to the poor so that the merit may be transferred to the deceased. This act of giving to the poor effectively serves to complete and seal the sacrifice (Chapter 5). As the food is meant to assuage the hunger of the poor, consuming it personally is an infringement of their right to the food, thereby depriving the deceased of the benefit they could have derived from this act of generosity. By sacrificing food in order to transfer merit to the dead, the living intercede on the former's behalf and alleviate the agony of their afterlife. In her study of a langar (communal distribution of food) at the Ghamkol Sharif shrine in Pakistan, Pnina Werbner (2002) outlines the structure of sacrificial giving. She distinguishes between the sacrifices/gifts given to God directed 'upwards' through saints, and those directed 'downwards' through the poor (103–4). Referring to such forms of giving as 'hierarchical gift economies', she draws our attention to the distinction made in the Punjabi gift economy between balanced giving among equals, unidirectional gifting from a superior to an inferior, tribute from an inferior to a superior, and finally gifting to God through communal giving (Werbner 1990). While a voluntary donation directed downwards to the poor is referred to as *sadqa*, the tribute to members of the highest castes such as Sayyids (regarded to be descendants of the Prophet) is considered *nazraana* (Werbner 1990). The nature of sacrifice, therefore, determines the recipient of the sacrifice/gift. Like *niyaz* and *fateha*, the purpose of the langar too is to earn merit for oneself while offering food to others. The act of animal sacrifice among Durrani Pashtuns is similarly an acknowledgement of the believers' indebtedness to God which gets articulated through the communal sharing of food and its underlying implication of social equality within the community (Tapper and Tapper 1986).

In addition, *niyaz* and *fateha* perform the semiotic function of signifying and communicating Barelwi identity. Borrowing from Zellelew's (2015) examination of the Christian and Muslim knife as a synecdoche of their respective slaughtering rituals, I attempt to analyse the food rituals of Barelwis as a synecdoche of their eschatological beliefs. The relationship of *niyaz/fateha* and Barelwi identity is not merely symbolic or indexical but is both metonymic and synecdochal. The metonymic association is clearly signalled in the use of the term *niyaz-nazar waale* (those who indulge in the practices of *niyaz* and nazar)[9] to refer to Barelwis. To engage in these practices (or conversely, to disparage them) is to performatively announce one's identity because the rituals derive structurally and theoretically from the theological beliefs that index Barelwi identity. If one were to try and decode the 'grammar of foods' in this case, the importance and rationale of these food practices would indicate their significance for the self-conception of Barelwis (Barthes 1997: 22).

The principle of *isal-e sawab* is premised on the act of transfer. This transfer could be examined through the lens of exchange rituals by interrogating the nature of transactions, but I am primarily interested in drawing attention to the ontological shift effected by these exchanges. The link between *duniya* (this world) and *àkhirat* (the hereafter) is operationalized through the transactions conducted across the two domains. Although the two worlds are separated conceptually, spiritually and temporally, there is constant communication between them. The mediation between the two is conducted through saints, shrines, relics, prayers and religious merit. In the context of giving away *qurbani* meat, Werbner also draws our attention to this 'communication' that is achieved 'indirectly, via the poor, through the act of giving' (Chapter 5, p. 129). Based on the principle of *isal-e sawab*, the *niyaz* and *fateha* rituals serve to establish a relationship with saints and the deceased, and in doing so they sanction an alternative organization of time that is structured by the Islamic calendar and centres on the moment of their departure from this world.

Niyaz/fateha: alternative temporalities

Niyaz is offered over food for a particular saint or holy man in order to invoke Allah's blessings and transfer merit to them and in the process to earn it personally too. The *niyaz* of different saints is usually observed at different times of the year, normally coinciding with the time of their *visaal* (departure from this world) and is traditionally associated with the preparation of different items of food, for many of them; for instance, *niyaz* is offered during Muharram for Hussain (the grandson of the Prophet) and those martyred at Karbala. The *niyaz* for Muharram is traditionally offered over *khichda*, which is a dish made of a variety of cereals, grains and mutton/beef cooked over a long, time-consuming period of time and therefore considered a specialty. By providing a ritually potent break in the temporal organization of everyday life, *niyaz* also serves as a calendrical marker around which life is organized.

The Islamic calendar or the Hijri calendar begins from 622 CE from the time of the Prophet's *hijrat* (migration) from Mecca to Medina, a definitive event in the history of Islam. It follows the lunar cycle and consists of twelve months – *Muharram, Safar, Rabi ul-Awwal, Rabi ul-Thani, Jamaad ul-Awwal, Jamaad ul-Thani, Rajab, Shábán, Ramzan, Shawwál, Zul Qaadah* and *Zul Hijjah*. Among Barelwis, the months of this calendar are often identified by the *niyaz* that fall within them instead of their proper names, for instance, *Safar*, the second month of the Islamic calendar, is called *Chehlum ka mahina* (the month of *Chehlum*) because the twentieth day of *Safar* marks the end of the forty-day mourning period for the martyrs of the Battle of Karbala.

In his study of culinary practices and ethnic identity among Maghrebian Jews in France, Bahloul (1995) points out the significance of the food calendar. He posits an opposition between 'food of ritual and food of daily life' that corresponds respectively to the time of the self, which is embedded in the religious ethnic identity and the time of the other (493). We cannot extrapolate this opposition to Barelwis in its entirety because it is based on the immigrant experience and the Maghrebian Jews' struggle for preservation of their culture while at the same time attempting to integrate with the dominant French culture. However, it might be helpful to use the terms of his opposition and his theorization of them. The Barelwi ritual calendar punctuated by *niyaz* of different saints is surely analogous to Bahloul's 'register of the sacred' (493). Much as Jewish gestures signify that one enters sacred time, *niyaz* organizes ritual time for Barelwis. It also demands that 'a special code of culinary gestures, of recipes, of odours and flavors, of table manners is instituted. Thus, sacred time is a time for difference' (493). The Barelwi calendar is not merely marked by annual and monthly *niyaz*, but the week is also organized in accordance with sacred temporality. *Jumeraat* (Thursday) is considered a particularly significant day for *niyaz* and for visiting shrines and the graves of relatives. Most of the shrines in Bareilly have the highest number of visitors on Thursdays. This tradition does not have scriptural valence but enjoys widespread popularity, as has been noted in many ethnographies of shrines (see, for instance, Shurreef 1863; Saheb 2002: 72; Werth 2002).

Muharram is the first month of the Islamic calendar and is significant because the Battle of Karbala (680 CE) was fought in that month.[10] Apart from the *niyaz* offered over *khichda*, items like *doodh ka sharbat* (sweetened milk and water) and *maleeda*[11] are almost exclusively associated with Muharram. Food is, indeed, central to the imagination of Karbala because of the conditions in which the battle was fought. There, Yazid's army cut off Hussain and his troops from the source of water, thereby causing scarcity of food and water in order to starve them into surrender.[12] The imagination of the battle and the hardships suffered by the family of the Prophet are articulated through the physical torment of hunger and thirst. This association is so strong that the name 'Karbala' itself becomes, in everyday speech, a metaphor for deprivation of food and water. Therefore, the observance of Muharram is associated with langar (communal distribution of free food) and setting up of *sabeel* (arrangements for dispensing drinking water or other drinks). People set up stalls for distributing *sooji* halwa (sweet semolina pudding) or rusk and biscuits. These items are also sometimes distributed within mosques to those who come to pray. By ensuring an abundance of food and water, the deprivation suffered by the family of the Prophet is remembered, mourned and reversed.

Imam Jaafar Saadiq (702–65 CE) was an alim of renown in Arabia and was also the great-great-grandson of the Prophet. His *niyaz* is observed in the month of *Rajab* (seventh month of the Islamic calendar) and involves the tradition of *koondhe bharna* (ritually serving food on earthenware). *Koondhe* are earthenware platters which are filled with deep fried sweet griddle cakes called *meethi* poori, for performance of the *niyaz*. The association of the month of *Rajab* with this *niyaz* is so strong that the month is commonly referred to as *koondhon ka mahina* (the month of *koondhe*). Even in homes where earthen vessels are not filled with food in accordance with custom, the preparation of *meethi* poori is the norm. The pooris are consumed by members of the family and also distributed among neighbours and friends. Many Barelwi households follow the tradition of not removing the vessels from their locations once they have been filled and *fateha* has been recited over them. The vessels are placed on a clean surface, usually covered with a cloth and guests are taken to them. Reversing the norms of hospitality that characterize the everyday, guests are not served where they are seated and instead are taken to the food being offered. The *adab* (etiquette, respect) of the food consecrated by the *niyaz* is expressed through the way in which it is consumed. People cover their heads and eat carefully from the *koondha*, trying not to spill anything lest it show an attitude of disrespect towards the consecrated food.

Shab-e Barat is the fifteenth night of *Sha'ban*, the eighth month of the Islamic calendar. It is significant because it is believed that it was the night when the Qur'an was given to the angels. It is also believed to be the Night of Judgement when a list is drawn up of all those who are to be born and those to die the following year. Believers spend the night praying and seeking God's forgiveness because they believe that sins are also pardoned on this night. As a respondent told me, God's grace is supposed to be on the lower skies on this night, thereby emphasizing contiguity to the sacred and the power of the night. It is said that on this night Allah himself asks if there is anyone who he should pardon (*hai koi jisey main baksh doon?*), and a person has only to ask for forgiveness for it to be granted. The occasion of Shab-e Barat is, therefore, a particularly auspicious night for the transfer of merit, and it is therefore considered desirable to spend it in prayer. In the evening, after *maghrib* prayers, men visit graveyards to offer prayers for the dead.[13] The *niyaz* for Shab-e Barat is traditionally offered on halwa.

Believed to be linked to religion, the tradition of associating certain foods with different *niyaz* is often justified by pointing to religious events in the past. There are indeed a multiplicity of stories in circulation which provide a rationale for the preparation of prescribed items on different *niyaz*, some of which are completely dismissed by the ulema, while they cast doubt on the veracity of many others. The reason for preparing halwa on Shab-e Barat is popularly attributed to an anecdote. A respondent told me that the halwa is a testimony to Amir Hamza's immense love for the Prophet. Amir Hamza (568–625 CE) was the paternal uncle of the Prophet as well as his Companion. He received the news that a tooth belonging to the Prophet was martyred (shaheed) in the Battle of Uhud.[14] Not knowing which tooth of the Prophet this was, Amir Hamza proceeded to smash all his teeth. It is, therefore, believed that halwa is prepared on Shab-e Barat because it is soft in texture and can be eaten by people without teeth. The very respondent who told me this also claimed that the banana was sent to earth on that very night for the same reason. These accounts, although very popular in Bareilly, are contested or their authenticity doubted by most ulema. Another anecdote often offered as a rationale for the preparation of *khichda* on Muharram is that after the Battle of Karbala, the women and children who were left behind by the men when they left for battle were driven to desperation by hunger. In order to assuage their hunger, the women collected all the remnants of food in their houses and brought them together. All the grains and other items were mixed before being cooked together, which is claimed to be the origin of *khichda*.

The *niyaz* of *giyarhvin sharif*[15] is offered for Sheikh Abdul Qadir Jilani of Baghdad (1077–1166 CE), popularly referred to as *Ghaus paak* (helper of the needy) and arguably the most important saint in South Asia. Sanyal (2010: 145) examines Ahmad Raza Khan's devotion to Abdul Qadir Jilani and argues that although Ahmad Raza ranked the latter below the Prophet in the hierarchy of saints, he placed him above all others. Barelwis obviously follow his lead in revering Abdul Qadir Jilani over all others. He left the world on the eleventh of *Rabi-ul Àkhir*, the fourth month of the Islamic calendar. Not only is his *niyaz* offered by some believers on the eleventh of every month, but it is referred to as *giyarhvin ki niyaz* irrespective of when it is offered. It is usually recited over biryani (rice and meat preparation) or *qorma* (a special meat curry).[16] Another *niyaz* associated with Sheikh Abdul Qadir Jilani is *toshè ki niyaz*, which is offered when a vow is fulfilled. It entails the preparation of a particular halwa, using exact proportions of specific ingredients. The custom of using specified proportions of cooking ingredients is also followed for the *niyaz* of Bu Ali Shah Qalandar

(1209–1324 CE), an Indian saint of the Chishti order, and it is recited over a meat curry called *sai muni sharif*. The name derives from the exact measure of items that go into its preparation. *Sai* means three and *mun* is a measure of weight (1 *mun* is approximately equal to 37 kg or 81 lbs). Hence, around 37 kg each of clarified butter, mutton, and yoghurt is used to prepare the curry for offering *niyaz*. The preparation is also mentioned by Shurreef (1863: 183) in his study of Muslim rituals in colonial India.

The role of women

It is primarily women who keep track of the different *niyaz* and make the requisite preparations for them. Many contributors in this volume highlight the gendered nature of domestic duties and its implications for women's piety (Sengupta, Engelmajer, Khan). Whether domestic chores come in the way of women's efforts to cultivate pious routines (Khan, Sengupta) or confer soteriological agency by making them responsible for the act of giving (Engelmajer) is a question that cannot be definitively answered because of the multiplicity of ways in which women reconcile the seemingly conflicting demands of the domestic and religious universes. The lives of Barelwi women offer a similar conundrum, but they resolve it differently from the women who figure in Khan's ethnography (Chapter 10). Owing to the significance of ritualized food production, distribution and consumption for Barelwis, the domestic becomes an extension of the religious. Indeed, in some ways it offers opportunities for the appropriate fulfilment of significant religious duties. For Barelwi women, the expression of piety entails not only the observance of *niyaz* and *fateha* but participation in a range of shrine-based rituals. Indeed, the significant role that women play in shrine-based practice has been well documented (Mernissi 1977; Betteridge 1985; Tapper 1990; Malik 2002; among others). The reason why women form a majority of shrine-goers is attributed to their exclusion from active participation in the public sphere of religion (Kamalkhani 2010). Denied entry into mosques in most places, women find ways of participating more fully and productively in various capacities at shrines (Trimingham 1971; Abbas 2002). Trimingham (1971: 232) posits a dualism between 'male and female religion' that is brought to the fore on Fridays when the men congregate and participate in the communal, ritual prayers and the women visit saints' tombs and graveyards to make vows and offerings. Tapper (1990) also notes the frequency of women's visits to shrines and the disparaging attitude of the men towards this. She points out that women seem to be more conscious and mindful of shrines and graveyards or the 'sacred geography' of the town than men (247).

Additionally, the rituals and practices at shrines provide a rich, sensorial experience that serves as the basis for alternative forms of communitarian identities for women, whose lives are believed to be relatively monotonous (Malik 2002). It would, however, be erroneous to characterize the role of women at shrine-based rituals as passive (Abbas 2002). While excluded from the mosque, women find it possible to participate more fully and productively at shrines. They do so in their capacity as mystics, poets, mothers, mentors, patrons, musicians, preservers of legend and guardians of Sufi tradition (Abbas 2002). Mernissi (1977) also explores the role of the shrine as a space of women's solidarity against a society that excludes them from political and economic power. Their association with shrines and relationships with saints grant them a measure of power at a place where they can exercise their will and attempt to a degree to control events. Ironically, however, by channelling the grievances of women to the divine, saints and shrines also serve to sap them of their disruptive potential (Mernissi 1977).

For Barelwi women, shrine-based practice and food rituals provide the means to be pious and allow them to forge a relationship with the divine which is relatively unmediated and intensely personal. Because they are marginalized in the public religious sphere, women's piety finds expression in alternative social contexts, especially in the domestic realm (Kamalkhani 2010). Also, through their constant awareness and mindfulness of a parallel, sacred temporality, they inhabit Bahloul's (1995) 'sacred time' simultaneously with ordinary time. For most Barelwi women, the rhythm of everyday life and domestic routines is attuned to the ritual calendar. In addition, women embody the Barelwi ethic through attentiveness to an attitude of *adab* towards food in the everyday, with regard to handling, storage, preparation, consumption, distribution, and disposal of items of food. Indeed, the consecrated food requires extreme care in its handling to ensure that the possibility of inadvertent *be-adabi* (disrespect) is minimized. It is recommended that only those food items be used for *niyaz* and *fateha* which can be eaten in their entirety and do not contain anything that will be discarded later, for instance, bones or seeds. Sanyal's study further offers us a glimpse into the process of inculcation of an attitude of *adab* in young girls at the madrasa, who would presumably be responsible for domestic duties later in life (Chapter 9). Women seek to ensure *adab* of consecrated food not only because they are responsible for its preparation but because, as believers, they identify closely with such rituals.

Apart from their instrumental role in the management and preparation of food, women are also believing subjects in their own right who articulate their piety through the idiom of food. In doing so, they seem to embody an agency that a critique like Rokeya Hossain's (Chapter 2) or Rehmat Apa's (Chapter 10) denies them. While women's labour in the kitchen does, indeed, take on an aspect of devotional practice, it does not necessarily crowd out other, more 'appropriate' forms and objects of devotion, as Hossain argues (Chapter 2). Instead, it enables adherence to traditional forms of devotion while also expanding the scope of what is implied by devotion itself.

It must be noted that while shrines are visited primarily by women from the middle class or the economically underprivileged sections of society with low levels of literacy, the rituals of *niyaz* and *fateha* are mostly followed by women across all social classes. The significance of these rituals in Barelwi households ensures that women are socialized into these practices from an early age. Children too young to be given any responsibility of organization and preparation are nonetheless actively encouraged and involved in the process of recitation and mindful consumption of the food items. These occasions mostly have a festive air, and young boys and girls often sit alongside the primary reciter of *niyaz* and *fateha* out of eagerness to consume the food items once the recitation is finished. Mindful of the sacredness of the occasion, both boys and girls learn at an early age to cover their heads, sit quietly during the ritual and make personal supplicatory prayers at the completion of the recitation. At a later age, when girls are gradually inducted into domestic responsibilities, they assume responsibility for the practices and continue to observe them in their marital homes as well. Werbner (2002) also notes the 'generative organising capacity' of the langar at the Ghamkol Sharif shrine and the manner in which it enables women to play a significant role in the process.

While it is women's responsibility to organize and prepare food for these rituals, men are involved in the rituals after the preparation of the food, as also seen in Werbner's study of Indonesian *slametan*s (Chapter 5). However, there are frequent exceptions because some households hold *niyaz* on a much larger scale in the form of open-house celebrations, which necessitates the use of professional cooks for the occasion. These professionals are invariably men, and the responsibility of the organization and preparation of food in such cases shifts to the men of the household. Even when the ritual is organized in the domestic realm, men are involved in the recitation, mindful consumption and distribution of the consecrated food. It would, therefore, be erroneous to understand these practices as being solely the preserve of women.

As mentioned earlier, Qur'anic verses are recited over food for *niyaz* and *fateha*. As believers, both men and women can recite the prayers and donate merit to saints and the deceased, but the usual practice is for men to be given that responsibility. Counihan (1999: 15) observes that it is the right of men to intercede with the supernatural in patriarchal cultures, whereas relatively egalitarian cultures allow women the power to mediate with the divine. Van Esterik (1985) notes the role of Thai Buddhist women in managing food transactions with both the human and the supernatural. They possess pragmatic knowledge of Theravada Buddhism, which enables them to offer the appropriate foods to humans, deceased humans, monks and deities. The experience of Buddhism for men and women in some way parallels the distinction of a mosque-based formalized male sphere and a shrine-based intimate, personalized Islam where women form the majority, as evident from Engelmajer's discussion in Chapter 6 as well. However, such an analogy has its limitations and should not be overstated.

Besides *niyaz* and *fateha*, there are other food rituals in which Barelwi women participate, for instance, in offering food items for vows and dedications made for wish fulfilment. The term *piyàli bharwaana* (to fill bowls) refers to the preparation of kheer (sweet rice pudding) or pooris and serving them in earthenware bowls, which are distributed among family, neighbours and the needy. The custom is so closely associated with wish-making that *piyàli bharwaana* becomes a metaphor for vow fulfilment.[17] Many Barelwi women also follow the tradition of offering *phal ka sehra* (chaplet of fruits) or *mewa ka sehra* (chaplet of dried fruits) on *taziya* (replica of Hussain's grave, mounted and displayed in processions) during Muharram. *Sehra*s are often promised in return for wish fulfilment. It is common practice to make wishes on the *taziya* even though the ulema forbid the practice. Naazera, a young woman, once made a *mannat* (vow) for a childless friend of hers. Her friend was desperate because her husband had decided to take another wife in order to bear children. Naazera tied a *kalewa* (coloured thread used for ritual purposes) for her friend at the *taziya*, and the woman soon conceived and gave birth to a boy. The second marriage was cancelled, and the woman offered *niyaz* of *mewa* (dried fruits) in return.

Neither *nàjaayaz* nor *wàjib*: navigating shariat

The debates around the prescribed form of ritual performances are usually aligned with theological differences between schools of thought. One of the most significant points of contention is the practice of people keeping food in front of themselves while reciting *fateha*. Traditionally, this is the practice, and when on occasion the food is not ready, a glass of water is kept in front of the reciter as a sign that he may begin the recitation. Such practices are disparaged by the ulema because it is not a compulsory condition for offering *fateha*. The issue is further complicated by the approach of the other schools of thought that condemn this Barelwi practice and believe it to be a *bidat* (innovation). Barelwi ulema are, therefore, hard-pressed to explain that this is not an illegitimate practice. In fact, the ulema declare as sinners all those who consider such food haram and *nàjaayaz* (illegitimate), because the food has been consecrated in the name of Allah and Allah's saints, while also distancing themselves from the common Barelwi belief that *fateha* cannot be recited without food.

The arguments in defence of the practice invoke shariat to establish that anything not considered illegitimate by legal standards is, by the same token, acceptable. To recite Qur'anic verses over food cannot possibly be illegitimate when the food is legitimate and the verses are drawn from the Qur'an. Being well within the bounds of shariat, the practice is not *nàjaayaz*. At the same time, to consider it obligatory is also wrong because it is not enjoined by shariat, and such a belief enables their detractors to denigrate and scorn Barelwis.[18] Rouse and Hoskins (2004) cite the racial antagonisms and identity politics articulated through cuisine in the case of African Americans after the Great Migration when millions of them relocated from the rural South to urban centres in the northern states. Associated with poor health, southern cuisines were criticized in newspaper articles, thereby reinforcing 'binary divisions between north and south: white and black, civilized and uncivilized, educated and uneducated, good and bad' (234). The practices of *niyaz* and nazar similarly draw upon and reinforce the binary divisions between unreformed Islam and reformist Islam, or popular and orthodox interpretations. Routinely condemned as 'unreformed' and 'popular' precisely on the basis of such food practices and other shrine-based rituals, the Barelwi interpretation of Islam is ranged in opposition to other schools of thought considered 'reformist'.

Ulrich (2007) draws our attention to the polemics around food that determine dietary practices and transactions. She studies the dietary polemics in Buddhist, Hindu and Jain literature in south India between the sixth and eleventh centuries and illustrates the way in which these texts 'attacked other religious communities on the grounds that they ate the wrong things or in the wrong way' (230). The polemics around Barelwi rituals are similarly based on arguments and counterarguments regarding popular rituals. As mentioned in

Maulana Ashraf Ali Thanvi's *Bihishti Zewar*, Deobandis[19] consider objectionable the performance of *fateha* and *niyaz* in order to seek assistance from saints. Indeed, it is argued that such beliefs are akin to idolatory (Metcalf 1990: 150). Also, the custom of setting aside days for *teeja*, *daswa* and *chaleeswa* after a death is criticized by Thanvi because they are not sanctioned by shariat and, therefore, constitute *bidat* (152).[20] Ulrich (2007) argues that rather than being aimed at convincing their opponents, the role of polemical literature in south India was to construct a common identity for their community in opposition to the others. The polemics around food among Barelwis appear to serve the same purpose. Deobandi ulema lay claim to a reformist position through their polemics against traditional practices, while Barelwi ulema defend these by invoking shariat and attacking their opponents. By not considering *fateha* food *nàjaayaz*, they attempt to articulate an identity distinct from that of their detractors, and by declaring it not *wàjib* (obligatory), they lay claim to textually grounded shariat-based piety.

Transacting with the divine

Belief in the afterlife and the existence of heaven and hell is an essential aspect of Islamic eschatology. The believer is continually urged to remember that his time in this world is limited and only a fraction of the time that he is destined to spend in heaven or hell. Such eschatological concerns are, therefore, bound to shape everyday life and imbue all activities that a person pursues with the prospect of redemption or its denial. The boundaries isolating this world from the next are revealed to be largely porous for the purpose of the transfer of intangibles such as merit or spiritual benefit. Indeed, it is only when a person establishes such a relationship with the hereafter that s/he can transcend corporeal limitations. The principle of *isal-e sawab* foregrounds the transactions that constantly bridge the spiritual distance between the two worlds. These transactions can be regarded as 'sacred commerce' based on 'self-interested exchanges between the human and the divine' (Eade and Sallnow 1991: 24) or a form of gift-exchange with it (Betteridge 1985). Both arguments have merit in the way they characterize the transactions but both have their limitations, and I argue that understanding *niyaz* and *fateha* only through these perspectives obscures the nature of the link between the human and the divine, which is marked not by rupture but by continuity.

Betteridge (1985) examines the tradition of gift giving in Iran in formal and intimate contexts. She includes the processes of making and fulfilling vows in the latter category because she emphasizes the intimacy of the relationship between the saint and the believer and the personalized nature of the rituals that contrasts with the ritualized performance of prayers, fasting and pilgrimages prescribed by religion. While agreeing with her characterization of the relationship, I wish to question further the nature of exchange that is effected through it. Betteridge examines the process of gift giving to saints, which appears to be a bargain, but she argues that actually the *nazri* or gift offered following the fulfilment of a vow illustrates an ideal gift: 'It is not given in the hope that a relationship will be formed or persist in a particular fashion, but to assert and celebrate the existence of that relationship' (198). Such a view is also espoused by Werbner (2002), who characterizes gifting to God as unilateral, 'given without expectation of return'. On the other hand, Eade and Sallnow (1991: 24) emphasize the underlying 'market ideology' that structures the relationship between believers and the divine. They view pilgrimage shrines as 'transformation stations' where pain and suffering are exchanged for spiritual merit and sins are written off through penance and piety (24). In addition, they point to the implausibility of selfless, disinterested acts of giving, particularly in the context of religions offering salvation, because all offering ultimately benefits the giver materially or spiritually. That is why they consider the motivation for securing favours to be extremely significant for pilgrims to a shrine. Such a view is in stark contrast to Betteridge's (1985) 'pure gift' that is premised not on reciprocity but on the celebration of a relationship.

In her study of the langar at Ghamkol Sharif, Werbner (2002: 115) stresses that the experience of the pilgrimage to the saints' *urs* (death anniversary of a saint) goes beyond 'calculus and communitas'. In other words, the experience of the pilgrim must be understood not only as a self-interested calculated exchange in return for wish fulfilment but alongside the other forms of sacrifice and gift giving in Islam. She emphasizes the metonymic (and metaphoric) transformation of the pilgrim and argues that the experience of 'voluntary labour and sacrifice' cannot merely be understood as 'sacred commerce' (115). Nancy Tapper (1990) introduces a gendered reading of the rituals of reciprocity and draws a distinction between the kind engaged in by men and women. She argues that women are excluded from participation in the '"pure gift" economy of salvation' expressed through public forms of ritualized religion which is available to men (252). Besides, they lack control over economic resources and therefore cannot undertake charitable work and participate in the market economy. Hence, women 'combine muted elements of both' (252).

In all the readings of shrine-based practices mentioned above, the nature of exchange between the human and the divine is interpreted as selfless or motivated or a combination of both. In a way, *isal-e sawab* for the deceased appears to be a 'pure gift' that can never be reciprocated. It therefore appears to be neither a gift that must be repaid (Mauss 1966) nor a gift that must not be repaid (Parry 1986). Indeed, it seems to be a gift that simply *cannot* be repaid. At the same time, however, the subject does hope for reciprocity at a later time. Faced with the inevitability of a person's own death when s/he will similarly be dependent on the efforts of another to earn merit for him/herself, the subject is invested in the gift, thereby making it, more appropriately, a 'generalized' form of exchange rather than a 'pure gift' (Sahlins 1972: 193). The possibility of receiving merit through such generalized exchange is reassuring and therefore a source of much moral succour that I refer to as the privilege of intercession. Whether this privilege is an impediment to personal piety or a distinctive prerogative is a matter far from settled, as expressed in theological debates and in the position of different scholars regarding the issue of personal responsibility of believers (see Metcalf 1982: 297; Sanyal 2010: 164–5).

Through an exploration of Barelwi transactions with the divine, I wish to draw attention not to the motivational logic behind the exchange but what the act of exchange tells us about the way the world is conceived. According to the eschatological principles of Islam, the end of life is not death but the afterlife. The continuity between the two is mirrored in the conception of a transient *duniya* and an eternal *àkhirat.* It is further exemplified through the concept of *sadqa-e jàriya* (perpetual charity),[21] which enables the believer to earn merit for him/herself till the Day of Judgement. Certain activities such as supporting the construction of mosques and schools or teaching someone to recite the Qur'an are considered so meritorious that they allow the believer to earn merit eternally for their act.[22] The advantage of such a clause becomes clear when we take into account the eternal afterlife following a person's physical death when s/he is powerless to earn any personal merit. *Sadqa-e jàriya* allows the believer to transcend such corporal limitations by enabling him/her to store merit for a time when s/he will be physically incapable of earning any. The idea of everlasting merit enables the subject to transcend the restrictions of the distinct temporal zones of this life and the afterlife.

The concept of *sadqa-e jàriya* evades categorization in terms of relationships of exchange. Just as *sawab* is donated to others, here it is given to the self in perpetuity. Analogous to the langar at Ghamkol Sharif, which is a form of 'perpetual sacrifice' maintained through an apparently endless supply of meat freely given to the saint and his shrine (Werbner 2002), *sadqa-e jàriya* is a perpetual gift to the self. Here, finally is a gift that is free from the demands of reciprocity, both direct and generalized. At the same time, given that the recipient is also the giver, can it be considered a gift at all or does it constitute a self-centred transaction? Mick and Demoss (1990) examine the phenomena of gifting to the self and find that 'self-gifts are a form of personally symbolic self-communication through special indulgences that tend to be premeditated and highly context bound'. It must be remembered, however, that their research is based on material gifts, whereas our concern is the intangible merit that the recipient accumulates for his life after death.

Whether *sadqa-e jàriya* constitutes the ultimate 'pure gift' or symbolizes the most self-interested exchange of all is not consequential for the argument here. What *sadqa-e jàriya* does point to is a transcendental relationship that enhances the scope of believers' ability to earn merit for themselves as well as others. Physical acts of charity, prayers, food practices, recitation of Qur'anic verses, material sacrifices, saints and shrines all serve as the medium for otherworldly communication. In the case of shrines, Eade and Sallnow (1991: 25) emphasize its transactional ethic as having a greater appeal for pilgrims than its redemptive aspect. While not rejecting the existence of a transactional ethic, I argue that the redemptive capacity of the shrine is not tangential to such a function. Indeed, the shrine emerges as a transactional and transformational space precisely because of its intersectional nature. It symbolizes and embodies the link between the earthly and heavenly realms by housing the saint who is, in this context, a liminal being par excellence. The relationships established and transacted between this world and the next are constitutive of and constituted by an imagination of the *duniya* and *àkhirat* as interrelated spheres of existence.

The very idea of mediation or intercession is premised on the existence of distinct spheres, and *duniya* and *àkhirat* are indeed distinct, but they are also contiguous and proximate. Werbner (2002: 108) notes the contrast that believers and saints draw between the 'greed and corruption of the "world" (*dunya*) and the purity of the lodge as a place of true religion (*din*)'. *Duniya* is, in this case, contrasted with *din* – embodied by the shrine – notwithstanding the lodge/shrine being physically located in the former. The conceptualization of both *duniya* and *àkhirat* is in terms of spiritual dominions rather than tangible spaces. These spiritual dominions employ the generative capacity of the link between them to position themselves as contiguous and continuous. Throughout their existence in the *duniya*, believers are exhorted to be mindful of the *àkhirat*. The existence of the other world and their positioning in relation to it informs their entire lives and routine activities in the everyday. Transactions with this world occur continually through prayers, rituals, gestures and intentions, thus establishing and sustaining a relationship of reciprocity with it, thereby transcending the space and time of both dominions.

Notes

1 The '*Bismillah*' is an Arabic phrase that means 'In the name of Allah, the most beneficent and most merciful'. It is recited by devout Muslims at the beginning of any new endeavour.

2 There is a substantial anthropological literature on the significance of food as an expression of culture and identity (Buckser 1999; Mannur 2004; Williams-Forson 2010). A range of identities are forged through food and cuisines: national (Visser 1999; DeSoucey 2010; Hale 2012), ethnic (Keen and Zeitlyn 2007; Trecchia 2012), religious (Rouse and Hoskins 2004; Ulrich 2007; Rosenblum 2010; Freidenreich 2011; Zellelew 2015), cultural (Bahloul 1995; Beoku-Betts 1995; Wilk 1999) and class-based (Johnston et al. 2012), among others.

3 In her study of the Dar ul-Uloom madrasa at Deoband, Barbara Metcalf (1982) traces the historical conditions that shaped Muslim intellectual thought in the nineteenth century that forced Muslims into a period of reform, as exemplified by the Deoband seminary that represents one such 'reformist' school of thought. Francis Robinson (2001) examines the role of the ulema at Firangi Mahal in dealing with the challenge of reformism within Islam, while in parallel negotiating with the British administration and increasing Western power. The Ahl-e Hadith argue in favour of direct access to texts and sources of Islamic authority, while eschewing reliance on schools of law and saints in order to be religious (Metcalf 1982). Yohanann Friedmann (2003) examines the Ahmadi movement, which is vehemently attacked by other schools of thought among Sunni Muslims for their belief in the prophetic status of the founder, Ghulam Ahmad Qadiyan, which challenges the finality of the prophethood of Muhammad.

4 The patronymic Barelwi derives from the city of Bareilly in north India where Ahmad Raza Khan lived. His shrine is in Bareilly and is managed by his descendants.

5 The Urdu term '*visaal*' is used to refer to the departure of a saint from this world. It literally means communion or meeting, signifying the union of their soul with Allah, thereby shifting the emphasis from this world to the next.

6 *Qur'an khwani* is conducted for a range of reasons: health, if someone is unwell; transferring merit to the dead; to mark auspicious occasions or in fulfilment of vows taken earlier. Werbner explores these reasons in detail as well as the structure of the ritual in this volume.

7 While the term *fateha* (rather than *niyaz*) can be employed to refer to the *isal-e sawab* for a saint, the converse is almost never the case. *Fateha* may thus be understood to be the wider term. In this chapter, however, I have used the conventional meanings throughout, keeping *niyaz* and *fateha* separate.

8 The utterance of particular ritually charged speech acts during slaughter transforms the animal's flesh, 'for Christians the *BaSeme Ab waWald waMenfes Qedus Ahadu Amlak* ("In the name of the Father, the Son, the Holy Spirit, One God"), and for Muslims the *Bismillah al-rahman al-rahim* ("In the name of Allah, the passionate and the Merciful")' (Zellelew 2015: 62).

9 Nazar is a variation of the Arabic word *nazr*, which means an offering. It refers to the act of offering a gift, either material or immaterial, in return for the fulfilment of a vow.

10 The Battle of Karbala was fought between Hussain, the grandson of the Prophet, and the Umayyad caliph Yazid. The family of the Prophet and his Companions were massacred by Yazid's army on the tenth day of Muharram (*Ashura*). Because of this, it is considered a day of mourning.

11 *Maleeda* refers to a sweet preparation made of crumbled dough, clarified butter and sugar. It is almost never prepared on occasions other than Muharram.

12 In order to fight against the wrongful assumption of the caliphate by Yazid, Hussain went to Kufah in Iraq. However, the people of Kufah reneged on their promise to support him and eventually Hussain, his family and supporters were surrounded by a huge army led by Umar Ibn Sa'd at Karbala in Iraq. 'Cut off from water for eight days, he parleyed with the Caliph's troops until at length the parties fought … Finally, Husayn mounted his horse and went into battle where, weakened by thirst, he was killed' (Glasse 1817: 163).

13 According to Barelwi ulema, women are not permitted to enter graveyards.

14 The Battle of Uhud took place in the third year of the Hijri calendar on the outskirts of Medina. In the battle, the Prophet was struck by the enemy, and two nails of his helmet impaled his face. Finally, one of his Companions, Abu Ubaidah, pulled the nails out of his face and when he did so, a tooth fell out with each nail (Hughes 1964: 381).

15 The term *giyarhvin* derives from the Urdu/Hindi word *giyarah* (the numeral eleven), referring to the date on which Shaikh Abdul Qadir Jilani left the world.

16 Both biryani and qorma are prepared on special occasions. Before weddings became lavish in Bareilly, the standard wedding menu among Muslims consisted of only one or both these items.

17 In his compilation of Muslim rituals in colonial India, Shurreef (1863: 179–86) lists the vows, oblations and dedications that women make in the name of Allah, the Prophet or a particular saint, followed by offerings in return of the fulfilment of their vow.

18 Following the same logic, many practices like filling *koondhe* are considered legitimate but not binding.

19 Deobandis are adherents of the school of thought upheld by the Deoband seminary in north India, which represents a 'reformist' school of thought (Metcalf 1982).

20 It must be remembered that there exists the possibility of Deobandi followers not adhering strictly to Thanvi's objections. The stance of the ulema is sometimes at variance with the practices of their followers, and it is possible that the latter are not as averse to these practices as Thanvi's text argues.

21 *Sadqa-e jariya* refers to a particular kind of *sadqa* (sacrifice). I would like to distinguish it from Werbner's *sadqa*, which is a form of sacrifice through substitution (see Chapter 5). Both are kinds of sacrifice, but they differ in form.

22 Such initiatives can also be undertaken in somebody else's name, with the express intention of *isal-e sawab*.

References

Abbas, Shemeem Burney. 2002. *The Female Voice in Sufi Ritual: Devotional Practices of Pakistan and India*. Austin: University of Texas Press.

Azmi, Maulana Amjad Ali. 1999. *Islàmi Akhlàq-o-àdàb: Bahàr-e-Shariat* (Part 16), trans. Mohammad Mehtab Ali. Bareilly: Ala Hazrat Darul Qutub.

Babb, Lawrence A. 1970. 'The Food of the Gods in Chhattisgarh: Some Structural Features of Hindu Ritual'. *Southwestern Journal of Anthropology* 26(3) (Autumn): 287–304.

Bahloul, Joèlle. 1995. 'Food Practices among Sephardic Immigrants in Contemporary France: Dietary Laws in Urban Society'. *Journal of the American Academy of Religion* 63(3), Thematic Issue on Religion and Food (Autumn): 485–96.

Barthes, Roland. 1997. 'Toward a Psychosociology of Contemporary Food Consumption'. In Carole M. Counihan and Penny Van Esterik (eds), *Food and Culture: A Reader*. New York: Routledge.

Beoku-Betts, Josephine A. 1995. 'We Got Our Way of Cooking Things: Women, Food, and Preservation of Cultural Identity among the Gullah'. *Gender and Society* 9(5) (October): 535–5.

Betteridge, Anne H. 1985. 'Gift-Exchange in Iran: The Locus of Self-Identity in Social Interaction'. *Anthropological Quarterly* 58(4), Self and Society in the Middle East (October): 190–202.

Buckser, Andrew. 1999. 'Keeping Kosher: Eating and Social Identity among the Jews of Denmark'. *Ethnology* 38(3) (Summer): 191–209.

Bynum, Caroline Walker. 1987. *Holy Feast and Holy Fast: The Religious Significance of Food to Medieval Women*. Berkeley: University of California Press.

Counihan, Carole M. 1999. *The Anthropology of Food and Body: Gender, Meaning and Power*. New York: Routledge.

DeSoucey, Michaela. 2010. 'Gastronationalism: Food Traditions and Authenticity Politics in the European Union'. *American Sociological Review* 75(3) (June): 432–55.

Douglas, Mary. 1972. 'Deciphering a Meal'. *Daedalus* 101(1), Myth, Symbol, and Culture: 61–81.

Eade, John, and Michael J. Sallnow (eds). 1991. *Contesting the Sacred: The Anthropology of Pilgrimage*. Urbana: University of Illinois Press.

Freidenreich, David M. 2011. *Foreigners and Their Food: Constructing Otherness in Jewish, Christian, and Islamic Law*. Berkeley: University of California Press.

Friedmann, Yohanan. 2003. *Prophecy Continuous: Aspects of Ahmadi Religious Thought and Its Medieval Background*. New Delhi: Oxford University Press.

Glasse, Cyril. 1817. *The Concise Encyclopedia of Islam*. San Francisco: Harper & Row.

Hale, Elizabeth. 2012. 'James Bond and the Art of Eating Eggs'. *Gastronomica* 12(4) (Winter): 84–90.

Horwitz, Liora Kolska. 2001. 'Animal Offerings in the Middle Bronze Age: Food for the Gods, Food for Thought'. *Palestine Exploration Quarterly* 133(2): 78–90.

Hughes, Thomas Patrick. 1964. *A Dictionary of Islam*. Lahore: Premier Book House.

Johnston, Josèe, Alexandra Rodney and Michelle Szabo. 2012. 'Place, Ethics, and Everyday Eating: A Tale of Two Neighbourhoods'. *Sociology* 46(6) (December): 1091–108.

Kamalkhani, Zahra. 2010. *Women's Islam: Religious Practice among Women in Today's Iran*. London: Routledge.

Keen, Anne Elise, and David Zeitlyn. 2007. 'Language, Diet, and Ethnicity in Mayo-Darlé, Adamaoua, Cameroon'. *Anthropos* 102(1): 213–19.

Malik, Jamal. 2002. 'The Literary Critique of Islamic Popular Religion in the Guise of Traditional Mysticism, or the Abused Woman'. In Pnina Werbner and Helene Basu (eds), *Embodying Charisma: Modernity, Locality, and the Performance of Emotion in Sufi Cults*. Taylor & Francis e-Library.

Mannur, Anita. 2004. 'Food Matters: An Introduction'. *The Massachusetts Review* 45(3), Food Matters (Autumn): 209–15.

Mauss, Marcel. 1966. *The Gift: Forms and Functions of Exchange in Archaic Societies*. London: Cohen and West.

Mernissi, Fatima. 1977. 'Women, Saints, and Sanctuaries'. *Signs, Journal of Women in Culture and Society* 3(1), Women and National Development: The Complexities of Change (Autumn): 101–12.

Metcalf, Barbara Daly. 1982. *Islamic Revival in British India: Deoband, 1860–1900*. Princeton, NJ: Princeton University Press.

Metcalf, Barbara Daly. 1990. *Perfecting Women: Maulana Ashraf 'Ali Thanawi's Bihishti Zewar, Partial Translation with Commentary*. Berkeley: University of California Press.

Mick, David Glen, and Michelle Demoss. 1990. 'Self-Gifts: Phenomenological Insights from Four Contexts'. *Journal of Consumer Research* 17(3) (December): 322–3.

Naeemi, Mufti Ahmed Yaar Khan. 2008. *The Obliteration of Falsehood*. Translated by Maulana Omar Dawood Qadri Moeeni. Bolton, UK: Maktab-e-Qadria.

Ohnuki-Tierney, Emiko. 1993. *Rice as Self: Japanese Identities through Time*. Princeton, NJ: Princeton University Press.

Ortner, Sherry B. 1978. *Sherpas through Their Rituals*. London: Cambridge University Press.

Parry, Jonathan. 1986. 'The Gift, the Indian Gift and the "Indian Gift"'. *Man*, NS 21(3) (September): 453–73.

Robinson, Francis. 2001. *The Ulama of Farangi Mahall and Islamic Culture in South Asia*. Delhi: Permanent Black.

Rosenblum, Jordan D. 2010. '"Why Do You Refuse to Eat Pork?" Jews, Food, and Identity in Roman Palestine'. *Jewish Quarterly Review* 100(1) (Winter): 95–110.

Rouse, Carolyn, and Janet Hoskins. 2004. 'Purity, Soul Food, and Sunni Islam: Explorations at the Intersection of Consumption and Resistance'. *Cultural Anthropology* 19(2) (May): 226–49.

Saheb, S. A. A. 2002. 'A "Festival of Flags": Hindu–Muslim Devotion and the Sacralising of Localism at the Shrine of Nagore-e-Sharif in Tamil Nadu'. In Pnina Werbner and Helene Basu (eds), *Embodying Charisma: Modernity, Locality and the Performance of Emotion in Sufi Cults*. Taylor & Francis e-Library.

Sahlins, Marshall. 1972. *Stone Age Economics*. Chicago: Aldine.

Sanyal, Usha. 2010. *Devotional Islam and Politics in British India: Ahmad Riza Khan Barelwi and His Movement, 1870–1920*. New Delhi: Yoda Press.

Scheid, John. 2011. 'Sacrifices for Gods and Ancestors'. In Jòrg Rùpke (ed.), *A Companion to Roman Religion*. Blackwell, UK: Wiley.

Shurreef, Jaffur. 1863. *Customs of the Mussulmans of India*. Translated by G. A. Herklots. Madras: J. Higginbotham.

Tapper, Nancy. 1990. '*Ziyaret*: Gender, Movement and Exchange in a Turkish Community'. In Dale F. Eickelman and James Piscatori (eds), *Muslim Travellers: Pilgrimage, Migration, and the Religious Imagination*. Berkeley: University of California.

Tapper, Richard, and Nancy Tapper. 1986. '"Eat This, It'll Do You a Power of Good": Food and Commensality among Durrani Pashtuns'. *American Ethnologist* 13(1) (February): 62–79.

Trecchia, Patrizia La. 2012. 'Identity in the Kitchen: Creation of Taste and Culinary Memories of an Italian-American Identity'. *Italian Americana* 30(1) (Winter): 44–56.

Trimingham, Spencer. 1971. *The Sufi Orders in Islam*. London: Oxford University Press.

Tuzin, Donald F. 1972. 'Yam Symbolism in the Sepik: An Interpretive Account'. *Southwestern Journal of Anthropology* 28(3) (Autumn): 230–54.

Ulrich, Katherine E. 2007. 'Food Fights'. *History of Religions* 46(3) (February): 228–61.

Van Esterik, Penny. 1985. 'Feeding Their Faith: Recipe Knowledge among Thai Buddhist Women'. *Food and Foodways: Explorations in the History and Culture of Human Nourishment* 1: 197–215.

Visser, Margaret. 1999. 'Food and Culture: Interconnections'. *Social Research* 66(1), Food: Nature and Culture (Spring): 117–30.

Werbner, Pnina. 1990. 'Economic Rationality and Hierarchical Gift Economies: Value and Ranking among British Pakistanis'. *Man*, New Series 25(2) (June): 266–85.

Werbner, Pnina. 2002. 'Langar: Pilgrimage, Sacred Exchange and Perpetual Sacrifice in a Sufi Saint's Lodge'. In Pnina Werbner and Helene Basu (eds), *Embodying Charisma: Modernity, Locality and the Performance of Emotion in Sufi Cults*. Taylor & Francis e-Library.

Werth, Lukas. 2002. 'The Saint Who Disappeared: Saints of the Wilderness in Pakistani Village Shrines'. In Pnina Werbner and Helene Basu (eds), *Embodying Charisma: Modernity, Locality and the Performance of Emotion in Sufi Cults*. Taylor & Francis e-Library.

Wilk, Richard R. 1999. '"Real Belizean Food": Building Local Identity in the Transnational Caribbean'. *American Anthropologist* 101(2) (June): 244–55.

Williams-Forson, Psyche. 2010. 'Other Women Cooked for My Husband: Negotiating Gender, Food, and Identities in an African American/Ghanaian Household'. *Feminist Studies* 36(2), Re-inventing Mothers (Summer): 435–61.

Zellelew, Tilahun Bejitual. 2015. 'The Semiotics of the "Christian/Muslim Knife": Meat and Knife as Markers of Religious Identity in Ethiopia'. *Signs and Society* 3(1) (Spring): 44–70.

5

Between *khatm-e qur'ans* and *slametans*: Gender and class in South Asian and Indonesian interdomestic rituals

Pnina Werbner

Introduction

The historiographies of South Asian and Indonesian Islam – both regions on the periphery of the Muslim heartland – highlight the way scholarly traditions gloss over apparently quite different, yet startlingly similar, traditions of ritual practice and belief. As regional conversations develop over time, however, a convergence may emerge where previously difference was stressed, and along with this revised scholarly recognition of resemblance, the disclosure of actual historical connections may come to replace earlier disjunctions.

The present chapter interrogates this process by drawing a comparison between two commonplace everyday rituals in Indonesia and Muslim South Asia – the *slametan* and the *khatm-e qur'an*. At stake in this comparison, I shall argue, is not only the place of gender in these rituals but of class as well.

It is worth reminding ourselves at the outset of Clifford Geertz's (1960: 1) original insight into what he describes as a 'core' ritual:

> At the centre of the whole Javanese religious system lies a simple, formal, undramatic, almost furtive, little ritual: the *slametan* … [it] is the Javanese version of what is perhaps the world's most common religious ritual, the communal feast, and, as almost everywhere, it symbolises the mystic and social unity of those participating in it. Friends, neighbours, fellow workers, relatives, local spirits, dead ancestors, and near-forgotten gods all get bound, by virtue of their commensality, into a defined social group pledged to mutual support and cooperation.

In Geertz's ethnography, the *slametan* is depicted as primarily a neighbourhood, household-centred ritual attended and convened by men; held in the front of the house, it consists of an appeal to a range of indigenous spirits and ancestors to whom food and incense are dedicated, before the men partake of some of the food and then, wrapping it in banana leaves, carry it to be consumed in their own houses nearby with their families. In Geertz's *The Religion of Java* the *slametan* is conceived of, above all, as a ritual held by the 'Abangan' peasantry, still immersed in pre-Islamic beliefs in spirits. The ritual virtually disappears in the book when Geertz turns to discuss the *Santri*, the urban reformist Muslims, and the *Prijaji*, the urban elites and aristocracy who command Javanese high culture and art. If the *slametan* is a 'furtive' little village ritual, it virtually vanishes from sight among educated townspeople, men and women (though we are told everybody still convenes it).

Equally furtive, perhaps, despite similarly being a core ritual, *khatm-e qur'ans* are virtually absent in scholarly writings on Pakistan and Muslim South Asia.[1] I first encountered the ritual in Manchester, United Kingdom, in 1975, and, much like Geertz found in Java, observed that it was repeatedly convened in response to a myriad of occasions, from dangerous accidents to thanksgiving or fulfilment of a vow. It was also, as in Indonesia, a domestic ritual, convened by a family or household. This set it off from other public ritual observances, though *khatm-e qur'ans* are also held in the mosque when a person has died. In South Asia, as elsewhere in the Muslim world, the mosque is above all the domain of men and serves as a backdrop for the performance of communal rituals and festivals, for theological punditry and for political-cum-ethnic organization. Domestic rituals are held in the home and are often dominated by women. The congregation attending these rituals is selected by the conveners and represents, as in Indonesia, their significant circle of friends, kinsmen and neighbours.

In the present chapter, I argue that there are striking similarities in the way that both the *slametan* and the *khatm-e qur'an* rituals allow for the creation of an everyday interdomestic domain controlled in large measure by women and based on female networking. Class and gender intersect in such networks, leading to different configurations of interhousehold relations in villages, neighbourhoods and urban contexts.

The *khatm-e qur'an*

Of all domestic rituals convened at home, perhaps the most central is this relatively simple, unelaborated ritual that most resembles the *slametan* in Indonesia. It is known as *khatm-e qur'an*, the 'completion' or 'sealing' of the Qur'an, or *qur'an sharif*, the 'noble', 'beautiful' Qur'an. In times of danger, thanksgiving or transition, Pakistanis in Britain convene their fellow migrants for a ritual of formal prayer and commensality. Like the *slametan* for the Javanese (cf. Jay 1969: 188–238), this seemingly simple ritual lies at the heart of Pakistani religious observance and may be regarded as a 'core ritual' (cf. Geertz 1960: 1). It is performed by a congregation composed mostly of women who are gathered in the house of the ritual convener. Between them the assembled guests read the entire Qur'an in one sitting. Each of the participants reads one or more parts (*sipara*s) out of the thirty in the Qur'an. The reading is dedicated to the person convening the event and is regarded as a service performed by the readers for the convener and his or her family. After the reading of the Qur'an has been completed at least once, a *du'a* (supplication) is uttered over an offering of food, which is distributed to the guests. In Pakistan a share of the food is set aside for the poor as charity (*sadqa*), but this is not done in Manchester as 'there are no poor people here'. By custom, the Qur'an should be read with absolute accuracy, so as not to confuse Arabic words which vary only slightly in their spelling. A high degree of ritualism thus characterizes one part of the proceedings. Otherwise, the structure of the ritual is very simple, and it contains little figurative elaboration.

Despite this apparent simplicity, however, the ritual embraces central religious and moral ideas and forms the basic model for a series of other rituals, all concerned with the two themes of sacrifice and prayer. The analysis of labour migrants' perceptions of the ritual and of related rituals brings into sharp focus what they consider are the fundamental features of the rites. It thus highlights the crucial elements of sacrifice and offering from a novel angle, lending some credence to certain approaches in the general debate about sacrifice and offering.

Khatm-e qur'an gatherings constitute important loci of interhousehold women-centred sociability. Along with weddings they constitute the 'interdomestic domain', mediating between the purely domestic and the public domains. The performance of *khatm-e qur'an* was a feature of migrant life mostly absent during the all-male, initial phase of migration and was only introduced into Britain with the arrival of wives and families. The form of the ritual is very widespread and appears in different variations from North Africa, throughout the Middle East and South Asia, to Indonesia. It has Hindu and Sikh variations (on one form of this ritual; cf. Hayley (1980)). Its structure is essentially the same almost everywhere, with a sacred book being read first, often in an esoteric language, followed by a meal or fruit offering. In the Hindu version, this food is first offered to an image of a god or goddess, but this act is, of course, absent in the Islamic form of the ritual. Despite its ubiquity, there appear to be few anthropological accounts of the ritual and its sociological or symbolic significance.

Symbolically, the moral attachment of a family to its current home and surroundings is tangibly expressed during *khatm-e qur'an* through a transformation of secular into sacred space. One room in the convener's house – and, by extension, the whole house – assumes, temporarily, certain features of a mosque. Shoes are taken off at the threshold to the room, and people read the Qur'an seated on the ground. Along with the burning of incense, these observances serve to define the space as holy or sacred.

The food prayed over at the completion of a Qur'an reading consists, usually, of water, milk, a sweet dish, rice and fruit. The fruit is distributed first, immediately after the reading is completed, while the readers are still seated on the floor. The selection blessed is representative of abundance, purity and the essential ingredients of a meal. The portion of the food prayed over is distributed first in order to ensure that it is entirely consumed and none thrown away.

The countering of misfortune

Occasional *khatm-e qur'an* gatherings are held in order to ask for forgiveness (*bakhsh*), thanksgiving (*shukriya*) and divine blessing (*barkat*, or *baraka* in Arabic). Although the three notions appear at first glance to be different, the ideas surrounding them are closely linked (cf. also Hubert and Mauss 1964: 14). The emphasis depends on the occasion. If the *khatm-e qur'an* is held to celebrate recovery from an illness, it is held for *shukriya* or thanksgiving. Since, however, there has been, it is believed, an unwanted intervention by God or spirits, a sin possibly committed either knowingly or unknowingly, an act of expiation is also involved. The convener is thus seeking to rid himself of the condition which caused the misfortune or affliction (*bala, musibat*) while at the same time seeking *barkat*. Hence, the ritual is intended to transform the state of the convener from that induced by negative intervention or lack of divine protection into one of *barkat* – endowed through positive divine intervention. *Barkat* is thus the obverse of affliction. This opposition is expressed in the formal structure and permutations of different offerings or sacrifices Pakistanis make.

The *khatm-e qur'an* ritual is divided into two key phases: in the first phase the Qur'an is read. This is the phase of consecration. In the second phase, food, which constitutes, in part at least, an offering, is presented to the assembled congregation. The two phases, although closely linked, represent two separate religious acts, each surrounded by a set of theological and cosmological beliefs.

The central feature of the first ritual phase is the recitation of the Qur'an. This recitation is considered to have immense power. The divine force invoked in the recitation has the power to expel evil spirits and protect against them. The reading of the Qur'an also evokes *barkat*, which is then imparted to the food served. *Barkat*, or *baraka* in Arabic, is a 'beneficent force, of divine origin, which causes superabundance in the physical sphere and prosperity and happiness in the psychic order' (*Encyclopaedia of Islam* 1960: 1032). The text of the Qur'an is charged with *barkat*. A *khatm-e qur'an* is intended to transform the state of the convener into one of *barkat*, which is also shared by those reading the Qur'an in his or her name. The complete recitation of the Qur'an, especially if done in a short time, is considered a meritorious achievement. Pakistanis say they read the whole Qur'an because they 'cannot be quite sure what particular passage suits the occasion', and this is particularly so where danger is present. The Qur'an, they say, includes a saying for every type of occasion, but the location and meaning of these passages are known only to God. By reading the Qur'an in its entirety, they ensure that they have read the appropriate passage. In this way they hope to influence God, which is the intention of the *khatm*.

This type of explanation clearly stresses the substantive or magical power of the Qur'an in invoking God and influencing the spirits. The Qur'an objectifies the power of God, and the stress is on this objective power which is contained in the word or text of the Qur'an and is transferred metonymically to the convener and the congregation. This objectification is indicated by the great emphasis placed on accurate reading. There must be no change of *zabar* or *pech* (vowel marks in Arabic), for this might change the meaning of the word. Indeed, the Qur'an is read in Arabic, which few Pakistanis understand (although most migrants have, of course, read the Urdu translation of the Qur'an).

In an alternative explanation, the morality of the Qur'an is emphasized. The Qur'an contains 'all the laws and sayings needed to live a good life'. When moving to a new house, I was told, it is right that the whole Qur'an be read. Where the Qur'an has been read, one is reluctant to sin or, if one does sin, one feels guilty about it.

Although the Qur'an is the book most commonly read in Manchester, on different occasions different books may be read. In one variation, held exclusively by women, stories of Fatima are read. In another variation known as *milad* various sayings of the Prophet (*hadith, kalma, gyarvin sharif*) and stories about the life of the Prophet are read. Usually one person leads the reading, while in between passages proverbs and *nats* (praise poems) are sung by the congregation. *Milad*s are usually held on joyful occasions. Whatever the script read, the attendant women must be ritually pure (*pak bilkul*), that is, they must not be menstruating, and they must have performed their ablutions before the reading. I witnessed a *milad* in Pakistan held by Sayyid women at the beginning of a saint's *'urs* (festival).

Sacrifice and the mediation of the poor

Going against the objective power of the Qur'an as a book containing *barkat* is the notion of intention or *niyat* (*niya* in Arabic) central to Islamic religious observance. While much emphasis is placed on the accurate reading of the Qur'an, the reading is followed by a prayer over the food asking God for forgiveness for any errors made in the proceedings. Pakistanis are clear that the intention supersedes the ritualistic aspects of the event. Perhaps the most important difference between the two phases of the ritual – the Qur'an reading and the offering made – relates to this distinction. Paradoxically, perhaps, the reading of the Qur'an represents the more ritualistic phase, while the commensal meal and the associated offering given away to the poor are closely tied to the intention of the convener. Moreover, the difference between the way in which offerings are made is linked to subtle differences in intention rather than in the form of food or money given away. Was the *khatm* held for *shukriya* (thanksgiving), for *barkat*, during illness, to consecrate a new house? The intention is all-important.

The problem of how to manage misfortune or deal with affliction is at the heart of all these observances. Pakistanis tell me that, according to Islam, nothing happens without the will (*raza*) and knowledge of God. Hence, their view of affliction and misfortune is closely related to their view of the moral order, of good and evil in the eyes of God. A serious illness or misfortune is believed to be caused by the intervention of evil spirits, and these can only be exorcised with God's help. Indeed, they should not have afflicted a person in the first place unless he or she lacked divine protection. In cases where *khatm-e qur'an* or sacrifices are performed for a person who is seriously ill or has a chronic illness or an unnatural condition (such as barrenness in women), or in times of misfortune or trouble (*bala*), the ritual is held for the explicit purpose of expelling evil spirits through the recitation of the Qur'an and through almsgiving. Some migrants, who deny the presence of evil spirits even in the case of serious illness, talk instead of the presence of misfortune or danger caused, in their view, by sin. It is the misfortune, *musibat* (or *bala*), of which a person rids himself through almsgiving and prayer. Reading the Qur'an is seen both as a protection against such misfortune and as a means of exorcising evil spirits or jinns.

Not all *khatm-e qur'an* rituals are associated, however, with exorcism, or even primarily with expiation since, as we have seen, many are intended to seek divine blessing or as thanksgiving, after the danger has departed. As will be seen, the ritual stress dictates the ritual form. In de Heusch's (1985: 213) terms, is the intended effect 'conjunction' (e.g. communion) or 'disjunction' (e.g. exorcism)?

A crucial feature of offering or sacrifice in this regard has to do with what parts of a sacrificial victim or offering are consumed and what parts are given away or destroyed. In substituting a 'sacrificial schema' for a prior evolutionary model of sacrifice, Hubert and Mauss recognized the highly complex but nevertheless ordered variation in sacrificial procedures, even within a single society. Crucial to this schema was a distinction between sacrifices of sacralization and desacralization, and although de Heusch (1985: 213) has recently criticized this contrast, it remains – perhaps in modified form – fundamental for an analysis of the transformation through sacrifice of relations between the gods, the sacrificer and the congregation participating in the ritual.

From this perspective, the significance of the commensal meal following the Qur'an reading cannot be understood apart from other practices of Pakistani sacrifice. Hence, true sacrifice, that is, the ritual slaughtering of an animal, may take a number of different forms. In Manchester, many Pakistani migrants perform animal sacrifices locally on two main occasions: at the annual Eid Zoha festival and after the birth of a child, particularly a son. The first sacrifice is known as *qurbani*, the second as *haqiqa*. The structure of the *qurbani* sacrifice represents an explicit model for the proper division of an animal in personal sacrifice, where the ritual act is intended to be both piacular and for the sake of divine blessing.

Qurbani sacrifices are performed to commemorate the binding of Ismail by his father Ibrahim (the Islamic version of the binding of Isaac by Abraham in the Old Testament). This myth, whether in its biblical or qur'anic form, exemplifies the principle of substitution of a life for a life in sacrifice. According to Islamic tradition the *baqra* (sacrificial victim) is supposed to be divided into three equal parts, with a third shared by the family of the sacrificer, a third by kinsmen and friends and the final third given away to 'the poor'. In Manchester, since 'there are no poor', two-thirds are given away to kinsmen and friends.

As performed locally, the sacrificial victim is slaughtered in the very early hours of the morning of the festival, either by the local Muslim butcher or by the sacrificer himself, who accompanies the butcher to the local abattoir. Often several families join in making a single sacrifice, usually a lamb. The sacrificial victim is then cut up by the butcher and divided into portions. After the morning prayers members of a family gather for a midday meal, and in this a third of the victim is shared. The sacrificer distributes the rest of the meat, usually divided into two-pound portions, among his neighbours and friends living in Manchester. Usually, he knocks on the door of each house he visits and hands the meat over to the person on the threshold, telling him or her that it is *qurbani*. If the people are close friends, he enters the house, but if they are mere acquaintances he will usually hand over the meat on the threshold to whoever opens the door. In some cases I found that people were not quite sure of all the families who had presented them with *qurbani* that year. It may happen that the meat is handed over on the doorstep to one of the children who does not remember the name of the donor. Knowing who brought *qurbani* is not very important, for no expectation of reciprocity is implied, and no debt has been incurred. The sacrifice is made in the name of God (*khuda da nam*) by the sacrificer and his family, in order to gain merit or to expiate sin.

The choice of persons to whom *qurbani* is given is not, however, arbitrary or accidental, but follows a similar pattern to the choice of partners in other rituals which migrants perform. In the central residential cluster – where neighbours are usually known – they receive a fair share of the meat. Among businessmen and professionals living in the inner suburbs *qurbani* is distributed among friends. Other migrants, among those living on the periphery of the central cluster, avoid performing *qurbani* locally altogether. Instead, they send money for it to be performed in Pakistan.

The *qurbani* sacrifice contrasts significantly with another form of personal sacrifice known as *sadqa* (from the Arabic *sadaqa*, a term also used for almsgiving in general). *Sadqa* sacrifices are always performed in Pakistan. They are preceded by a *khatm-e qur'an* and are held, I am told, 'for the life'; if someone is mortally ill or has escaped a very bad accident, a *sadqa* sacrifice is made. The idea appears to be one of substitution, and the unusual aspect of this type of sacrifice for Pakistanis is that the animal is given away to the poor in its entirety. Neither the sacrificer nor any of his kinsmen are supposed to partake of the sacrificial victim. To do so would be to detract from the efficacy of the ritual act. In cases of abnormal illness, I was told, the meat is not even given to the poor, but is thrown away.

Two beliefs are implicit in *sadqa* sacrifice among Pakistanis. On the one hand, as the name of the sacrifice – *sadqa* – indicates, the sacrifice is an extreme act of almsgiving. On the other hand, it is also an act of expulsion of evil spirits or misfortune. For Pakistanis there is no belief that a sacrifice should be burned or destroyed, nor is there an explicit view that the 'life of the flesh is in the blood' (Lev. 17.11). There is, moreover, no sacred altar or shrine. The idea that God is partaking directly of any tangible substance, such as the blood of the animal, is abhorrent (cf. Weir 1908). The blood of a sacrificial victim is for Muslims *haram*, that is, prohibited and sacred. Their view is that the flow of blood signals the intention and removes all impurities before the animal is shared and consumed. In other words, the flow of the blood is a purificatory element of the sacrifice.

Islam recognizes, moreover, no priestly order. Nor do the poor constitute scapegoats, bearing or accumulating the sins of the donors (Parry 1980). The gift to the poor completes and seals the act of offering or sacrifice (for a structural analysis of the processual form of a sacrifice, cf. Richard Werbner (1989)). Communication in sacrifice is therefore achieved for Pakistanis indirectly, via the poor, and through an act of giving. Who are 'the poor' (*lokan gharib*)? For Muslims the poor may include any person, even members of one's own kin group or village, such as widows or orphans. They do not form a clear category of outsiders, and this is made quite explicit in the Qur'an. The notion of 'the poor' cuts across the categories of family, friends and fellow villagers, such as low caste or landless labourers, to embrace the widest humanity Pakistanis recognize: the beggars around saints' tombs, or the residents of orphanages, leper homes and so on. I was frequently told that I could not imagine real poverty, living in Britain. There are, moreover, no persons in Britain willing to define themselves as poor and take the remains of a commensal meal or sacrifice. It is worth noting here that although the part of the meal given away to the poor is the equivalent of the *juts*, or leftovers, given among Hindus to lower castes, the Islamic idea of giving to the poor is not as clearly predicated on a notion of intrinsic inequality. It does, however, presume the existence of hierarchy. It implies real inequalities in wealth and property as a 'natural' feature of society. Thus it is that offering and sacrifice fit into a more general pattern of a hierarchical gift economy I have described elsewhere (Werbner 1990).

Pakistani labour migrants universally direct their almsgiving via the mosque or various charities towards Pakistan. If they hold *khatm-e qur'an* offerings, *qurbani* or *haqiqa* in Manchester, it is because they feel that the further crucial social category of friends is present here. Without sharing among friends, there is no commensal meal, no *barkat*, no communication with the divine. It is possible to hold all these rituals by proxy, through kinsmen at home, in Pakistan. The sacrificer sends the money for a meal to be prepared or a beast slaughtered in his name. Many migrants, especially more recent arrivals of village origin, virtually always perform these rituals at home. Perhaps for them, more than for middle-class, urban migrants, the poor are a known and personalized group. The village or home neighbourhood remains the focus of their significant relations; they remain rooted back home, symbolically, emotionally, experientially. Yet over time, they too come under increasing communal and social pressure to reconstitute a moral universe in Britain. Like the *slametan* in Indonesia, the ritual 'symbolises the mystic and social unity of those participating in it' (Geertz 1960: 11).

South Asia and Indonesia compared

I have described the *khatm-e qur'an* ritual in some depth in order to tease out its comparability with the *slametan*, before going on to analyse its gendered and classed dimensions. A striking feature elided in the early historiographical accounts of the ritual in Indonesia relates to the belief in evil spirits, jinns and the like. In fact, such beliefs are common in both Indonesia and South Asia, although in South Asia a multitude of invisible agents is regarded as part of Islam, even mentioned in the Qur'an, whereas in Indonesia, as argued by Geertz, for example, these spiritual agents are defined as indigenous and pre-Islamic.[2]

Even beyond this, the contrast between the rituals in South Asia and Java seems stark at first, even if in both rituals a commensal meal is preceded by a *du`a* (supplication): on one side is a ritual predominantly convened by women, centred on a holy book, the Qur'an, in which all the congregants present participate in the reading and the host's intention is often not declared publicly. On the other side is a male-dominated ritual in which a single person chants an Islamic prayer and pronounces a statement on behalf of the hosts regarding the food and intention of the ritual.[3] In the *khatm-e qur'an* a portion of food blessed should be dedicated to the poor if it is to constitute a proper offering rather than merely a feast. In the *slametan* the spirits are said to partake of the fragrance of the food and incense.

More recent scholarly revisions of earlier interpretations of the *slametan* have recuperated its Islamic dimensions and with it, its direct connection to South Asia, particularly south India. Mark Woodward (1988: 55) in particular has argued that rather than being understood as a synthesis of animism, Hinduism, Buddhism and Islam, in which animism is numerically and conceptually predominant, the *slametan* can be seen to be derived directly from Sufi texts and interpretations. Like others, Woodward rejects the tripartite division between the *Abangan, Santri* and *Prijaji* in Java in favour of a simple distinction between *santri* and *kejawen*. Instead, he argues, 'the distinction between *santri* and *kejawen* is a culturally specific instance of the recurrent tension between *shari'ah*-minded and mystical interpretation characteristic of Sunni Islam. Both derive from the Qur'an and the emulation of Muhammad, claiming to capture the true meaning of Islam' (56). The *santri* support the less knowledgeable *kejawen*, as one *santri* told Woodward: 'I take pity on Javanese people because they don't know any Arabic and cannot pray properly. I want to help them so I pray for them at slametan and when they die' (62). Indeed, according to Woodward both groups consider the *slametan* to be a Muslim ritual. Against Geertz's view, not only are ritual meals characteristic of Islam and authorized by the scriptures, but the hadiths, the sayings of the Prophet, mention feeding the poor as meritorious and indeed, according to Woodward (1988: 63), 'Kejawen Muslims take pains to invite poor people to *slametan* or, at least, to send them some of the food. Many also donate uncooked rice and other foods to augment the small amounts of sacred food distributed at the ritual'. They regard spontaneous piety as of greater value than that regarded by the shari'ah.

At this point in his article Woodward (1988) draws an explicit connection between the *slametan*, also known as *kenduri*, and the Indo-Persian *kanduri*, also practiced elsewhere (Malaysia, Aceh). Meaning feast, it derives etymologically from the Persian word for incense (64). Woodward adds: 'With the exception of rites required by the *shari'ah* the *kanduri* is the most common ritual in Malay, Achenese, and South Indian Islam. In all these societies the *kanduri* is remarkably uniform. Like the *slametan* it includes recitation of portions of the Qur'an, the distribution of blessed food, and prayers for saints and the local community' (65). John Bowen (1993: 230 fn.) describes the *kenduri* in Gayo, Sumatra, similarly to the *slametan* and even draws a comparison with the *khatm-e qur'an*. In light of the reach of the *kenduri* ritual, Woodward (1988) comments, the *slametan*, while being local, may also be regarded as part of a much wider transcultural tradition paralleling that of the sharia. Furthermore, he argues, the *slametan* is not primarily a village ritual and is not limited to the *kejawen* community. Indeed, most royal rituals are elaborate *slametans*, suggesting a strong link between court and village community (85). There are many other resemblances across vast geographical areas: of the ritual aim of peace and blessing for the community following a supplication, and even the kind of foods offered (mainly rice in various forms). Hence not only scriptures but also such local rituals can 'travel' from one place to another.

The intersection of gender and class

Alongside this revision of the Islamic nature of the *slametan* has come a revision in the role played by women in the *slametan*, from being an all-male affair to something a lot more complex. The *khatm-e qur'an* obviously demands a certain proficiency and literacy in reading Arabic. Most Pakistani women in Manchester do not know Arabic, but they have been taught to read the Qur'an accurately. This accuracy signifies the magical power of the Qur'an: it is not the meaning of the text that is salient but the text's sacred effectiveness to ward off evil spirits and bring *barkat* (*baraka*, blessing) to the hosts and the assembled congregation. Although reading Arabic is an accomplishment not found among women in village Java, in other respects the rituals enable female-centred networks of sociality much in the same way as among Pakistani women. In a 2007 article, Jan Newberry rejects the view of contemporary *slametan*s in Java as male-dominated rituals. As she says,

> The *slametan* has been described as a ritual focussed on the male head of household as the formal and public representative of a co-resident family group. Hosted out of the main front room of the house, the conventional description of the *slametan* supported a structuralist reading of the house as split into a front, male, public space and a back, female, private space (Rassers 1960; cf. Keeler 1983). By taking the role of the house seriously in the staging of a *slametan*, we can see this plan of the house is less apt than one that figures its role as conduit to community exchange relationships managed by both males and females. (1311)

For a start, Newberry says, people attend *slametan*s as couples. Both men and women can officially host the ritual. Moreover, female labour underpins even the smallest *slametan*. This may require many days of planning. A large ritual requires the mobilization of kinswomen and neighbours beyond the immediate household, the helpers arriving through the back door. This is where people laugh and joke, by contrast to the solemnity of the front room. Women can also be mobilized through the back door to cope with any food shortages and the like. Food is also distributed according to established channels defined by female labour. As Newberry says,

> A focus on the front door and the people fed during the slametan is only a partial picture; it is the flow of women, resources, services, and food through the back door – before, during, and after – that makes the slametan possible. And this reciprocal, mutually reinforcing flow of resources and aid defines houses less as discrete structures than as nodes and conduits in a network of neighbourly exchange and connection. (1314)

Ann Stoler (1977: 86) argues in similar vein that in Kali Loro, a village in Central Java,

> focusing our attention on the distribution of food, rather than the symbolic aspects of ritual, it becomes clear that the real mediators of interhousehold relationships in the *slametan* are the women and not the men. The women buy, cook, and make the decisions as to how the food will be distributed, the latter a task often more complex than Geertz's description might imply.

Although this leads Newberry to define the '*slametan*' as a 'community' ritual, my own argument, as presented elsewhere in detail (Werbner 1990/2002) is that such rituals establish a separate domain between the public and the purely domestic. I have called this the 'interdomestic domain', a domain of sociality and of ritual and religious celebration focused on familial, friendship and neighbourhood networks. Among Pakistanis it is a social domain perpetuated and reproduced through the extension of personal gifts and services, and through hosting and feasting on domestically important occasions. Within this domain the gift economy flourishes (for a similar domain of gift exchange in Java, see Asmussen (2004)). Others too have noted the centrality of women in preparations for *slametans* (see, e.g., Hefner 2008: 147, citing Bianca Smith). For Malaysia Judith Nagata (1974: 97) says it is the 'domain of women' to be involved in preparations of *kenduris*. *Khatm-e qur'an* do not entail an obligation to reciprocate but they tend nonetheless to mirror these networks, based on gifting and reciprocal exchanges.

Whereas the official, public, communal sphere is almost exclusively an adult male domain, involving at any one time only a small segment of the adult population, the interdomestic domain catches up almost everyone, men and women alike; and it is mostly women who dominate here through the managing of ritual, labour and gift exchange networks. Through these interdomestic networks, equality and inequality, friendship, caste, *biradari* and class find their daily expression. A man's status thus remains for most men who are not active politically, crucially anchored in this interdomestic realm, in large measure controlled by his wife.

Women, literacy and Islam

Most of the Pakistani women I knew were able to read the Qur'an in Arabic, though without understanding its meaning, and could thus participate in *khatm-e qur'an* rituals. For Pakistani women who cannot read the Qur'an, however, equivalent rituals are substituted, much as in the *slametan*, relying on a leader to lead the religious part of the ritual. For example, in a ritual known as 'the story of Bibi Fatima' (*bibi fatima ki kahani*), the leader tells the story of miraculous events in the life of Fatima, the Prophet Muhammad's daughter. Pakistani women, including middle-class literate women, also convene *mahfil al-milad* gatherings to recite poems praising the life of the Prophet Muhammad, with the audience joining in refrains following the main reciter (see also Qureshi 1986: 53–5).

As Islamic reform movements have spread from the Middle East to South Asia, there are those who reject the familiar Pakistani *khatm-e qur'an* ritual on the grounds that the readers don't understand the words of the Qur'an in Arabic. In other words, the magical quality of the Qur'an as an efficacious sacred object with the agency to protect, heal and bless is challenged by the reformists. Instead, reformist women told me, they hold a *dars* in which a leader reads and interprets verses from the Qur'an, often in front of a mixed audience of men and women (middle-class *khatm* rituals were often mixed in the past as well). This is followed, I was told, in the usual way, with a *du'a* and a meal which constitutes a food offering.

Throughout Southeast Asia too, female literacy, and with it the capacity to read the Qur'an, have become common. In Malaysia, for example, one author reports that the *kenduri* has changed from being male centred in the rural context to having exclusively female rituals in the urban context, called *majlis doa* (Cederroth 2004: 4). There are ceremonies in Malaysia for the completion of reading the Qur'an called *khatam Qur'an*, as in Pakistan (see Nagata 1974: 94), but Malaysians do not seem to convene separate *khatm* rituals. In Jakarta, Indonesia, Anne Rasmussen (2010) has studied events convened by elite women in which, as one reviewer of her book sums up the argument, the women 'embody, encode, and enact the sound of the recited Qur'an in ways that transmit knowledge of Islamic texts and aural experiences of the divine through female subjectivities' (Silverstein 2012: 105). Though Rasmussen connects the holding of *khatam Qur'ans* in Indonesia to Arab rather than South Asian sources, the events she describes resemble their Pakistani counterpart in that the Qur'an is recited as a collective oral performance; in this case by thirty *qari'a*s (female reciters) in under an hour, in a 'tapestry of human voices' (Rasmussen 2010: 83) that produces 'heterogeneous textures of sound' (Silverstein 2012: 106).

The resulting 'dense cacophony' of voices described by Rasmussen (2010: 83) differs, however, radically from the soft murmur of the Qur'an reading characterizing Pakistani *khatms*. Like in them, though, through such recitations women are said by Rasmussen to create a 'gendered sphere' (Silverstein 2012: 106). The author links the emergence of *khatam* celebrations in Jakarta to the broader rise of Islamic feminists in Indonesia. Despite similarities, the one *khatam Qur'an* event Rasmussen describes in detail, however, differed from the usual Pakistani *khatm-e qur'an*: it was an elite event in which the Qur'an was recited by accomplished female expert Qur'an reciters, dedicated to several causes simultaneously: thanksgiving for the health of one woman, blessing the child of another, praying for the health of a third, celebrating the circumcision of a woman's son and 'many many other reasons' (Rasmussen 2010: 82). Although not mentioned, one can only assume that the reading is followed by a prayer and a ritual meal.

Concluding remarks

Beyond the differences between *slametans*, *khatm-e qur'ans* and other domestic rituals centred on a single household throughout South Asia and Indonesia, I have pointed in this chapter to the striking similarities scholars have identified in the way that such rituals allow for the creation of an everyday interdomestic domain controlled in large measure by women and based on female networking. Class and gender intersect in such networks, allowing for different configurations of interhousehold relations in villages, neighbourhoods and urban contexts. If the *slametan* was an extension of south Indian *kenduri* celebrations, the contemporary spread of communal Qur'an readings to Indonesia highlights the continuing interconnections across the Muslim world as these affect women's capacities to network beyond the constricted, restricted domestic domain.

Notes

This chapter was first presented at a conference on 'Islam, Gender Relations and Women's Agency: An India-Indonesia Comparative Study' at the Australian National University convened by Kathryn Robinson. I am grateful to Kathy and the conference participants for their comments. It draws on my earlier book, *The Migration Process* (Bloomsbury, 1990/2002), which was based on long-term research on the Pakistani diaspora in the United Kingdom. A version has been published in *Intersections: Gender and Sexuality in Asia and the Pacific*, issue 43, 2019 (http://intersections.anu.edu.au/issue43/werber.html).

1 The one exception I found was in an article by Regina Qureshi (1986: 56–8) on Canada in which she calls the *khatm-e qur'an qur'an khwani*.

2 In this regard it is instructive to compare contemporary beliefs in Pakistan and Indonesia documented in the 2012 Pew Foundation survey. According to the survey, belief in jinns is higher in Pakistan (77 per cent to 53 per cent), and they are somewhat lower on sorcery (50 to 69), higher on the evil eye (61 to 29) and much higher on the use of talismans and other charms (41 to 4). Virtually all Pakistanis and Indonesians display Qur'anic verses in their homes (90 per cent and 88 per cent, respectively), while slightly more Pakistanis use traditional healers (55 per cent vs 38 per cent). Only 7 per cent in Pakistan and 20 per cent in Indonesia have witnessed an exorcism of evil spirits. See http://www.pewforum.org/2012/08/09/the-worlds-muslims-unity-and-diversity-4-other-beliefs-and-practices/ and https://en.wikipedia.org/wiki/Superstition_in_Pakistan (both accessed 11 April 2015).

3 According to van den Boogert (2017: 354), before the prayers the host delivers an *ujub*, 'an opening speech in which he states the purity of his intentions, the specific purpose of the slametan (for example, the seventh month of the pregnancy of his daughter), and apologizes for his lack of eloquence and the inadequacy of the food'.

References

Asmussen, Vibeke. 2004. 'Constructing Gender and Local Morality: Exchange Practices in a Javanese Village'. *Indonesia and the Malay World* 32(94): 315–29.

van den Boogert, Joachem. 2017. 'The Role of Slametan in the Discourse on Javanese Islam'. *Indonesia and the Malay World* 45(133): 352–72.

Bowen, John R. 1993. *Muslims through Discourse*. Princeton, NJ: Princeton University Press.

Cederroth, Sven. 2004. 'Plurality, Tolerance and Change in Southeast Asian Islam'. *NIAS* 4: 4–5.

Encyclopaedia of Islam. 1960. Ed. H. A. R. Gibb, J. H. Kramers, E. Levi-Provencal, and J. Schacht. Leiden: E.J. Brill.

Geertz, Clifford. 1960. *The Religion of Java*. Glencoe: Free Press.

Hayley, Audrey. 1980. 'A Commensal Relationship with God: The Nature of the Offering in Assamese Vaishnavism'. In M. F. C. Bourdillon and Meyer Fortes (eds), *Sacrifice*. London: Academic Press, 107–26.

Hefner, Robert W. 2008. 'Review: Islam in Indonesia, Post-Suharto: The Struggle for the Sunni Center'. *Indonesia* 86: 139–60.

de Heusch, Luc. 1985. *Sacrifice in Africa: A Structuralist Approach*. Bloomington: Indiana University Press.

Hubert, Henri, and Marcel Mauss. 1964 [1898]. *Sacrifice: Its Nature and Function*. London: Cohen and West.

Jay, Robert R. 1969. *Javanese Villagers: Social Relations in Rural Modjukoto*. Cambridge: MIT Press, 188–238.

Nagata, Judith. 1974. 'Adat in the City: Some Perceptions and practices among Urban Malays'. *Anthropologica* XVI: 91–109.

Newberry, Jan. 2007. 'Rituals of Rule in the Administered Community: The Javanese Slametan Reconsidered'. *Modern Asian Studies* 41(6): 1295–329.

Parry, Jonathan P. 1980. 'Ghosts, Greed and Sin: The Occupational Identity of Benares Funeral Priests'. *Man (N.S.)* 15: 88–111.

Qureshi, Regula B. 1986. 'Transcending Space: Recitation and Community among South Asian Muslims in Canada'. In Barbara Daly Metcalf (ed.), *Making Muslim Space in North America and Europe*. Berkeley: University of California Press, 46–64.

Rasmussen, Anne. 2010. *Women, the Recited Qur'an, and Islamic Music in Indonesia*. Berkeley: University of California Press.

Silverstein, Shayna. 2012. 'Women, the Recited Qur'an and Islamic Music in Indonesia (Review)'. *Journal of Middle East Women's Studies* 8(2): 105–7.

Stoler, Ann. 1977. 'Class Structure and Female Autonomy in Rural Java'. *Signs* 3(1): 74–89.

Weir, T. H. 1908. 'Sacrifice (Islamic)'. In James Hastings (ed.), *Encyclopaedia of Religion and Ethics*. Edinburgh: T.H. Clark.

Werbner, Pnina. 1990. 'Economic Rationality and Hierarchical Gift Economies: Value and Ranking among British Pakistanis'. *Man (N.S.)* 25(2): 266–85.

Werbner, Pnina. 1990/2002. *The Migration Process: Capital, Gifts and Offerings among British Pakistanis*. 2nd edition with new preface. Oxford: Berg.

Werbner, Richard P. 1989. *Ritual Passage Sacred Journey: The Process and Organization of Religious Movement*. Washington, DC: Smithsonian.

Woodward, Mark R. 1988. 'The Slametan: Textual Knowledge and Ritual Performance in Central Javanese Islam'. *History of Religions* 28(1): 54–89.

6

Buddhist women and food-gifting to monks

Pascale F. Engelmajer

Buddhist women's roles have traditionally been restricted to those of wives and mothers, and their religious aspirations have mostly been framed within that context. Rita Gross (1993) described the functions associated with these roles as 'enabling', in the sense that when women fulfil them, they enable the men around them to pursue their own goals, and therefore the focus is on men as Buddhist followers rather than on women followers. She furthermore argues that these laywomen, wives and mothers, who are praised and celebrated as role models in Buddhist texts, are merely an 'androcentric creation' that cannot serve as 'usable role models' for contemporary women (50–1). This statement implies that the religious activities of laywomen are perceived as less worthwhile and meaningful than those of female monastics. This is an unrecognized bias in Buddhist studies: on the one hand, it devalues lay religiosity in general and women's traditional religiosity in particular and, on the other, it seems oblivious to the fact that the majority of women do not wish to become renouncers. They choose to live their spiritual and religious lives outside the monastic path, and even sometimes as wives and mothers, just as the majority of men do not wish to become monks. It is undeniable that it is crucial and indispensable that women be allowed to become full monastics if they so desire. But supporting this goal must not imply the devaluation of the lay role and of the traditionally female functions that it entails.

This attitude may in part explain why there is little research on women's religiosity within ordinary traditionally female activities such as preparing and providing food.[1] Yet, even today, as a brief survey of contemporary practices will show, in Theravāda Buddhism, whether in Sri Lanka or Southeast Asia, women typically manifest their religiosity through daily food offerings to the Buddha, monks and others. These activities must be recognized and examined in their full religious settings based on the textual study of the Pāli canon and on the understanding of the role of the lay community in Buddhism. This will allow us to distinguish the profound religious and spiritual value of the ordinary daily activities that are a conspicuous part of women's roles as wives and mothers and a major way through which they achieve religious agency in the lay context.

As Nirmala Salgado (1997: 216) notes, in contemporary Sri Lanka women are still expected to fulfil their roles of wife and mother, and she emphasizes that 'there is little tolerance for those [women] who desire an alternative path conflicting with their traditional roles'. She describes in her study of a Buddhist hermitage how the Buddhist nuns there had either faced fierce opposition from their families or 'fulfilled [their] duties as wi[ves] and mother[s]' before finally becoming nuns, an attitude that is reflected in the resistance to reinstating female ordination in Theravāda countries such as Sri Lanka and Thailand. In that context, women's religiosity can be manifested in a socially acceptable way in their daily activities as wives and mothers.

Gombrich and Obeyesekere (1990 [1988]: 234), writing in the 1970s, observe that as Donors' Committees (*Dāyaka Sābhava*) were formed in Sri Lanka to organize food donations to their local temples, their 'officeholders [were] usually men even if their wives [did] the work'. Juliane Schober (1996: 201) mentions similar organizations administered by men in Burma, in which 'women, though responsible for preparing the food offered before the Buddha images, rarely take an active role'. On the other hand, Nancy Eberhardt (2006: 49, 107) describes the active involvement of Shan women who make merit every morning by bringing food to the village monastery. They also sponsor, plan and organize the preparation and distribution of food during the village ordination ceremonies (138–9, in particular). In a 2007 documentary on Lao funeral rituals, women are similarly responsible for the preparation of foods to be offered to monks (Ladwig and Kourilsky 2007). Rita Langer's work in Sri Lanka shows that women appear as the primary, if not always unique, preparers of food. In her work on Buddhist funerals, only women are involved in the preparation of food to be served to the monks who perform the funerary rituals (Langer 2007). In Langer's 2015 documentary work, while the uncharacteristic man sometimes participates, it is still almost entirely women who are seen preparing food, whether it is to be offered in puja to the Buddha, morning-alms given to monks or rice offerings presented to urban crows. This documentary work emphasizes the importance of women's function in food preparation and offerings in a religious context, and furthermore, it brings to our attention the fact that, as she mentions in the description of the videos, the 'voices of those who prepare the food are rarely heard, their expertise as religious specialists seldom acknowledged'.

As these practices show, at least one of women's manifestations of religiosity focuses on food preparation and giving. Yet, besides what I have mentioned here, and as far as I am aware, there is very little ethnographic material on how women conceptualize their food preparation and giving within the larger Buddhist framework. How does the Buddhist tradition itself understand these activities? Is there evidence for their soteriological value in the textual sources that would support the claim that women gain religious agency by preparing and offering food?

The Theravāda Buddhist tradition practiced in Sri Lanka and Southeast Asia (Myanmar, Thailand, Laos and Cambodia) is based on a set of texts, which was transmitted in Pāli, a Middle Indian language. According to tradition, the texts that form the canon were recited by the Buddha's closest disciples in the presence of a council of five hundred monks (*bhikkhus*), who had reached awakening (*nibbāna*) (Von Hinüber 1997: 5–6). It is said that the canon, referred to as the three baskets (*tipiṭaka*), was transmitted to Sri Lanka by Emperor Aśoka's son Mahinda, in the third century BCE. It is generally accepted that in its present form the canon was closed in the fifth century CE by Buddhaghosa, a monk from the Sri Lankan monastery of Mahāvihāra (Collins 1990: 96). While the contexts in which the canon was transmitted and received were not identical and unchanging, they were similar and stable enough that a Theravāda cultural landscape, based on what Steven Collins (1998) has referred to as the 'Pāli imaginaire', had emerged by the fourteenth century, constituting an environment in which texts and stories, values and ideals were, and still are, shared in the form of carvings and paintings, in popular accounts (today they are commonly found in comic book form), in songs and theatrical performances. They are well known by all, lay and monastic alike, and their values and ideals pervade social, cultural and political life.

In those texts, Buddhism presents itself as a renouncer's tradition that rejects the householder's lifestyle in favour of an ascetic, peripatetic, spiritually focused existence whose only purpose is the attainment of *nibbāna*. In this light, activities related to the production and preparation of food seem antithetical to the pursuit of its highest goal and its associated lifestyle that requires that one give up the amenities of the worldly life, including growing, storing and preparing food for oneself. Accordingly, the Buddhist sangha – the monastic community – operates within the framework of a close, even symbiotic, relationship with the lay community, because it is entirely dependent on its offerings for its physical livelihood. *Dāna*, the offering of the four requisites of food, robes, medicine and lodging to monks and nuns, is the most crucial aspect of the laity's religious life, and generosity epitomizes both the first step and the culmination of the Buddhist path. While the laity is composed of men and women, in the texts women are those most often represented as making offerings of food. Today's world, of course, is vastly different from the world in which the Pāli texts were composed and compiled. Yet, in countries in which Theravāda Buddhism is practiced, women's social roles and soteriological options have changed little, and I wish to argue that the reading of the Pāli texts I am offering is applicable to contemporary Theravāda Buddhist women in South and Southeast Asia today.

First, it is important to acknowledge that women were a very minor concern for the compilers of the canon: undeniably, the texts were intended for an audience of monks and were little concerned with lay life in general and with women in particular, except as a threat to the celibate lifestyle or, significantly, as a source of alms. Female monastics appear in the canon, but they do not figure prominently: only one *sutta* is addressed to them directly by the Buddha, and only fourteen passages of the four main *Nikāya*s explicitly identify nuns (it may be worth mentioning that this body of texts consists of thousands of pages). Unlike the men in the canon, few women are characters with names and a personal story. Most references to women are to generic females in lists and metaphors that describe the social world in which the Buddha and his followers lived, and the most common and most important female characters are laywomen – by comparison, the most common male characters are monks.

A thorough examination of these female characters reveals that the Pāli texts provide continuity with the ancient Indian context in which women's social functions are restricted to their roles as wives and mothers. For example, the oft-cited excerpt that 'a woman … may turn out better than a man' explains that her potentially surpassing a man resides in fulfilling her functions of wife and mother, in particular being a 'devoted wife' (*patibbatā*) and producing a son (*Saṃyutta Nikāya* I 86).[2] Indeed, these two roles are not only predominant in descriptions of women, but they seem to constitute the essence of womanhood.

A woman's destiny is inevitably that of a wife and mother, as emphasized when the Buddha highlights the five sufferings peculiar to women, all of which are related to women's reproductive function and their role as wives. A woman is said to suffer because she 'goes to live with [her] husband's family' (*daharova samāno patikulam gacchati*) and is separated from her birth family; and she 'is made to serve a man' (*purisassa pācariyam upeti*) (S IV 239). Furthermore, women menstruate (*utunī*), they become pregnant (*gabbinī*) and they give birth (*paraṃ vijāyati*) (S IV 239).

The *Uggaha Sutta* is representative of how the texts describe the wife's functions – a wife's main duties revolve around her husband and his affairs. Her duties include, among other things, preparing and serving food. That this is a crucial aspect of a wife's duties is highlighted in the instances in which a woman's interaction with her husband is set at the moment when she serves him food (e.g. S I 160). But she does not serve only her husband: she is also responsible for distributing food to the servants of the house according to their merit. Many other stories, which I will describe in more detail below, depict women handing out food to various recipients.

There are no similar instances of texts focusing on the mother's functions, although a description of parents' care for their child is found in a passage of the *Anguttara Nikāya*[3] that emphasizes how parents care for their children, especially by nourishing (*posakā*) them. The terms (*āpādakā* and *posakā*) used, in the feminine, refer to a milk-nurse or foster-mother (A I 132, also at A II 70).[4] These terms are used in particular to describe what Mahāpajāpatī, the Buddha's foster-mother, did for him, and how she essentially saved his life by nursing him when his biological mother died seven days after his birth (*Dīgha Nikāya* II 1 and *Jātaka* I 49–53).[5] In this passage, the giving of milk to the infant Bodhisatta epitomizes the function of motherhood.[6]

Both in descriptions of wives and mothers, the two most prominent roles for women in the Pāli canon, the giving of food appears to be their most important function. As noted earlier, the giving of food to renouncers and monks, including the Buddha (or the infant Bodhisatta as in the case of Mahāpajāpatī), is an action taken within the confines of a woman's ordinary duties, which are the usual setting within which the act of offering is described. Yet this act is a soteriological deed that, the texts explain, will have positive consequences for the woman involved. One striking example is that of Mallikā, a poor street-seller, who made an offering of unsalted gruel to the Buddha and as a result, was chosen by Pasenadi, the king of Kosala, to become his chief queen by the 'force of merit earned by her donation to the Buddha' (Scheible 2014: 15).

But the results of giving *dāna* are not limited to this life. There are countless examples of the good consequences of almsgiving, especially giving to the Buddha. In fact, one collection of such stories is contained in the *Vimānavatthu*,[7] a canonical text that shows how meritorious actions result in rebirths in heavenly realms. The *Vimānavatthu* includes two sets of accounts: a shorter set dedicated to thirty-five men, and a longer one dedicated to fifty women, the only Pāli text in which women are more numerous than men. According to the tradition, both volumes describe Mahāmoggallāna, one of the Buddha's chief disciples, who is said to have obtained supernatural powers through meditative practices, as he was visiting the *devaloka* (gods' realm) and meeting with its inhabitants (Vim-a I 2–3). He marvelled at their wonderful circumstances and questioned them on the action that resulted in their being reborn in such conditions.

The men's *Vimānavatthu* describes a variety of meritorious activities such as listening to the *Dhamma* – the teachings of the Buddha – or giving one's needle kit to the Buddha, or adorning the stupa of a former Buddha with flowers. In the women's *Vimānavatthu*, however, the stories focus mostly on the giving of food and drink and, as James Egge (2013: 86–7) has pointed out, the stories are more developed and descriptive of the women's intentions. Women are depicted as giving meals to elders, water or 'fragrant drinks' to parched monks, and even to the Buddha himself. The actions are described as part of these women's ordinary daily activities, within which they take the decision to make the act of offering. However, the focus, as usually the case with the soteriological path of women, is on rebirth and not on attaining the ultimate Buddhist goal of awakening. This implies that women may not enter the Buddhist path as easily as the lines quoted above suggest. Indeed, there is evidence in the canon that the renouncer's status is seen as a last resort for women, after they have fulfilled their social roles of wives and mothers (Engelmajer 2014: 103–4).

However, it must be emphasized that through this act of giving, women achieved a level of soteriological agency that they did not have in the religious context of ancient India, in which their salvation rested with their husbands, requiring that they be married and fulfil their wifely duties. The *Mānavadharmaśāstra*,[8] a Brahminical text composed around the first century CE, strongly emphasizes women's lack of soteriological agency, admonishing that 'apart [from their husbands], women cannot sacrifice or undertake a vow or fast; it is because a wife obeys her husband that she is exalted in heaven' (MS 5.155).

Keeping the ancient Indian context in mind allows us to understand how the *Vimānavatthu*'s detailed descriptions of the soteriological consequences of women's ordinary activities such as giving food were radical because they recognized that women's religious agency was independent not only of their husbands but also of their wifely duties. While it is undeniable that these stories also serve a normative purpose by emphasizing what the proper role of a woman is, at the same time it is exactly by describing these as ordinary women's activities that they could be accepted by the contemporary socio-religious milieu because, at least on the surface, they did not challenge that milieu.

However, as I have mentioned previously, this seems to focus on obtaining a better rebirth rather than achieving *nibbāna* and therefore to deny women the ultimate Buddhist goal of pursuing awakening. Women prepare and give food or drink within the course of their daily activities and as a result, they are reborn in heavenly realms. While they achieve agency and autonomy through these actions, they seem to remain separate from what is usually seen as the proper sphere of Buddhist religious goals. But it would be inaccurate to interpret it in this way: in fact, canonical commentaries have understood it within a properly 'Buddhist' context. Through these actions, women are not simply seeking to be reborn in heavenly realms, but they are actually aiming for *nibbāna* itself. For example, in the commentary to the *Dhammapada*, remarkably the emphasis shifts and the ultimate goal is made explicit: the goal of merit-making is no longer a better rebirth, but *nibbāna* itself.

A story tells us of Uttarāmāta, a poor farmer's wife, who is on her way to bringing her husband his lunch when she meets Sāriputta, one of the chief disciples of the Buddha, on his alms-round. Debating with herself, she decides to use her husband's lunch rice to make an offering to Sāriputta, so that she may 'be a partaker of the Law which [he] had himself beheld' (*Dhammapada-aṭṭhakathā* iii 304).[9] In another account, Puṇṇa, a servant-girl, makes an offering of a rice-cake made of broken rice bits to the Buddha 'so that the Truth he [has] beheld be of avail' to her also (Dh-a iii 323). Both women give up the little bit of food they have in order to have direct access to the Buddha's Dhamma. In the *Saddharmaratnāvaliya*, the thirteenth-century Sinhalese translation of this commentary, the women make the offering so that 'by this Act of Merit, [Uttarāmāta may] enjoy the extremely sweet taste of *nibbāna*', and Puṇṇa 'obtain the sweets of *nibbāna*', clearly indicating that the tradition understands that the purpose of these acts of food offering is the highest Buddhist goal (Obeyesekere 2001: 192, 200). Most strikingly, Uttarāmāta, by giving away her husband's lunch, is not only disregarding her wifely duties but gaining spiritual agency. The text is explicitly describing a wife who can achieve her own spiritual salvation independently of her husband. It is true that the radical nature of the situation is immediately mitigated by describing how Uttarāmāta rushes back home to cook another lunch for her husband and, as she brings it, warns him not to be angry with her so as 'not to bring to [nothing] what [she] had done that morning' (Dh-a iii 305). One can surmise that the text sought to assuage any fear that it may be encouraging women to abandon their wifely duties in favour of exclusively feeding the sangha.

These canonical and para-canonical texts clearly establish the soteriological role of food offerings and give us a powerful theoretical framework through which to understand and valorize the act of food preparation and giving by women. These acts must be recognized as profoundly religious and as providing women religious agency within the context of their daily roles. By preparing and giving food, activities which women routinely perform, they undertake the foundational practice of the Buddhist path – generosity. Further ethnographic research, along the lines of that undertaken by Rita Langer and Nirmala Salgado in Sri Lanka, which I described earlier, is required to better understand how contemporary women view their food preparation and giving activities in the wider Buddhist framework that I have explored in this chapter.

Notes

1 An additional explanation is that it is more difficult to research women's traditional activities than public rituals or religious texts.
2 *Saṃyutta Nikāya* (translated in Bodhi et al. (1995)), hereafter 'S'.
3 *Anguttara Nikāya* (translated in Woodward (1995 [1932], 1995 [1933])), hereafter 'A'.
4 In Pāli, *bahukāra … mātāpitaro puttānaṃ, āpādakā posakā imassa lokassa dassetāro*. The *Pāli English Dictionary* gives the following translations: *āpādakā* – one who cares for a child; *āpādikā* – nurse, foster mother; *posaka* – nourishing; *posikā* – nurse.
5 *Dīgha Nikāya* (translated in Walshe ([1987] 1995)), hereafter 'D'; *Jātaka* (translated in Cowell (1957)), hereafter 'J'. The *Mahāpadana Sutta* (D II 1) and the *Jatāka-nidāna* (J I 49–53) both describe the paradigmatic life of the Bodhisatta and his mother.
6 Bodhisatta is the term that refers to the Buddha before his awakening – it means a 'being intent on awakening'.
7 *Vimānavatthu-aṭṭhakathā* (translated in Masefield (2007)), hereafter 'Vim-a'.
8 *Mānavadharmaśāstra* (translated in Doniger (1991)), hereafter 'MS'.
9 *Dhammapada-aṭṭhakathā* (translated in Burlingame ([1921] 1995)), hereafter 'Dh-a'.

References

Bodhi, Ven, Bhikkhu Ñāṇamoli and Bhikkhu Bodhi (trans.). 1995. *The Middle Length Discourses of the Buddha: A Translation of the Majjhima Nikāya*. Boston: Wisdom Publications.

Burlingame, E. W. (trans.). 1995 [1921]. *Buddhist Legends*. Oxford: Pali Text Society.

Collins, Steven. 1990. 'On the Very Idea of the Pāli Canon'. *Journal of the Pali Text Society* 15: 89–126.

Collins, Steven. 1998. *Nirvana and Other Buddhist Felicities: Utopias of the Pali Imaginaire*. Cambridge, UK: Cambridge University Press.

Cowel, E. B. (ed.). 1957. *The Jātakas or the Stories of the Buddha's Former Births*. London: Pali Text Society.

Doniger, Wendy, with Brian K. Smith (trans.). 1991. *The Laws of Manu*. London: Penguin Classics.

Eberhardt, Nancy. 2006. *Imagining the Course of Life: Self-Transformation in a Shan Buddhist Community*. Honolulu: University of Hawaii Press.

Egge, James. 2013. *Religious Giving and the Invention of Karma in Theravāda Buddhism*. London: Routledge.

Engelmajer, Pascale. 2014. *Women in Pāli Buddhism: Walking the Spiritual Paths in Mutual Dependence*. London: Routledge.

Gombrich, Richard, and Gananath Obeyesekere. 1990 [1988]. *Buddhism Transformed: Religious Change in Sri Lanka. Delhi: Motilal Banarsidass*. Princeton, NJ: Princeton University Press.

Gross, Rita. 1993. *Buddhism after Patriarchy: A Feminist History, Analysis, and Reconstruction of Buddhism*. Albany: SUNY Press.

Ladwig, Patrice, and Gregory Kourilsky. 2007. *Caring for the Beyond: Two Lao Buddhist Festivals for the Deceased*. Vientiane: Lao Art Media Production.

Langer, Rita. 2007. *Buddhist Rituals of Death and Rebirth: Contemporary Sri Lankan Practice and Its Origins*. Critical Studies in Buddhism Series. London: Routledge.

Langer, Rita. 2015. *A Buddhist Cosmology in Food*. Documentaries series. University of Bristol. Available online: http://research-information.bristol.ac.uk/en/publications/a-buddhist-cosmology-in-food(608fc065-f687-4d92-82ee-67a1295345a4).html.

Masefield, Peter (trans.). 2007. *Elucidation of the Intrinsic Meaning So Named the Commentary on the Vimāna Stories*. Lancaster: Pali Text Society.

Obeyesekere, Ranjini. 2001. *Portraits of Buddhist Women: Stories from the* Saddharmaratnāvaliya. Albany: SUNY Press.

Salgado, Nirmala. 1997. 'Sickness, Healing, and Religious Vocation: Alternatives Choices at a Theravāda Buddhist Nunnery'. *Ethnology* 36(3) (Summer): 213–26.

Scheible, Kristin. 2014. 'The Female Householder Mallika'. In Todd Lewis (ed.), *Buddhists: Understanding Buddhism through the Lives of Practitioners*. Chichester, Malden: Wiley Blackwell.

Schober, Juliane. 1996. 'Religious Merit and Social Status among Burmese Buddhist Lay Associations'. In Cornelia Ann Kammerer and Nicola Beth Tannembaum (eds.), *Merit and Blessing in Mainland Southeast Asia in Comparative Perspective*. Yale University Southeast Asia Studies. New Haven: Yale University Press.

Von Hinüber, Oskar. 1997. *A Handbook of Pali Literature*. New Delhi: Munshiram Manoharlal.

Walshe, M. (trans.). 1995 [1987]. *The Long Discourses of the Buddha: A Translation of the* Dīgha Nikāya. Boston: Wisdom Publications.

Woodward, F. L. (trans.). 1995 [1932]. *The Book of Gradual Sayings* I. London: Pali Text Society.

Woodward, F. L. (trans.). 1995 [1933]. *The Book of Gradual Sayings* II. London: Pali Text Society.

Part Three

Everyday life, power and agency

7

Women's ritually shared bodies and food-penance in rural Maharashtra

Deepra Dandekar

Women's participation in Maharashtra's political arena has been inadequately theorized, except for their involvement in the right wing (Sarkar and Butalia 1995). My chapter demonstrates how food sharing between women and goddesses can be experienced as political in the Marathi rural context. The location of gender, female reproduction and child mortality at intersections of agrarian patriarchy complicates notions about women's sexual and reproductive pollution (*viṭāḷ*) and their entitlement to food within marital clans and castes. My chapter examines how women's practices of eating and the exigencies of childbirth are ritualized to produce a shared political space between female bodies and village goddess worship that mediates the birth of male heirs and constructs food and women's eating as politically marked. Since male heirs in rural agrarian clans are viewed as inheritors and representatives of dominant-caste property, their birth and its ritualized celebration compares women's motherhood to food consumption, culturally linked with agrarian fertility and their entitlement to partake in agrarian produce. Therefore, women's inability to conceive a child after marriage imposes ritual periods of fasting on them, since the lust for food is considered to be a contaminating agent that prevents conception, pregnancy, childbirth and the healthy longevity of male children. Women believe that ritual fasting produces a shared and ritualized 'one-body' existence between them and goddesses as they dedicate rich and nutritive food items to goddesses at village shrines. This dedication and simultaneous abstention affect the bodily transfer of their contaminating lust to goddesses in the form of the very food that objectifies it. The notion that the goddess 'eats' this dedicated food as well as the contaminating 'lust' conjoins both evil and good in an ambivalent image. The draining away of women's lust, absorbed by the goddess through food, now produces the latter as free of contamination and sin (*vāsanā*). The woman is now considered passive and fertile, like agrarian soil that awaits fertilization and the birth of a male heir. However, ritualized body sharing also takes place within caste-based contexts. Since goddess worship mediates childbirth and inheritance among dominant-caste agrarian clans, the birth of 'pure' children and the ritualized 'purification' of mothers reproduces the rural capitalistic culture of dominant-caste clan agrarian inheritance.

Introducing affliction avoidance

Women's participation in caste and clan politics and their entitlement as agrarian consumers within their marital village is tied to the birth of male children, as their bodies become enmeshed in a variety of domestic-reproductive labour that perpetuates agrarian ownership, yoked to the production of inheritors, in return for ritualized food entitlements. Most childbirth and motherhood rituals in rural Maharashtra that involve food-penance and food dedication concern a village goddess named Saṭvāī, and she presides over the birth of male heirs among village clans. Many of my respondents believed that the goddess Saṭvāī protected their marital clans like a mother or mother-in-law by disciplining new and 'sinful' daughters-in-law given to immaturity, who resisted motherhood and marital responsibilities. While this 'neglect' (*durlaksha*) of marital responsibilities always remained euphemistic, my respondents qualified *durlaksha* by describing new daughters-in-law as foolish and far more interested in personal consumption of material goods and enjoyment than in providing for the family.

This distinction became clearer with the etymology of the goddess Saṭvāī that village women described, since my respondents believed the Saṭvāī to consist of the souls of women who had died while giving birth to sons. Many of her worship rituals also resembled Hindu death rituals or the *pinda-dān* ritual that is commonly observed at Varanasi (Parry 1994). Scholars have generally equated childbirth goddesses in the anthropological context with the Sapta-Mātṛkās (Kinsley 1986), and the Saṭvāī is often compared with goddess Ṣaṣṭhī mentioned in the Prakṛti Khaṇḍa of the *Brahmavaivarta Purāṇa* (Sen 1974); she is also considered the malevolent younger sister of the Brahminical Marathi goddess Jīvatī (Śarmā 2012: 475–8), while the Jñāneśvarī compares her to the Satī (Panse 1952). Besides these, there are many other disease-related village goddesses in the Deccan, such as the Mari-āī, Reṇukā or Yellammā (Hiltebeitel 1988), whose narratives bear resemblance to that of the Saṭvāi and other water goddesses such as the Sāti-āsrā (Brubaker 1978; Feldhaus 1995). Village women told me of how the Saṭvāī consisted of seven (*sāt*) ancestral mothers or *āyā* (plural) of representative village castes, who were worshipped in one composite village deity, the Sāt-āi. Another version of the same story described how the deity was a pure (*satv*) mother (*āī*). In both cases, the 'seven mothers' or 'pure mothers' were believed to epitomize courageous feminine and sacrificial motherhood (*vīrāṅganā*).

Predictably, as there are many relevant similarities between Satī and Saṭvāi worship (Harlan 1994), many in my field area considered the Saṭvāī to be another form of the Satī. I often encountered Saṭvāī shrines where Satī and hero-stones were worshipped. When I pointed this out to my respondents, it seemed that they considered no ontological difference between selfless wives who had died for their husbands (Satī) and selfless mothers who had died for their sons (Saṭvāī). Since both the Satī and the Saṭvāī epitomized feminine sacrifices upholding the duties of married life, women believed that the goddess became angry and enraged with 'lustful' village daughters-in-law and afflicted them in order to discipline them. Since the Saṭvāī – or if there were many such shrines near a village, the Saṭvāyā – were considered the generational mothers and protectors of village agrarian clans, new daughters-in-law were duty-bound to perform their rituals of food dedication and fasting that would help them transition and integrate into the status of pure 'wifehood' and 'motherhood' within their marital clans. This integration often provided them with political participation, power and an entitlement to consume and distribute food among relatives and friends in dominant-caste networks in the village.

I will exemplify my argument by discussing a prominent Saṭvāī ritual called the *pāṭā*. The ritual ceremony described below was one of the first I attended for a newborn boy in a dominant-caste Maratha family in village Shinoli, located in Ambegaon Taluka (District Pune) in November 2006.[1] However, before proceeding to describe the ritual ceremony, I would like to briefly highlight the role played by Saṭvāī ritualists in women's ritual integration with their marital families as wives and mothers that gained the latter food entitlements (cf. Dandekar 2016a,b).

One of the things that immediately became clear to me from the beginning of my fieldwork was how Saṭvāī affliction, in terms of childlessness, was limited to upper- and dominant-caste women, since agrarian clans and castes were primarily concerned with the inheritance and ownership of agrarian property. Sometimes women used the interpretation of childlessness as Saṭvāī affliction, as markers of upward mobility and their belonging to dominant castes.[2] The reason was that Saṭvāī affliction visited on lower-caste women often entailed a ritual period of illness until they acquiesced to undertaking ritual tasks that facilitated the reproductive integration of dominant-caste women into their marital clans. Therefore, lower-caste women were known to contract Saṭvāī afflictions only if they resisted caste-based ritual duties that aided dominant-caste women, just as the latter became afflicted when they resisted their clan duty of childbirth that facilitated agrarian inheritance.[3] Saṭvāī ritualists therefore did not undertake food-penance, as the discourse of reproduction and subsequent food intake upheld by Saṭvāī afflictions did not include ritualists within the ambit of concepts such as lustful sin and hungry eating. Since most Dalits did not inherit agrarian property in the same way that dominant castes did, but only inherited the right to perform and practice their caste duty in the village (*bālūtedārī*), childlessness among Dalits wasn't included within the ambit of the Saṭvāī's affliction.

When I asked Saṭvāī ritualists about the nature of their ritual intervention that helped dominant-caste women become wives and mothers, they spoke of the necessity of their presence at childbirth ritual contexts as both ambivalent and powerful. They viewed themselves as gluing agents (*chiktāvṇe*) at Saṭvāī childbirth rituals, as those who were simultaneously important and insignificant; without them, dominant-caste women could not bond and integrate with their marital clans, and yet they were just glue, utilized and fed by dominant castes, who became insignificant as soon as dominant-caste women became stable as mothers and wives. My respondents from the dominant castes viewed the body of the Saṭvāī ritualist as having an 'absorbent' quality (*śoṣṇe*). Dominant-caste women were of the opinion that the Saṭvāī ritualist 'absorbed' their childlessness-producing lust within ritual contexts and therefore acted as conduits or mediums of the Saṭvāī. Such ritual contexts always became spaces for marked food dedications not only to the Saṭvāī but to her ritualist as well. The ritualist's food entitlements were viewed as a return and recognition of the caste duties she performed for her clients (*yajmān*) and for helping dominant-caste women gain their food entitlements in recognition of childbirth. Here, it is important to note that both dominant-caste wives and Saṭvāī ritualists remained ensconced within the frameworks of their marital clans and the official mandates of their clients, respectively, as these clients and clans were dominant and powerful within the village. Neither Saṭvāī ritualists nor dominant-caste wives ever felt united in an imagination of feminist sisterhood (Hiltebeitel and Erndl 2000). Rather, individual interests ran high on both sides. While wives and new mothers negotiated for maximum integration, power and stability within their marital clans, Saṭvāī ritualists negotiated for maximum ritual networks with dominant-caste clients so that they would be repeatedly invited to convene rituals of integration.

Individualized 'devotee–client' relationships with deities in India have hitherto been compared with Bhakti, just as food offerings are compared with *prasād*. Although afflicted women individualize food-penance within Saṭvāī rituals, I am uncomfortable about grouping the obvious diagnostics of Saṭvāī affliction or sexual/reproductive impurity (*viṭāḷ*) and the shame and stigma of childlessness among dominant-caste women that is considered to ensue from lust, with Bhakti. Such a comparison would render the position of Saṭvāī ritualists meaningless, as they hardly 'heal' in formats suggested by anthropologist-psychologist Sudhir Kakar (1982) or Joyce Flueckiger (2006). Neither are Saṭvāī ritualists mere shrine servants and cleaners. Apart from 'absorbing' the 'heat' (*uṣṇa*) released from encounters between 'lustful' women and their clans, thereby facilitating the goddess's own actions of absorption, the ritualist negotiates the client's clan mandate to her individual benefit. Her absorption of dominant-caste 'sin' is as much caste-based labour as is dominant-caste reproduction of the male heir. However, the fact that Saṭvāī ritualists are unable to ascertain fixed and structural positionality does not cause them to be socially absent or politically inactive. The absence of a fixed position allows Saṭvāī ritualists to negotiate their individualized role in ways that may be powerful and that vary across clan and client, though they never go outside the perimeter of caste hierarchy.

The *pāṭā* ritual

The ceremony took place very late in the evening, as do all *pāṭā* rituals planned between the fifth night and sixth day postpartum. This ritual is therefore also referred to as the child's *pācī*, or the fifth. I was introduced to the family, and accompanied there by a Saṭvāī ritualist named Maya (who was also the midwife in that case) and her husband from nearby Dimbhe village. All three of us rode into Shinoli packed astride Maya's husband's motorcycle that functioned mostly on kerosene, arriving in a cloud of smoke. Maya had an interest in attending the *pāṭā* ritual, as she was going to receive some gifts for officiating as midwife. These gifts included the ritual food offered to the goddess. She also had the opportunity of continuing to work for the family during the first forty days of ritualized birth impurity that involved washing menstruation clothes and bathing the newborn, until all childbirth rituals had been properly discharged. She would be offered everyday food with the family in exchange during the period that she worked with them, and extra food grains to take home with her at the end. Her continuing presence during birth impurity in the family was understood to prevent any possible danger to the child. Her body (as a Matang-caste ritualist and midwife) was understood to 'absorb' any accidental affliction incurred by the mother that angered the goddess Saṭvāī, for which she was remunerated with cooked food, ritual goods (food grains, a piece of soap, a comb, a mirror, a small towel, a pair of slippers and a marriage necklace or *mangaḷsutra*), everyday ornaments (glass bangles, forehead decoration or *bindi* and eye kohl), cosmetics used by married women (turmeric and vermillion) and clothes (usually a blouse piece of good material).

While some of my ethnography with Maya for the Shinoli case took place in the form of spluttered shouts on her husband's motorcycle on our bumpy ride between Dimbhe and Shinoli amid kerosene fumes, the rest of the ethnography, along with participant observation of the ritual, is the result of collective information resulting from the contributions, cacophony and interjection of the many women who were present that evening. I suddenly realized that Maya was treated as 'lower', once we were amidst 'them': Maratha women easily interrupted and corrected Maya's explanations and jostled with each other to give me 'correct' and 'authentic' descriptions of Saṭvāī rituals in 'good' clans such as theirs.[4] I was the stranger from the city and their guest, and I was to realize that no ethnographic context could be produced as 'natural'. They refused my requests to pretend that I wasn't there and just allow me to observe. They said that it was more important that I understand the ritual 'in principle', in its perfect, most pristine and purest form, rather than in its 'adjusted', practiced or lived version that differed from family to family in the region. Later in the night they pushed me into a six-seater motorized rickshaw, and I wasn't able to find an opportunity to debrief with Maya any longer. She and her husband returned to Dimbhe, and I heard later that she had found work with the family for their birth impurity period. I did not therefore put her into a loyalty quandary with her clients by asking her for any insider information.

A grinding stone is called a *pāṭā* in Marathi. It is a common cooking utensil owned by every rural Marathi clan for grinding spices into a paste. Each clan has its own *pāṭā* that reflects its unified domesticity: its ownership of the agrarian economy, translated into 'purified' acts of cooking its 'own' food that entitled coparceners to eat together in a kitchen presided over by household shrines. For Maya, the *pāṭā* represented the Parvati-counterpart of Lord Shiva and the very plinth of the temple, where the goddess Saṭvāī's temple rested. For her, the dedication of ritualized food to the Saṭvāī was both to the temple plinth and the temple idol, as both Lord Shankar and goddess Parvati were inseparably united in the act of reproducing the cosmos. For her, their inseparability marked the Saṭvāī temple's function as reproductive, and produced her own personal role to the goddess as a ritualist who facilitated childbirth. For the agrarian clan, however, the *pāṭā* was 'their own' grinding stone that they would never lend to outsiders, though they were permitted to donate food prepared on it. According to them, their *pāṭā* was only used for 'insiders' to the clan, and its use marked those it was being used for, as 'insiders' to the clan. Using the household *pāṭā* for childbirth rituals was therefore a way of awarding clan honour to a mother and her baby.

The pestle was dressed like a baby for the ritual: it was anointed with turmeric and attired in attractive baby clothes, gold ornaments and a little frilly cap. Called the *gōpā* (or *bāḷ gōpāḷ*), it was placed along with the *pāṭā* as a ritual offering for the goddess so that she would encounter it when she entered the house at night to accept and inspect the food and ritual offerings. The clan hoped that she would then nurse the *gōpā* as her own and disregard the real baby. Once the goddess was satisfied with the obeisance paid her, she would lose all interest in issuing punishments. But until then the clan had to be careful. The newborn wasn't allowed to wear proper baby clothes (called *bāḷote*) or ornaments until the goddess Saṭvāī had first had the chance to nurse her *gōpā*. Until such time, the infant was swaddled in a long piece of cloth and made indistinguishable from a bundle of clothes. Sometimes sleeping male infants were covered with girls' clothes or blouses so that the goddess would lose capricious interest in them. The *bāḷote* had special significance for witchcraft-avoidance. Witches were understood to have the power to kill babies with *bāḷote* when they found it. They could burn the baby clothes and eat a pinch of burned *bāḷote* ash every day. With every pinch, the baby's health was understood to get weaker, until one day the *bāḷote* ash ended, and the baby expired.

It was not just the *gōpā* that accompanied the *pāṭā*. Every Saṭvāi *pāṭā* ritual also required a stone lamp 'owned' by the family for its female coparceners. Since the goddess Saṭvāi was imagined as an entourage of many, or at least a minimum of five sisters (all belonging to different castes), small lamps made from cooked dough were filled with oil, lit up and placed at five corners of the *pāṭā* (these small lamps were distributed to neighbourhood children the next day). The stone lamp representing the goddess's chief and unshakable principle was lit and placed at the triangular end or head of the grinding stone, its flame shielded from the infant's eyes as the mother holding the infant bowed to the *pāṭā*. It was feared that the child might grow blind or cross-eyed if it looked at the flame directly, as this was its first Saṭvāī ritual and its first confrontation with the goddess. However, the goddess, who was hungry for propitiation, was imagined to be waiting for the mother's first mistake, so she could take the child from her.

The *pāṭā* ceremony was always performed at the birthing corner of the house. This corner was especially prepared near the bathroom of the house, and Maya told me of how in earlier times bathrooms would be especially prepared and dug in birthing chambers. The placenta, which was earlier kept under a basket in the corner of this special bathroom, was now buried in the bathroom floor. The placenta was considered the infant's first and blood mother, and it was kept 'alive' for the first five days after childbirth by making small food offerings and the daily offering of a lamp. It was believed that water from the placenta that trickled onto the child or its proximity to the child, as the latter bathed in the bathroom, represented the blood mother's love for the newborn that the baby required in its first five days postpartum. Once the placenta basket was buried, the *pāṭā* was placed on top of its burial stone for rituals to the goddess Saṭvāī.

While the placenta was the child's first and blood mother, its human mother would then become its milk mother – a relationship she would share with other agnatic women. All of them would produce clan heirs as collective and clan property, while the goddess Saṭvāī became the child's *dharma* mother and village ancestor. The 'heat' and 'impurity' of grief produced by the biological severing of the child from its blood mother (the placenta), the entire birthing process and the placenta's death/burial required Maya's presence. Her presence 'absorbed' any illness which might be generated through 'impurity'; the impurity of resisting dharma manifested by the expression of pain in the social production of motherhood. She was the one to place the grinding stone over the placenta grave, and then to draw twelve anthropomorphic figures around the bathroom, the front door and back door of the house. These, according to the women, were called *Baḷi-rāna*.[5] Soon they were offered food dedications (a small piece of bread, lentils and vegetables), anointed with turmeric and vermillion and shown a small lamp to 'enliven' them. The *Baḷi-rāna* were said to guard the mother and baby until the next childbirth ritual on the twelfth day postpartum. The family would wipe away one *Baḷi-rāna* figurine from the wall each day, as the Saṭvāī, who would visit the home to see whether any taboos had been broken, took one *Baḷi-rāna* as her propitiatory offering every day. One of the older women attending the ritual that evening recounted how dangerous it was in earlier times to keep the door open for the goddess, who was believed to take the form of a cat, in the night. Villages were not industrialized then, and there were no proper roads. Moreover, many villages were nestled next to small forests or large sugarcane plantations. She recounted one *pācī* ritual when a small leopard (very commonly encountered in rural western Maharashtra known as *bibṭyā*) had wandered into a home, finding the door open and smelling food. The family was petrified when they saw the leopard and naturally did not dare to make a sound. However, the leopard seemed relaxed and roamed around for a while, foraging in the corners for food. It then wandered out, at which the child's grandmother leapt up to lock the doors and windows from the inside. It had been twenty years since this incident, but the boy (who had grown up to be a young man) had always been teased in the village for having a 'special' Saṭvāī.

The *pāṭā* was used as a platform to make food offerings to the goddess. Only after this offering could the mother eat normal, everyday food. Before that, the goddess retained her first claim over the food, while the mother fasted, ate a variety of porridge and breast-fed simultaneously, waiting for her uterus to contract (a painful condition called *vāyū-gōḷā*),[6] which sometimes lasted for over a month. During this period of birth impurity, the goddess Saṭvāī kept a close watch on mothers and babies, both of whom needed great care. One of these care-taking measures was for the mother-child duo to sleep on a mattress that had dried stalks of grass under it that crackled as they moved, so that the Saṭvāī was reminded that they belonged to an upper-caste agrarian clan that she was sworn to protect. Another effort involved placing an iron sickle and winnowing fan near the mother and child's bed, so that the Saṭvāī, on seeing these agricultural implements, would be reminded of their upper-caste agrarian clan. A third preventive measure I encountered was a paste of asafoetida (or *hīṅg*) that mothers and babies applied on their foreheads.[7] Women also hung up leather footwear at the entrance to their homes (as a mark of belonging to agrarian caste society) and iron horseshoes outside their homes. Many women were unaware of the significance of the horseshoe as a preventive measure against the goddess. Some men I interviewed told me that during the Maratha rule, homes that regularly paid their taxes were marked on their doorjambs with hobnailed horseshoes across the lintel to demonstrate allegiance. Although one can deduce the antiquity of the goddess Saṭvāī and her traditional agrarian roots through such practices, the continuation of this political history of taxation in ritualized forms of paying tribute to the goddess is merely conjecture.[8]

On the fifth day after childbirth, on the day of the *pāṭā* ritual, the goddess Saṭvāī is offered food and other ritual objects on the grinding stone. She is known to come to the house during the night in the form of a cat to accept the food, inspect the ritual offering, nurse the *gōpā* and take one of the *Baḷi-rāna* as sacrifice. After finding everything to her satisfaction, she is known to write the fate (or longevity) of the newborn on its forehead before departing. Once satisfied, the goddess is 'cooled' and becomes distant and benevolent towards the child and its mother, retreating from the home and allowing the child to thrive. In effect this is a message that declares the mother to be virtuous and above reproach.

Five small pebbles, signifying the multiplicity of the goddess Saṭvāī, are placed at the centre of the *pāṭā* after it is decorated with the stone lamp, dough lamps and the *gōpā*. Coloured and black string (representing the clothes and hair of the goddess) are laid alongside these stones, as these goddesses are thought to be dressed in multicoloured clothes and be long-haired. Five or more wild plants (known as *pāc-pālavī*), commonly worshipped as clan totems or as insignia of the Maratha caste, are clustered around the *pāṭā*. These include: pieces of cactus, twigs of the pomegranate shrub and the cotton plant, twigs of the jujube berry and neem tree, twigs of the mango and fig tree, betel and pīpal leaves, twigs of the Jāmbhul (*Calyptranthes jambolana*) and twigs of the Sondad tree (*Prosopis cineraria*), known to keep witches away. Along with this foliage, some river sand is arranged near the *pāṭā* together with grass reeds that grow at the riverside. Food offerings of bread, rice, lentils, pulses, vegetables, fries, sweets and an animal sacrifice (if the family consumes meat and fish, it must first be offered to the goddess), along with the discarded umbilical cord from the child's body (considered medicinal), are dedicated to the goddess Saṭvāi (the five dressed pebbles). All the nutritious food that is considered especially beneficial for mothers and children is laid out on the *pāṭā* and dedicated to the goddess along with incense sticks.

Maya pointed out to me how the *pāṭā* ritual reconstructed the Saṭvāī temple in its entirety. While the grinding stone became the temple plinth, the five pebbles represented the Saṭvāī idols in a shrine, located under the open sky. The different plant dedications arranged around the grinding stone resembled the goddess's sacred grove. Traditionally many Saṭvāī shrines are located under a tree or in a little glade next to a stream or well. The arrangement of river sand and grass reeds also reconstructs a dry riverbed adjoining the temple, a scene commonly encountered near shrines. The lighting of the stone and dough lamps to the goddess is the perfect oblation, as her plinth located over the placenta grave signifies her superiority over biological blood relationships between mothers and children, giving precedence instead to dharma, caste and milk relationships that are an important means of learning clan loyalty, which unites agrarian ethics and land relationships.

Neighbourhood and clan women gathered for the ritual traditionally shared soaked gram or *ghugryā* between them after the ritual, as *ghugryā* represented the benevolence and cooled fertility of the goddess who no longer cause illness in children or afflicted mothers. The form of *ghugryā* was considered to represent the consistency of healthy excreta. The health of newborn infants who passed their first Saṭvāī milestone successfully and without affliction were marked by their healthy excretion. As the Saṭvāī becomes distanced, the child's health improved, and this was measured by its digestion. The child's excreta symbolized by the gram was shared among attending women as those who shared in the goddess's benevolence and fertility, which allowed children to thrive. The sharing of *ghugryā* also signified that the women were the child's superiors and the mother's agnates. Henceforth they stood in a mothering and reprimanding relationship with the child, through the sharing of Saṭvāī fertility, represented by gram that resembled its healthy, affliction-free and well-formed excreta.

An ethnographic framing of affliction

While most women respondents in the villages where I worked remained suspicious of my motives for studying Saṭvāī and childbirth rituals, especially as I was childless myself, I received more cooperation from men. Many women were uncertain about whether I would bring them bad luck as a childless woman or whether my 'research' constituted a subterfuge for rituals that I would later perform in secret to escape my own childlessness. Maya too, asked me whether I was researching Saṭvāī rituals in order to 'learn' them. Village men, however, viewed my work through a cultural and regional nationalist lens, seeing it as the recording of dying Marathi traditional-rural culture that would soon be erased by modernity, medical technology, clinical births and anti-superstition squads, who lectured women about the meaninglessness of rituals. While I was uncomfortable about my research being framed as a cultural repository of rural Marathi tradition, I was also uncomfortable about the possibility of anti-superstition squads deliberately disrupting the rituals. Though I was aware that the framing of Saṭvāī childbirth rituals as a cultural repository may function as a way of conserving tradition, I agreed that this conservation served a traditionalist and patriarchal purpose. There were really no clear answers, and I was to remain conflicted with this question until the end of my fieldwork. However, I was relieved that most of the men did not view me as a clandestine ritual learner.

Researching Saṭvāī rituals, I realized the thin boundary between childbirth rituals, which purified motherhood and ensured the child's safety, and child loss/childlessness, that was considered to result from women's lust (sin) and illegitimate eating that caused sexual pollution/impurity or *viṭāḷ*. My respondents explained how achieving purity and avoiding sin emerged from a fear of Saṭvāī affliction at puberty that continued as women performed Saṭvāī rituals to protect their motherhood and children at every stage of childbirth, from conception (the seventh month of pregnancy) to well within the postpartum period, until the children were weaned. Postpartum Saṭvāī purification rituals were performed until the child was able to subsist on its mother's milk, marking the fifth day (*pācī*), the twelfth day (*bārāvī*) and the first three months after childbirth (*jāwaḷ*). Motherhood and children were considered 'safe' only after the child had transitioned to cooked food and stopped depending on its mother's milk. Only after this would the child be taught his own name and treated as a separate person.

The fear of affliction and the introduction of lust as a pejorative concept converges with the onset of menstruation in women's lives. Women explained how the Saṭvāī primarily afflicted upper-caste (dominant, agrarian caste) menstruating women when the latter 'wandered' too close to their shrines. Since women belonging to the upper (dominant) caste were supposed to stay in seclusion during menstruation and await pregnancy, the goddess grew angry with them when she encountered them outside their allocated marital clan habitations. By doing this, women were breaking both gender and caste rules. Although women knew that the idea of conceiving during menstruation was irrational, they were simultaneously of the opinion that male heirs of value were conceived only during menstruation, as Saṭvāī affliction also took place during menstruation. They told me that Saṭvāī shrines were located on the outskirts of villages and at the intersection of agrarian spaces and impure spaces, where women's moral mistakes and sins were identified and where the Saṭvāī's shrine acted as a ritual 'police station' that 'arrested' errant, wandering menstruating women. If women conceived thereafter, the Saṭvāi was known to 'abort' the babies. Post facto ritual diagnosis worked the other way around, of course; if a young bride miscarried, she was ritually diagnosed as afflicted by the Saṭvāī for having 'wandered'.

As affliction diagnosis associated the lust for food with women's sexual lust and sin, and the absence of pure and passive wifely fertility that was deserving of pure motherhood, affliction diagnosis implicated women in witchcraft and ascribed to them cannibalistic potential. Women diagnosed as afflicted, who had lost their children, were often accused of having 'eaten' these children. The accusation of cannibalism became an extension of the discourse of lust and sin. The Saṭvāī's diagnosis that aborted the 'impure' baby therefore condemned it as a non-child who had come into illegitimate existence outside clan and caste boundaries, while its mother was 'wandering' and engaging in sin by breaking gender and caste rules. Many of my respondents told me that it was the goddess Saṭvāī who 'ate' the children, when she afflicted and possessed 'wandering' pregnant women. This description shared a very thin boundary with accusations of possessed, afflicted and sinful women as cannibals and witches.

Given that the implications of Saṭvāī affliction diagnosis were so dangerous for women, affliction cases were always individualistic and characterized by intense clan negotiations. Women's safety within these diagnostics and their outcome depended on the socioeconomic status of their clans in their marital and natal villages and the strength of their clan's caste networks within the wider region. In addition, negotiations in Saṭvāī affliction cases involved the convincing participation and performance of Saṭvāī ritualists and husbands. These complex personal negotiations surrounding Saṭvāī affliction always resulted in unpredictable outcomes, though they can be grouped in three broad categories. If diagnosed women were socio-economically well placed in secure clan and caste networks and well ensconced in their marital relationships, afflictions were characterized as childish mistakes (as the women had mistakenly walked near Saṭvāī shrines while menstruating). Because affliction diagnosis was always post facto, women forgiven for their mistakes were easily reinstated in their marital clans after performing the required fasting rituals. They would be declared innocent by not being considered guilty to start with, but just mistaken.[9] Other women battled lingering family conflicts such as dowry disputes, an increasing burden of domestic labour and negotiations surrounding sexual demands within intimate marital relationships through avenues provided them by affliction diagnosis. Familial dissatisfaction or spousal dissatisfaction was often expressed through Saṭvāī affliction diagnosis and its associated symptoms of 'selfishness', 'resistance' and 'lust'. Those who were disliked by their marital families and husbands battled domestic violence through the onset of Saṭvāī affliction diagnosis that was often interpreted as witchcraft. I learned to view the interpretation of Saṭvāī diagnosis as witchcraft as a sign of violent and abusive marriages in the village. Women considered allegations of witchcraft as serious. Such allegations usually signified the last stages of a marriage and led to its dissolution. However, since women competed so much with one another, they were more likely to fear each other than be sympathetic. They believed that as everyone was so alert about witches, the latter worked in secret and hid their tracks. They cannibalized their own children to hide their witchcraft from the world, as no one would believe that a mother could eat her own children. Once she had got away with eating her own children and fooling the world, she would then turn to her real goal: eating other children in the clan and village. Women dealing with 'witch' accusations faced intense domestic violence, abandonment and repeated insults about how unlucky, evil and afflicted they were as witches (*lāv*); many such women returned to their fathers' homes, underwent divorce litigation, were separated from their children and, finally, were supplanted by a new wife. Saṭvāī affliction diagnosis was therefore a constant danger that characterized women's precarious social position in agrarian and rural Marathi society.

The intense competition that Saṭvāi afflictions produced led to a further diversification of diagnostic categories suffered by women. These categories emerged as defences for coping with differences among them, mediating the personal outcome of their illness. Because some personally empowered women were viewed as childish and innocent, while others were viewed as malevolent and deliberate malefactors, the resulting jealousy and competition between women often led to a third layer of 'victimhood to witchcraft' among dominant upper-caste afflicted women. Dominant-caste women, aware of their own privilege, protected themselves from the competition and jealousy of women diagnosed as witches by utilizing the latter's diagnosis of witchcraft in their own favour. Many dominant-caste women I interviewed about Saṭvāī affliction diagnosis told me of the witchcraft worked against them by 'real witches' who were jealous of them. Women's groups were therefore very cautious and suspicious of including the less fortunate among them, lest this unfortunate friend become jealous of their good fortune and steal it away by working witchcraft against them. This was also one of the primary reasons why, as a childless woman, I had difficulty gaining entry into many women's groups.

Turning to the language used by women when describing afflictions and Saṭvāī rituals, while none of them clearly articulated 'lust' (*vāsanā*) as a reason and symptom of Saṭvāī affliction, their idea of incurred sexual and reproductive pollution (*viṭāḷ*) was greater than lust. Their concept of pollution associated gendered images of women's uncontrolled, feral and boundless hunger (*bhūk*) imagined as cannibalistic, with the women's sexual contamination (*vital*) and ensuing childlessness. Not only did these associations of being afflicted and possessed by the Saṭvāī conjure up images of demon-goddesses such as the A-Lakṣmī, who was kept away and separated from women to inaugurate the Lakṣmī within them, but the characteristics of A-Lakṣmī were considered dangerous and contagious. Childlessness, lust and sin were a part of every woman and could become a disease and her nemesis if not controlled and socialized through ritualized fasting that separated the Lakṣmī and A-Lakṣmī across multiple boundaries of morality, village structure and caste. Lakṣmī's virtuous fasting that purified women sexually separated the A-Lakṣmī's eating of food, the latter being represented by the Saṭvāī's shrine located outside village boundaries, in impure spaces that were sites of lower-caste habitation (Dandekar 2009).

Afflicted women offered various foods and ritual objects to the goddess Saṭvāī for her consumption at her shrines for a stipulated ritual period of five weeks: breads, rice, vegetables, pulses, lentils, sweets, fried foods, fruits, flowers, colourful clothes, cosmetics, bangles, articles of daily usage (such as slippers) and sometimes sacrificed animals (if their caste status so demanded). Importantly, during these five weeks, afflicted women abstained from consuming the ritually offered food and articles of personal use themselves (including colours/ materials dedicated to the goddess). Performing this penance left women with very little choice of food during ritual periods. Their hunger and publicly performed rituals reminded them of their affliction, as they felt embarrassed and ashamed of accusations of lust. All this caused in them and other women who beheld them an enduring fear of child loss and of the Saṭvāī shrine that they had learned to avoid. Women's entry path into the village after they had performed the ritual was always cleared of other people, as their encounter with the Saṭvāī was considered to have made them contagious to other women. They wouldn't accept food invitations from other village women during their social quarantine during the fasting period either, as they were afraid that jealous women in large gatherings might contaminate their food to try to reverse whatever purity they had achieved.[10] Childlessness was contagious and hinged centrally on women's consumption. Remembering Scheper-Hughes's (1993) ethnography on motherhood,[11] I witnessed how women from agrarian societies in rural Maharashtra felt unable to experience their grief at the death of their children or foetuses. Viewing themselves as objectified functions of caste-based, marital clan reproduction, they experienced the shame and terror of 'impurity' and Saṭvāī affliction that resulted in unending chains of food-penance and a systemic imposition of hunger balanced against the birth, health and longevity of sons.

Conclusion

Food cannot be accepted at face value in rural and agrarian Marathi communities, as eating is politicized. Food entitlements are gendered, ritualized and associated with 'pure' motherhood and therefore complicated by questions of legitimacy, women in the village being produced as consumers counterbalanced against their recalcitrant 'labour' (no male children or childless). The difference between dominant-caste clients and lower-caste ritualists is signified by the Saṭvāī's ritual distancing in childbirth rituals, and her proximity to the ritualist's immunity that enmeshes caste, gender and village boundary together with women's own understanding of body and purity. The Saṭvāī shrine at the village boundary represented not just spatial borders but also caste and gender boundaries between women. Many women in my field area were invested in the performance of purity and immunity. Several women from the dominant castes knew that they needed immune repositories like ritualists, who functioned like impure storehouses, to shed their own impure afflictions. Dominant-caste women (especially educated women) were also aware that the lower-caste ritualists' so-called immunity was an artificial construct that was similar to affliction; immunity was linked with purity and women's caste. Women from both sides of the caste divide were aware that they aided in providing village clans and castes, which they served as wives and ritualists, with offspring and inheritance (*kūladīpak*) in return for food and viewed themselves as the valorous feudatories (Mātṛgaṇa) of the goddess, performing tasks of dharma. Though I often asked my dominant-caste respondents whether it was fair to understand lower-caste ritualists as 'immune', as doing so belittled lower-caste poverty and experiences of illness and child loss, these suggestions were badly received. Poverty and hunger were a harsh and intersectional experience for women across the caste divide, as dominant-caste women faced morally and ritually induced hunger and impoverishment. They immediately plunged into narratives of how they invited women of the lower castes for sumptuous lunches whenever their children fell ill, so that this eating could transfer and absorb the children's illness. As this always had to be a sumptuous meal, it being considered inauspicious if the lower-caste invitee rejected the food, they dismissed my suggestions immediately. It was because the ritualist ate this food that the mother's own sinful lust was absorbed and turned away, even as the mother went hungry; this is how dominant-caste children remained healthy from a ritual perspective. Caste boundaries between village women, and the composite organization between caste differences that produced the close relationship between purity and immunity, was often described as represented by the body of the village goddess Reṇukā, Mari-āī or Yellammā, who was a composite goddess, made up of the conjoined heads and bodies of women from the upper and lower castes.

To conclude, there were two interconnected forms of illegitimate eating for women that were viewed negatively in Marathi agrarian society. The first, representing the Saṭvāī's own image, signified women's caste and gender boundaries. Her eating of the sacrificial *Baḷi-rāna* and the dedicated food was a complex and violent phenomenon for those who beheld it, as beholding the goddess while she ate rendered upper-caste women impure even as lower-caste women remained immune to the goddess's affliction. The second form of illegitimate eating was represented by the figure of the witch, who ate secretly to break gender and caste divisions instituted by the goddess Saṭvāī. Therefore, while the Saṭvāī ate to make the divide, the witch ate to break the gender and caste divide. While the Saṭvāī ate to foster purity and immunity that aided in childbirth, the witch ate to kill those children. The visual interconnections of illegitimate eating between the Saṭvāī and the witch were therefore linked as if in a mirror image, where the Saṭvāī ate only to control the witch and her eating. Women who did not want to be denounced as witches, fasted. While figures of expiating women formed the composite image of village goddesses like Reṇukā, the A-Lakṣmī became unmarked and ubiquitous. She was known to be contagious and live within every woman who had to fight lust and hunger to purify herself.

Notes

1 Duvvury (1991) has also researched childbirth rituals among upper-caste Tamilians with observations that have a startling similarity with those in Maharashtra.
2 The theory of Sanskritization (Srinivas 1987) was later applied to Rajputization (cf. Singh 2011), and Guha (2013) wrote of the discursive production of the Maratha caste.
3 Ritualists were central to my ethnographic fieldwork and method and their position as midwives has been studied by medical anthropologists (Chawla 1994).
4 I have elsewhere (Dandekar 2014, 2015) explored childbirth rituals in rural Maharashtra and developed a research methodology to discuss similar contexts.
5 Youngblood (2016) has described the importance of Baḷī or Baḷī-rājā within the context of Marathi agrarian society and agrarian social movements to denote the importance of the Dalit farmer and the assertion of his cultural and non-upper caste identity.

6 Chawla (2002) has also carried out ethnographic research on Hawa-gola.

7 There is an enduring association between goddesses in western Maharashtra and asafoetida. Scholarship on important goddesses such as the Tulja-Bhavani in Maharashtra (being tutelary goddesses for the Maratha Empire) being originally called Hingulja-Bhavani and being associated with the goddess Hinglaj in Sindh makes asafoetida an interesting ritualized food association for other rural goddesses that draw on Tulja-Bhavani's cult (Jansen 1995).

8 Cf. Gordon (1994) for exploring the political history of Marathas as tax-extracting marauders.

9 Many such cases of newly married girls and their afflictions have been explored by Freed and Freed (1993); similarly, questions of women's sexual empowerment and subversion have been explored by Raheja and Gold (1994).

10 Masilamani-Meyers (2004) has worked on guardian deities of Tamil Nadu using concepts of 'wilderness' and 'domesticated' in structural ways that have followed Mary Douglas's (2002) logic of how boundaries become spaces for negotiating power, important to the internal community.

11 Some important scholars who have researched relationships between maternity and midwifery traditions in South Asia include Rairkar (2007) and Sadgopal (2009).

References

Brubaker, R. L. 1978. 'The Ambivalent Mistress: A Study of South Indian Village Goddesses and Their Religious Meaning'. Unpublished PhD thesis, University of Chicago.

Chawla, J. 1994. *Child-Bearing and Culture: Women Centred Revisioning of the Traditional Midwife; The Dai as a Ritual Practitioner*. New Delhi: Indian Social Institute.

Chawla, J. 2002. 'Hawa, Gola and Mother-in-Law's Big Toe: On Understanding Dais' Imagery of the Female Body'. In S. Rozario and G. Samuel (eds), *The Daughters of Hariti: Theory and Practice in Medical Anthropology and International Health*. London: Routledge, 147–62.

Dandekar, D. 2009. 'Satvai and the Lives of Women in Ghodegaon'. In R. Badry, M. Rohrer and K. Steiner (eds), *Liebe, Sexualität, Ehe und Partnerschaft: Paradigmen im Wandel* (Love, sexuality, marriage and partnership: changing paradigms). Freiburg: Fördergemeinschaft wissenschaftlicher Publikationen von Frauen, 281–92.

Dandekar, D. 2014. 'Childlessness and Empathetic Relationships'. *The Oriental Anthropologist* 14(1) (Special Number on Fieldwork in South Asia, ed. G. Alex): 123–39.

Dandekar, D. 2015. 'Women's Śakti and the Satvāī: A Folk Goddess of Childbirth in Maharashtra'. In K. S. Rege, Suraj A. Pandit, Sunita Jeswani and Radha Sabnis (eds),

Śakti in Indian Archaeology, Art, Literature and Philosophy. New Delhi: Agam Kala Prakashan.

Dandekar, D. 2016a. 'The Baaravi Ritual, the Satvai and Female Ancestor Worship in Western Maharashtra'. In G. Alex and K. Polit (eds), *Childbirth and Its Accompanying Rituals*. Heidelberg: Draupadi Verlag.

Dandekar, D. 2016b. *Boundaries and Motherhood: Ritual and Reproduction in Rural Maharashtra*. New Delhi: Zubaan Books.

Douglas, M. 2002. *Purity and Danger*. London: Routledge.

Duvvury, V. K. 1991. *Play, Symbolism and Ritual: A Study of Tamil Brahmin Women's Rites of Passage*, American University Studies, Vol. 11. New York: Peter Lang.

Feldhaus, A. 1995. *Water and Womanhood: Religious Meanings of Rivers in Maharashtra*. New York: Oxford University Press.

Flueckiger, J. B. 2006. *In Amma's Healing Room: Gender and Vernacular Islam in South India*. Bloomington: Indiana University Press.

Freed, R. S., and S. A. Freed. 1993. *Ghosts: Life and Death in North India*, Anthropological Papers of the American Museum of Natural History, vol. 72. Seattle: University of Washington Press.

Gordon, S. 1994. *Marathas, Marauders, and State Formation in Eighteenth-Century India*. New Delhi: Oxford University Press.

Guha, S. 2013. *Beyond Caste: Identity and Power in South Asia, Past and Present*. Leiden: Brill.

Harlan, L. 1994. 'Perfection and Devotion: Sati Tradition in Rajasthan'. In J. S. Hawley (ed.), *Sati, the Blessing and the Curse*. New York: Oxford University Press, 79–90.

Hiltebeitel, A. 1988. *The Cult of Draupadi 1: Mythologies: From Gingee to Kurukshetra*. New Delhi: Motilal Banarsidass.

Hiltebeitel, A, and K. M. Erndl (eds). 2000. *Is the Goddess a Feminist? The Politics of South Asian Goddesses*. New York: NYU Press.

Jansen, R. 1995. *Die Bhavani von Tuljapur: Religionsgeschichtliche Studie des Kultes einer Göttin der Indischen Volksreligion* (The Bhavani of Tuljapur: Study in the history of religion of the cult of an Indian folk goddess) (Beiträge zur Südasienforschung, Südasien-Institut, Universität Heidelberg (Contributions to South Asia Research, South Asia Institute, University of Heidelberg), vol. 168). Stuttgart: Franz Steiner Verlag.

Kakar, S. 1982. *Shamans, Mystics and Doctors: A Psychological Inquiry into India and Its Healing Traditions*. New Delhi: Oxford University Press.

Kinsley, D. 1986. *Hindu Goddesses: Visions of the Divine Feminine in the Hindu Religious Tradition*. New Delhi: Motilal Banarasidass.

Masilamani-Meyer, E. 2004. *Guardians of Tamilnadu: Folk Deities, Folk Religion, Hindu Themes*, Neue Hallesche Berichte (New Reports from Halle), vol. 5. Halle: Verlag der Franckeschen Stiftungen zu Halle.

Panse, M. G. 1952. *Index Verborum of Jnanesvari*, Bulletin of the Deccan College Research Institute 10: 572–762.

Parry, J. P. 1994. *Death in Banaras*. Cambridge: Cambridge University Press.

Raheja, G. G., and A. G. Gold. 1994. *Listen to the Heron's Words: Reimagining Gender and Kinship in North India*. Berkeley: University of California Press.

Rairkar, H. 2007. 'Midwives: A Tradition on the Move in Maharashtra'. In J. B. Bernard Bell, B. Das, V. Parthasarathi and G. Poetevin (eds). *The Social and the Symbolic*, Communication Processes, vol. 2. New Delhi: Sage Publications, 413–72.

Sadgopal, M. 2009. 'Can Maternity Services Open Up to the Indigenous Traditions of Midwifery?' *Economic and Political Weekly* 44(16): 52–9.

Sarkar, T., and U. Butalia (eds). 1995. *Women and the Hindu Right: A Collection of Essays*. New Delhi: Kali for Women.

Śarmā, K. 2012. *Āplā saṃpūrṇa cāturmās*. 4th edition. Mumbai: Manoramā Prakāśan.

Scheper-Hughes, N. 1993. *Death without Weeping: The Violence of Everyday Life in Brazil*. Berkeley: University of California Press.

Sen, R. N. 1974. *Brahma Vaivarta Puranam (Part 1: Brahma and Prakriti Khandas), The Sacred Books of the Hindus*, vol. 24, part 1. New York: AMS Press.

Singh, U. 2011. 'Introduction'. In U. Singh (ed.), *Rethinking Early Medieval India: A Reader*. New Delhi: Oxford University Press, 1–44.

Srinivas, M. N. 1987. *The Dominant Caste and Other Essays*. New Delhi: Oxford University Press.

Youngblood, M. 2016. *Cultivating Community: Interest, Identity, and Ambiguity in an Indian Social Mobilization*. Pasadena, CA: South Asian Studies Association.

8

Eating and fasting as a complex professional strategy

Nita Kumar

There are four entry points into my topic. The first is that the people I am talking about can almost all articulate the narratives of their lives as characterized by a domineering patriarchy, where they had in most cases an early arranged marriage, moved into a joint family, coped with a new role of wife, daughter-in-law, sister-in-law and then mother, and then crafted out a balance for themselves between the demands of work and family. They are complicit in this patriarchy and celebrate it to different extents, quite echoing the literature on the subject, if not with a reflexivity about its various arguments (for instance, Ortner 1974; Mohanty 1984; Sangari and Vaid 1989; Kumar 1992; Kumar 1993). They also exercise agency and choice in a myriad of different ways.

The second is that teachers in India, especially women teachers, are not given a high status in contemporary society. They are aware of this and deal on an everyday basis with comments at home and in their community that belittle or question their commitment to their jobs, always striving to show their work as inferior to other possible jobs. Their self-image is not high, and they do not make references to their jobs that are complimentary, a self-recognition that is referenced in the literature (Batra 2005; Kremer et al. 2005; Jain and Saxena 2010).

The third is that, notwithstanding the low status of their profession, they are proud of their educational qualifications and their modernity. Many commute in their own *garis*, vehicles or scooters (or 'scooties'), and report on their lives with pride as being full of competent, well-managed responsibilities. A study of modernity in India shows that the modern person takes pride in distancing herself from the problems around – the *garbage*, literally and metaphorically – using education as the defining difference between herself and the uneducated or less-educated masses who are a brake on progress.

And fourth, they are lower middle-class women who earn between Rs 10,000 and 15,000 per month. Their husbands earn erratically, or earn less, or do not cover all the household expenses with their earnings and certainly do not cover their wives' personal expenses. The women's earnings are therefore of importance to them and not to be treated lightly or jeopardized by casualness. A self-consciousness about women's leadership roles is emerging in administration as well as teaching (Ahmad et al. 2008).

This group of self-consciously modern, low-status professionals who value their jobs but are also torn between two loyalties, one to their professional self and the other to their community self, may be better understood by looking at their relations with food, cooking and meals, and within this larger world of food, at their strategies of fasting, selective eating or refraining from eating. It was after years of research with teachers and puzzlement over their negotiations with professionalism and modernity that I took seriously the topic of this volume – food. It struck me that the key to their building of boundaries around themselves, to heighten their sense of power and identity, lay in their manipulation of eating and not eating at several levels.

This chapter carries on from my earlier research among lower middle-class and working-class women that sought to understand their lives in terms of power, autonomy and agency, all while they spent long hours involved with food and mentioned it voluntarily as central to their identities (Kumar 2006a). It was, I realized, a measure of their power insofar as they had autonomous control over their kitchens. They could decide how much time they gave to food and typically spun this time out in creative directions such as making and preserving condiments, exchanging recipes and occasionally experimenting with and sampling each other's preparations. They could decide on menus and serve others in the order and manner they wished. They could choose when and what to eat themselves. From the outside it seems that women are constrained by their family members' wishes in all these activities, but in practice they understand how to manage this autonomous world of food that they technically and practically have control over.

The present research swings into new directions, however, because teachers have strict work times and do not have the leisure to exercise the kind of control over food that I found in the case of homemakers. Second, I have a managerial role over a set of teachers in India and first became aware of women's fasts because there were two significant kinds of *trouble* caused by teachers' food practices. There was a retreat from partaking of the midday lunch compulsory for all teachers and staff, and there were an unusual number of applications of leave for days that were not school holidays but were days of fasting for the women teachers. My preferred anthropological approach of underscoring their agency is thus complicated by the employer's perspective of questioning their professionalism, and then comes back again to inspecting their strategy for deliberate (professional) manoeuvring again. My interest in studying their culture and lives is impacted by my other-professional interest in aiding their progress – a kind of layering that I have tried to problematize elsewhere (Kumar 2006b).

Let me start with the case of Mamta Upadhayay. Almost forty, Mamta is in a family of nine members: her son, husband, mother-in-law (*sas*), older brother-in-law (*jeth*), his wife (*jethani*), their two children and husband's sister (*nand*). She has a master's degree in Hindi from Banaras Hindu University (BHU) and is recognized as a competent teacher who can negotiate annually for a higher salary and earns, if not as high a salary as the government would give her, a respectable Rs 15,000 per month.

Mamta sighs when asked about her family. She gives some priceless quotes. Her *sas* has this to say about her need to go in on a day when the *sas* prefers that it be a holiday: '*Tumhara school to albela hai*' (Your school is weird/amazing!). Her sister-in-law does not understand why she would venture out on a hot day instead of taking it easy at home. '*Kyun haddi sukha rahi ho? Kam kya karne ki zaroorat hai?*' (Why are you wearing yourself out to a skeleton? What is the use of this job?) The sum of her family's comments is that she is perverse to be working instead of being a full-time housewife, and that she probably is doubly perverse in that she *pretends* to be working but is probably having fun. She is consistently the butt of sarcasm and verbal abuse from her in-laws. Her husband and son are non-supportive by simply refusing to share in the housework. Every morning Mamta cooks the breakfast and lunch and packs her own and her son's snacks before she leaves for her full-time eight-hour job a half-hour rickshaw ride away.

It is amazing to me that Mamta relates all this with a half-smile, though a resigned one, and that she does not directly criticize her in-laws, characterizing their thinking more objectively as 'rooted in certain *samskaras* (traditions) for so many days'.

Mamta explains why she needs to take leave on the days that she fasts. Since she is a strong woman I ask her directly why women cannot be more professional instead of creating trouble through this casual leave-taking which men employees never do. 'It's not the fast itself,' she replies. 'The fast is no problem. It's all the preparations that have to be made on that day. There is the *thikua* to be made to be offered to the Sun on Chhat. There are the *gujiyas* on Teej, the fruit to be washed and cut. All this has been done in our home for hundreds of years. We have to clean up, wash, wear new clothes, get many things ready. Everyone at home would not believe it if I left home: You have *school* today?' Mamta adds to help me understand further that her *sas* is illiterate and from a village, albeit living in the city for thirty years. There is a 'huge difference in our levels'. Mamta says that her solution is 'adjustment' and 'management', the first to her family, the second of her school. She *has* to 'adjust' to her family. She tells herself, '*Chalo, school to ham manage kar lenge*' (Okay, I will manage the school). In other words, in this 'controversy' (her word) between the school and the home, she feels that the school is more pliable and she can bend it to her will, but her home is intractable and needs to be obeyed. In both cases, I realized as I listened to her, her success is diluted by her having to listen to negative comments on the choices she makes.

Let us look at the case of Sunita Tripathi. Also about forty, Sunita's family consists of two brothers and their wives and two children, and their older widowed sister-in-law and her son. Sunita is the middle daughter-in-law. The parents-in-law and oldest son have died, '*tak-tak-tak*', says the oldest daughter-in-law, called Bhabhi. Her natal home is in a *qasba* (small town) near Allahabad; the other two daughters-in-law are both from Jaunpur, with a certain amount of moving around. In short, they are all from other places and came to live in Banaras after their marriage. The youngest has been married only ten years, the oldest twenty-five, Sunita nineteen. Each was married at the age of twenty-three or twenty-four: 'A good age to get married,' they agree.

How does one gauge what is 'a good age to get married'? For most women, the question is one of 'adjustment', in two parts. One is adjustment to the husband, not of an individual to another, but of a role to be played to another role that is being played. Never have I heard a man being analysed as being whatever he is because that is his personality, character or choice. Rather, his behaviour is described as '*ab vo to karenge hi; aadmi/pati hain na*' (He will, of course, do this. He is the man/husband, isn't he?). The usual occasion for such a description is when a criticism has to be made, supported or responded to.

With Sunita, I saw how such ascription to roles could be a strategy in not merely a critical dialogue but in one that celebrated patriarchy, paternalism and the purposefully submissive positions of women. The third daughter-in-law was perhaps too young to contribute as an equal, but the other two talked together to explain the ways in which hegemony operated.

'This family (*yah parivar*) is very, very good (*bahut hi achha hai*). They never say anything. They never tell you anything. They give you complete freedom to do what you like. They value daughters-in-law a lot. But they make it clear what you cannot do … So you yourself draw the line.'

They explained that education was valued, that learning and teaching were everyone's passion. Each of the three sons, as well as the father himself, had been in educational 'service'. There was 'something' about the family that was very 'good'. They did not use the word 'culture' – *samskriti, samskara* – but meant something like it.

Sunita verged on the specific, then retreated. I asked her when she was next going to Lucknow where her parents and brothers now lived. She laughed and said that she did not know. It was not easy. '*Kuchh hai, ki maike ka nam lete hi sabka munh phool jata hai*' (Something about saying you are going to your natal home makes people here sulk). She went on to explain that though she only planned to go once a year, in the summer holidays, even that was frowned upon. Bhabhi elaborated how when she was newly married, she was kept in her new home (her in-laws') for two years straight, without a break to visit her parents. She was laughing as she kept repeating, 'They just did not let me go!' It was a conspiratorial laugh and opened up the unsaid: that she, in turn, had created the same situation for her two younger sisters-in-law. 'Disciplining' was good for the soul and went around in a circle.

I did not ask her to explain why, but she took the initiative to explain the strong rationale for the activity. It was so that the new entrants into the family would get totally accustomed to the ways of the family and make no mistakes. Going home would be a distraction. Sunita, who was the most iconoclastic of them, said plainly, 'It's so we are not taught the wrong things by our own parents and families.' Wrong things? 'Yes, you know, to work less hard in our *sasural* (in-law' house), to become lazy, to think of other things but the family comfort.'

Sunita presented homemade samosas. That gave me an entry into the topic of food. She was celebrated as a great cook, and everything she ever made was declared to be wonderful. She also made it fast. I had telephoned her at 4.00 pm to say that I would be coming, and a feast was ready for me, made from scratch, at 6.00. But she had a 'disease', as she fondly, and then I, finally, with reservations, called it. She could not bear to eat anything anyone had touched, and definitely nothing from outside. It would simply not go down her throat. She felt that it was polluted, dirty and possibly infected with *kira*, which could translate as insects, bugs, germs, bacteria or a virus.

Was this her mode of resistance? To not be allowed to go home, to be always put upon for savoury snacks and great meals, to be expected to conform to an internal, magnificently hegemonic model of the ideal housewife, daughter-in-law, wife and mother? She simply would not eat as normal people did.

Sunita carried over this 'fasting' into her professional life. The school where she has worked for fifteen years has a cafeteria that provides a hot lunch every day to the staff. The cost of it is hugely subsidized and deducted at source, the idea being that everyone – and the staff are overwhelmingly women – should be free from the obligation of putting together and packing a meal in the morning. Rather, in the middle of their busy day, they should be given the treat of being *served* a nutritious, fresh-cooked, home-style meal. Sunita was the first to declare that she would *not* eat this meal and did not completely explain why. She came across as special and exclusive. Others followed her lead. Soon as many as a dozen staff members, out of some sixty, or 20 per cent, stopped eating the hot lunch. They then demanded fresh fruit, as money was being deducted anyway, and a little army of protesting fruit-eaters developed.

Dipti Bhattacharya is 34 and lives with her retired engineer father-in-law, now eighty-six, her electrician husband and their two sons, fourteen and eleven. Her younger brother-in-law and his family used to live with them but now live elsewhere. But they visit often, as do her father-in-law's three brothers and their families. Dipti rides a cycle to school, which takes her twenty-five minutes. We discussed how it is excellent for health and the environment, but that none of her teaching colleagues do it now – the three who cycled until recently have all acquired 'scooties', that is, scooters. Dipti is yet another teacher who gets up at 4.00 am, sweeps the floor, cooks lunch, makes breakfast, packs snacks, gives her father-in-law his medicine and leaves for work. On returning, she makes tea for her father-in-law and snacks for her son. She cleans up and relaxes. At 7.00 pm they have *nashta* or teatime snacks. At 10.00 or 10.30 they have dinner. Dipti's day is a cycle of cooking.

In answer to the question of how she balances work and family, Dipti says evocatively, 'You have to be *energetic*.' She moves directly to describing a Thursday fast that she keeps for Sai Baba. That fast has made her control her anger and acquire self-control. What was she angry about? Dipti said that she used to harbour the dream 'that someone should ask after me, should give me importance'. Now she is fine with the resolve that '*jo milega, le lungi, jo nahi milega, chalega*' (I'll take what I get, and what I don't get, I will not care for). Her family sounds supportive now, judging by her description, but she had troubles in the past, particularly when her husband's brother's family also lived with them and her children were younger. She had '*krodh*' (anger, even fury). '*Har chiz pe dukhi ho jate the*' (I would get broken-hearted at everything). She had a 'problem' (*problem thi*). The Thursday fast resolved it. Now she does not have the problem.

Right at the end of our conversation I chance upon the fact that she *also* keeps the typical Bengali household fast for Lakshmi, also on Thursdays. This, she told me, is a family puja, an old one, with an established procedure and the use of a Bengali prayer book. Dipti does not voluntarily ascribe any power or results to the Lakshmi fast.

Finally, after the example of three teachers who coincidentally all happened to be Brahmans, there is the case of two teachers who are Chauhans: Abha and Sangeeta (I will discuss only Abha here). Chauhans are high caste as well and like the other three, locals of Banaras, though Abha has lived for many years in Jhansi and Agra and Sangeeta grew up in Bombay. Sunita, let us remember, had come from Jaunpur via Lucknow, Mamta from Ballia and Dipti had Bengali origins in Calcutta. All their worlds are plural, along several dimensions. The experience of women, particularly in north India, of belonging to two homes, natal (*maika, pihar*) and conjugal (*sasural*), is a studied, but perhaps understudied phenomenon. It produces ideologies and manoeuvring of status, identity and authenticity that puts into question some of these very categories (Bagchi 1993; Burton 2003).

Abha, like the rest of them, gets up at 4.00 am. Her husband lives in Ahmedabad, and she lives with her seventy-year-old mother-in-law and two sons, fourteen and ten, in Banaras. Like Mamta, she decided to start working some sixteen years ago, to pay for a good school for her sons. Her husband does 'support' her, but it is her income that runs the house on a daily basis. She cooks a full meal of rice, dal and vegetables in the morning, makes a breakfast of parathas or sandwiches, packs her children's tiffin and her own and then leaves. She is one of the teachers who does not eat lunch in school and explains evasively that once she had surgery and was asked to be careful with her diet; after that, though fully recovered, she never came back to the school routine.

Abha's tale of adjusting to her in-laws, managing little children when her husband accepted a job far away and practicing increasing self-discipline in general is familiar, although she is not as articulate as some of the others. When asked to describe some of the difficulties she experienced, she does mention the initial differences in her in-laws' home compared to her own, including the food. She learned her in-laws' ways. She keeps no weekly fasts but does keep the annual Karva Chauth, Teej, Jyutiya and the first and last days of Navmi. For each of these she takes a holiday – not for the fast itself, but for the cooking, cleaning and readying of the puja.

Abha's refusal to eat lunch in school, even if she adds to her early morning work by making lunch for herself at home and packing it, savours of a protest, as did Sunita's. What could they be protesting? Maybe that Akash, the school sweeper, eats if not from the same plates, in the same spaces, exactly the same food? That he washes in the same place, the rule being for everyone to manually wash their plates? But I see a more interesting parallel. The women teachers are constructing a relationship whereby their natal home: their conjugal home:: their present (conjugal) home: their workplace. In each case, they are comfortable with the habits of one place and have to 'adjust' to or 'manage' the other. The parallels are as follows:

In their own home, they are asked after and given importance. In their *sasural* and workplace, they are not. In their own home they can make the rules. In their *sasural* and workplace, the rules are made for them or thrust upon them. Even in the friendliest, nicest *sasural* or workplace, where no overt rules seem to dominate, there is a sweet but firm drawing of lines between what is permissible and what is not. The home is a place where the individual voluntarily wishes to go. The *sasural* and the workplace are places to which she has to go and that try to prevent her from going home at chosen times. The home is a place where she has educated herself and grown in stature, and usually been supported in doing so. The *sasural* and the workplace may occasionally be a place of support in self-growth, but typically any learning is accompanied by a struggle.

In short, many women teachers, such as the four I describe above – Mamta, Sunita, Dipti and Abha – see their workplace much like their *sasural*, a place of benign but firm hegemonic domination, where they may be shown respect but the rules are inviolable and therefore imprisoning. In conceptualizing their workplace thus, they are shifting the understanding for themselves of their actual *sasural*. From the 'other' in their *sasural*, they become the insider, because now their othering is in their workplace.

Of the many questions I had for them, I will not go into the question here of the practices and meanings of their many fasts, which include Lakshmi Puja, Ganesh Chaturthi, Teej, Jyutiya, Karva Chauth, Nag Panchami, Bhaiya Duj, Dhola Chhat, Janamashtami, Durga Puja, and several others, but speak only of those that produced requests for leave (for Hindu fasts, see Pearson (1996); Pintchman (2005); McDaniel 2002, among many others). Muslim women teachers wanted to leave early during the month of Ramzan, and I have not described their similarities and differences to the Hindus here. I do want to broach one more topic here, even though I will not look at it in detail: the overlap of teachers' practices with that of the support staff. Almost all the above mentioned fasts kept by teachers were shared by the unschooled women support staff members as well. It became obvious that whatever the lines of division between the educated and uneducated, the modern and the non-modern women, keeping fasts was not one of them. However much women teachers and administrators drew a distinction between themselves, the urban, educated, professional and modern, and the supposed traditionalism and illiteracy of previous generations and non-working women, the distinction did not lie in a different attitude towards ritualism and mythology.

Four support staff members, Pushpa, Kanti, Chinta and Saira, may be compared with the four teachers I have discussed above. The three Hindus, Pushpa, Kanti and Chinta, are all from the *anusuchit jati* (Scheduled Castes), the first two being *chamar*, who call themselves Valmiki or Raidasi, named after the mythical author of the *Ramayana*, and the medieval poet-saint Raidas or Ravidas, respectively. Chinta is also *dalit*, her husband a landless labourer. Amazingly, these staff members have succeeded in *erasing* the difference between themselves and high-caste teachers with the instrument of food, both eating and fasting. Thanks to the school policy, the same meal is served to teaching and non-teaching staff. While the teachers I have discussed avoid eating it on several pretexts, one or the other of them may be observed bending over a desk together with a staff member to plan or discuss a menu or a recipe. At other times, the female staff ask for leave for the same ritual days such as Karva Chauth or Jyutiya, as do the teachers. Their fasts are indistinguishable from those of the Hindu teachers, although I do not mean to suggest that important differences may not exist between high-caste and low-caste interpretations of them, and between the high-class and low-class availability of resources for them.

The question I have focused on in this chapter has to do with the meanings, and the manipulation of meanings, of professionalism for the teachers and the uses of fasting and non-eating as strategies in this manipulation. The teachers never brought in issues about their children or family to the employer's attention. They resolutely kept the worlds separate. Only with fasts did they let the worlds seep into each other. They felt comfortable mentioning their fasts and making them the plank on which to seek leave. One important plank of their identity, their class-based and education-based difference from the poor and uneducated, was, if not erased, minimized. It is fascinating that food should have the power of difference-making and difference-erasing, of boundary construction and identity building, but also of confusing and straddling between boundaries. Why should food have that power?

One hypothesis that suggests itself from my research, and from the interpretations presented in this volume, is that food is polyvalent and powerful in that it consistently functions as both symbol and artefact, the two functions not separated from each other. The Brahman or Chauhan teacher who refrained from eating, or fasted, did so because she understood this as a tool to control her world, enabling her to rise from the status of victim to that of exemplary individual. At the same time, she made her choices of eating/fasting with a view to exercising power in a defined public sphere. The paradox inherent in food practices is that self-sacrifice, as embodied in fasting, is in truth self-interest and even more, self-aggrandisement. Used strategically, it gives power not only in the internalized, ascetic sense that imbues disciplinary meaning to the Hindu fast, but also in the externalized image of fasting, an image that seems to rise above the actual nature of the fasting person to construct an ideal type of a superior person. Such a person can manage, administer, run a business or state, exercise control. No one can blame a person for *fasting*, or accuse her of unprofessionalism.

It does not seem to matter that the fasting teachers were trapped in women's worlds. Even when they were the breadwinners and decision-makers in their households, the fasts they kept were for their husbands and sons and not reciprocated by their spouses or sons. They needed to stay home on fasting days not to rest – the very idea produced a laugh – but for more work. Special foods had to be made, baths taken, spaces readied, rooms cleaned up, preparations done and pujas planned for. The whole day could apparently go in doing this and was expected to. Of course there were some free days when they could avoid cooking or make a deliberately simple meal and toss it off by declaring, 'I work. I have no time.' But on the day of the fast particularly, there could be no excuses. Everything had to be just so, the day dedicated to it, the in-laws pleased; ironically, it was as if the gods themselves would be satisfied with only complete *samarpan* or commitment to the one job. All this, however, made for power – both an internal and an external one. The woman felt superior, and she was looked on as a superior being.

The paradox also appeared in the modern, professional identity the teacher was also trying to carve out for herself. The strategy of the fast belonged to the home. The woman's professionalism came to be penetrated by this home or community identity, entering, as it were, from the back door, because of the dualism that the woman's life was built on. At home her natal–conjugal home dualism was replaced by a new workplace–home division, and the tussle continued even when it had died out in its original form. In the workplace the struggle came across as the dilution of a professional identity.

This dualism could be a promise of strength if harnessed towards that 'power of tradition' model that a globalizing India is trying to project. I can imagine an advertising campaign in which the very smart, modern young woman approaches her boss and gets away with a day's leave for a fast, all the time looking and smiling as if she owned the globe. Back at home she changes from her trouser suit to a sari and bindi and is loved by all in her family for being the fulcrum of their world as it should be. She would be all the more playing roles, but they would be on her terms, as both the home and the workplace would recognize.

Let us end with the relationship I presented earlier whereby their natal home: their conjugal home:: their present (conjugal) home: their workplace. Is there perchance a new possibility for professional women that takes into account her rootedness in a family? It is possible that the workplace could reinvent itself to present itself for women workers as the 'home' and not the '*sasural*'. The home is where the woman is, idealistically speaking, supported, given importance, allowed to make her own rules and tolerated somewhat in her idiosyncrasies. As it stands, the workplace has lodged itself as the *sasural* in the home–*sasural* dichotomy and thus is resisted, protested, run away from and, even when 'adjusted to' or 'managed', is not loved. In my hypothetical replacement of the home by the workplace, I wish to end by emphasizing that in the women's narratives, the natal home has been presented in an idealized form. Thus, the workplace does not *actually* have to be a haven of love and security, it just has to come across as being such. The workplace and the worker could *together* construct a complex professional strategy. One could speculate as to what place food would have in this construction.

References

Ahmad, S. Waseem, Nilofer and Gazala Parveen. 2008. 'Women's Political Participation and Changing Pattern of Leadership in Rural Areas of UP'. *Indian Journal of Political Science* 69(3) (July–September): 661–72.

Bagchi, J. 1993. 'Socialising the Girl Child in Colonial Bengal'. *Economic and Political Weekly* 28(41): 2214–19.

Batra, Poonam. 2005. 'Voice and Agency of Teachers: Missing Links in the National Curriculum Framework 2005'. *EPW* (1 October): 4347–56.

Burton, Antoinette. 2003. *Dwelling in the Archive: Women Writing House, Home and History in Late Colonial India*. New York: Oxford University Press.

Jain, Manish, and Sadhana Saxena. 2010. 'Politics of Low Cost Schooling and Low Teacher Salary'. *Economic and Political Weekly* 45(18) (1–7 May): 79–80.

Kannabiran, Kalpana. 2004. 'Voices of Dissent: Gender and Changing Social Values in Hinduism'. In Robin Rinehart (ed.), *Contemporary Hinduism: Ritual, Culture, and Practice*. Santa Barbara: ABC-CLIO, 273–307.

Karlekar, Malavika. 1975. 'Professionalization of Women School Teachers'. *Indian Journal of Industrial Relations* 11(1) (July): 53–64.

Kelting, M. Whitney. 2009. *Heroic Wives: Rituals, Stories and the Virtues of Jain Wifehood*. New York: Oxford University Press.

Kremer, Michael, Nazmul Chaudhury, F. Halsey Rogers, Karthik Muralidharan and Jeffrey Hammer. 2005. 'Teacher Absence in India: A Snapshot'. *Journal of the European Economic Association* 3(2/3) (April–May): 658–67.

Kumar, Nita (ed.). 1992. 'Introduction'. In *Women as Subjects: South Asian Histories*. Calcutta: Stri Publications, 1–25.

Kumar, Nita. 2006a. 'The [No] Work and [No] Leisure World of Women in Assi, Banaras'. In Lina Fruzzetti and Sirpa Tenhunen (eds), *Culture, Power and Agency: Gender in Indian Ethnography*. Calcutta: Stri Publications, 52–89.

Kumar, Nita. 2006b. 'The Scholar and Her Servants: Towards a Postcolonial Anthropology'. *India Review* 5(3–4) (July–October): 519–50.

Kumar, Radha. 1993. *The History of Doing: An Illustrated Account of Movements for Women's Rights and Feminism in India 1800–1990*. Delhi: Kali for Women.

McDaniel, June. 2002. *Making Virtuous Daughters and Wives: An Introduction to Women's Brata Rituals in Bengali Folk Religion*. Albany: State University of New York Press.

Mohanty, Chandra Talpade. 1984. 'Under Western Eyes: Feminist Scholarship and Colonial Discourses'. *Boundary* 2(23:3/13:1): 333–58.

Ortner, Sherry. 1974. 'Is Female to Male as Nature Is to Culture?' In Michelle Rosaldo and Louise Lamphere (eds), *Woman, Culture, and Society*. Stanford: Stanford University Press, 67–87.

Pearson, Anne Mackenzie. 1996. *'Because It Gives Me Peace of Mind': Ritual Fasts in the Religious Lives of Hindu Women*. Albany: State University of New York Press.

Pintchman, Tracy. 2005. *Guests at God's Wedding: Celebrating Kartik among the Women of Benares*. Albany: State University of New York Press.

Sangari, Kumkum, and Sudesh Vaid (eds). 1989. *Recasting Women: Essays in Colonial History*. Delhi: Kali for Women.

9

Fasting, feasting: Social and religious food practices at a Barelwi girls' madrasa

Usha Sanyal

Madrasas for girls have been increasing in number in South Asia since the 1980s. Given the historical preference in South Asia for the education of boys over girls and the consequent lag in girls' education among all religious communities, the increase of girls' madrasas is a significant social trend, one that has so far received little scholarly attention (but see Jeffery et al. 2004, 2008; Winkelmann 2005; Borker 2018). In fact, some scholars report that as of 2000 there were more girls studying in madrasas than boys in the western Uttar Pradesh (UP) district of Bijnor where they did their fieldwork (Jeffery et al. 2004). While the reasons for this are complex, the most important ones relate to poor employment prospects for boys with a madrasa education, on the one hand, and better marriage prospects for girls with such an education, on the other. That Muslim men seem to prefer educated brides who know enough about Islamic ritual duties and obligations to raise children in accordance with Islamic norms is an interesting new development in itself, one with roots in changing patterns in household composition starting in late-nineteenth-century British India (see Khan 2016) as well as the rise of literacy in South Asia overall (on educational trends, see the Sachar Committee Report 2006, among others).

Given that Sunni Muslims in South Asia identify with different schools of thought (*maslaks*) led by the ulema, which differ from one another on the finer points of theology, and that boys' madrasas are identified with one *maslak* or another, it is not surprising that girls' madrasas also distinguish themselves in this way. The most important Sunni *maslaks* since the late nineteenth century have been the Deobandi, Tablighi Jama'at, Barelwi, Ahl-i Hadith and Jama'at-i Islami (on these identities, see, among others, Metcalf (1982); Nasr (1994);

Sanyal (2010); Darakhshan Khan (2018)). Each *maslak* has girls' madrasas of its own, catering to students of its orientation.

This chapter – which emerges from my larger project on Muslim girls' religious education in South Asia (Sanyal 2020) – is based on fieldwork at a Barelwi girls' madrasa in June 2012, when I had just started working at the site. It seeks to understand the importance to young students aged between twelve and sixteen of voluntary fasting at a time other than the holy month of Ramadan. The madrasa is a site of intense socialization in Islamic norms and practices, which leads over time to a gradual process of self-transformation. I argue in this chapter that the practice of undertaking voluntary fasting is a means of self-empowerment for some students.

Voluntary fasting at the madrasa

Jami'a Nur al-Shari'at, or Jami'a Nur for short (a pseudonym), is a girls' madrasa in the western UP town of Shahjahanpur. It was founded in 2003 by Sayyid Ehsan Miyan, a Barelwi scholar who keenly felt the absence of a Barelwi madrasa for girls in the area, as the only existing one was Deobandi. There is also a Jama'at-i Islami madrasa for girls in the neighbouring town of Rampur, which caters to middle-class girls and charges relatively high fees. The Jami'a Nur, by contrast, charges fees that are low by Indian standards (Rs 800 per month, or $15, in 2012), which covers room and board as well as tuition, as the madrasa is residential. It caters to lower middle-class and working-class families in the region. In 2015 it had 400 students, up from 250 the year before. (By contrast, the boys' madrasa next door, also run by Sayyid Ehsan Miyan, had a smaller and more stable student population of about 200.) Many of the Jami'a Nur students were from families in which the parents were minimally educated, often not higher than the eighth grade. Fathers worked as farmers or small businessmen, or in service jobs as bus drivers, car mechanics or imams at local mosques. In no case did the mother work outside the home.

In June 2012, with daytime temperatures at over 110°F in Shahjahanpur, I was visiting the madrasa for the first time. Luckily for me, there was a special event on one of the days of my visit. The event was Shab-i Miraj, the night of the Prophet's ascension to heaven, celebrated with student speeches and the recitation of *na'ts*, verses in praise of the Prophet Muhammad, from 10 p.m. to midnight. It takes place on the 27th of Rajab, the seventh month of the Islamic calendar.

The following day – or, by the Hijri calendar, the same day, as a day is counted from sun down to sun down – a number of students chose to observe a voluntary fast (*nafli roza*). According to the *Sunni Bihishti Zewar* (Sunni Heavenly Jewels), a women's advice manual taught at the madrasa, the virtues of fasting on this day are extolled in several hadith. It quotes one of them as follows: 'It is narrated by Salman Farsi that if a person observes the night in supererogatory (*nafl*) prayer and fasts during the day on a certain day in Rajab, he or she earns [the reward of] the equivalent of a hundred years of night prayers and a hundred years of fasts. That day is the 27th of Rajab' (Muhammad Khalil Khan Qadiri Barkati 2011: 181). Clearly, the religious benefits of fasting on this day are believed to be considerable.

The next day, some of the girls who had fasted fell ill, an unfortunate consequence of the intense heat. The warden with whom I was sharing a room was called at 11 a.m. to take a sick girl to the doctor, a short rickshaw ride away from the madrasa in one of the neighbouring streets. So she donned her burqa and left. When she came back, she told me that the girl had thrown up several times and had been given some medicine by the doctor. But despite her condition, she asked the warden if she could buy a samosa (a popular spicy, savoury snack) to eat on the ride back to the madrasa. Both the warden and the doctor firmly refused, saying she could have some yoghurt instead. That afternoon, the warden made another trip to the doctor with five more girls. It was another exceedingly hot day, and at the end of it the warden herself was not feeling well. Her home being in Shahjahanpur town, she decided to leave the madrasa at night and take a day off to recover. Meanwhile, another girl had become too ill to be treated by the local doctor, and the madrasa called her parents to come and take her home. She left during the day, crying profusely because she didn't want to go home.

Looking back, I remembered this string of events very clearly as the episode brought home to me something to which I had not given much thought before, namely, that Muslims fast not only during the month of Ramadan, but through the year as well. But these fasts are different, being voluntary. Why do they do it? How often? Do men do it too?

For the girls at the madrasa, as for all teenagers in a boarding school – *any* boarding school – food is very much on their minds.[1] The girls would have a little pocket money from home with which to buy snacks from the front office during evening recreation time, and they eagerly lined up to do so. They also had some food items in their personal trunks or suitcases (a practice which, not surprisingly, attracted mice). Seeing their enjoyment of these small pleasures centred around food, it seemed to me that it would require an enormous effort of will to go without food and water from sun up to sun down in 110°F heat. And thus I began to take an interest in the girls' practice and behaviour around food.

The *Sunni Bihishti Zewar* on the merits of fasting

The *Sunni Bihishti Zewar* is the Barelwi equivalent of the *Bihishti Zewar* (Metcalf 1990), the book for women – classified as 'advice literature' – by Maulana Ashraf 'Ali Thanvi (d. 1944), the famous Deobandi scholar about whom much has been written, including by several contributors to this volume (see, e.g., the chapters by Steele, Sengupta and Khan). The *Sunni Bihishti Zewar* was published in 1978 in Karachi. The author is Mufti Muhammad Khalil Khan Qadiri Barkati Marharwi (1920–1985), whose name tells us that he was affiliated with the Qadiri Sufi order and belonged to the Barkati family of Sufi pirs from the town of Marahra in Eta district, western UP (see Sanyal 2013). This was the family of pirs to whom Ahmad Raza Khan Barelwi (1856–1921) and his father had been affiliated, and being Sayyids, descendants of the Prophet, they enjoyed particular respect in Barelwi circles (Sanyal 2010). Maulana Khalil Khan Barkati migrated to Pakistan in 1951 and eventually settled in Karachi. It was there that he wrote this book in response to his felt need for a book for women. Before that, women's issues had been addressed in the encyclopaedic work *Bahar-i Shari'at* by Maulana Amjad 'Ali A'zami (1878–1948), alongside other issues that pertained to the Muslim community as a whole. This was the first Barelwi book written specifically for women. It was joined soon thereafter by a second work, *Jannati Zewar* (the title of which also translates as 'heavenly jewels'). This book is also taught at Jami'a Nur. *Jannati Zewar* was written by another Barelwi scholar from UP, though he was from east UP and chose to remain in India after Partition rather than migrate to Pakistan (Sanyal 2013).

At the madrasa, the *Sunni Bihishti Zewar* is classified as a work of jurisprudence (fiqh) and is taught in the first year (*'ula*) of the four- to six-year 'Alima course. Certain sections are taught, not the entire book, as is the case as well with other prescribed texts in the madrasa curriculum. It deals at length with the ritual duties of Muslims, particularly as these pertain to girls and women. The most important subject is considered to be ritual purification (*taharat*), which must precede the performance of each of the five daily prayers (namaz). Ritual pollution caused by bodily emissions of any sort must first be erased before one can begin the canonical prayer, for without this preliminary step the prayer would be rendered religiously invalid. Thus, one of the first things the students are taught is the well-known prophetic saying (hadith), 'The canonical prayer (*namaz*) holds the key to paradise (*jannat*), and ritual purification holds the key to canonical prayer.'[2] The subject of ritual purification has multiple levels of complexity and is therefore taught in more advanced classes as well. The academic year begins with this subject and students explore it in minute detail over several months.

To return to the question of voluntary fasting and why some young madrasa students choose to do it, there are several reasons. The simplest is to make up for missed fasts during the previous Ramadan. Muslims, both men and women, must keep track of the fasts they miss and make up for them before the next Ramadan the following year. Men and women may legitimately suspend the fast if they are travelling or sick, making up for it after they reach their destinations or get well (Qur'an 2:187). Old people who cannot fast when the month of Ramadan occurs in summer can make up for their missed fasts in the wintertime, or alternatively, if they have the means they may choose to travel to a cool place in order to fast in greater comfort during the regular fasting month. Women have to suspend their fasts during their menstrual cycles. Other conditions include childbirth and breast feeding a newborn.

Making up for a missed day by fasting on another by way of compensation is called *kaza* and is regarded as an obligatory (*fard*) religious duty.[3] In this sense, it is not strictly speaking 'voluntary', in that there is no choice in the matter other than in choosing on which day one will do it. According to Faiza Hussain,[4] many South Asian Muslim women conceal the days on which they were unable to fast during Ramadan because of the cultural prohibition against talking about menstruation even with female friends and family members. And when they undertake compensatory fasts they talk about them as being a means of following the sunna (prophetic practice) rather than for what they really are, namely, compensation for days they missed fasting during Ramadan because of their menstrual cycle. Her data are based on fieldwork at a girls' madrasa in Pakistan (personal communication, 2016).

I have no way of knowing, of course, whether the young girls at Jami'a Nur were undertaking to fast that day in June 2012 because, it being the seventh month of the Islamic/Hijri calendar, they were running out of time before Ramadan came around again (in the ninth calendar month), or whether they had other reasons. It seems unlikely that they would have chosen to wait until the height of summer to fulfil a duty that was obligatory. Rather more likely, I think, they would have followed the ulema's advice in books such as *Sunni Bihishti Zewar* and discharged their duty as soon as possible in order to lift the weight of this responsibility off their shoulders. One can speculate that they did have other reasons, because (as noted above) voluntary fasting is regarded as a highly meritorious activity in the religious sense.

The *Sunni Bihishti Zewar* has a whole section on the days and months of the year when God showers extra rewards on those who fast with the intention of pleasing him. Some of the days mentioned are specific, such as the 27th of Rajab noted above, or the 9th day of Zul-Hijja (the month of the annual hajj pilgrimage to Mecca, the twelfth month of the Hijri calendar) and the 10th day of Muharram (known as 'Ashura, this day is particularly holy to the Shi'a, being the commemoration of Imam Husayn's martyrdom in 680 CE);[5] students at the madrasa get a holiday on that day and everyone observes the fast.[6] The 15th of Sha'ban (the eighth month) and six days in Shawwal (the tenth month) are also recommended fasting days (*SBZ* 2011: 177–83). But other days are more general: for example, the book notes that fasting on Mondays and Thursdays is pleasing to God. Fasting on Wednesdays and Fridays is also full of merit, as is fasting on three consecutive days, especially the 13th, 14th and 15th of the month (*SBZ* 2011: 181). On all these days, God rewards the person who remembers him with immense reward in the hereafter. Hadiths are cited to support the merit of fasting on each of these days as a means of atoning for sins committed, whether intentionally or inadvertently.

All good deeds earn a reward in the hereafter in Muslim belief, whether this be through recitation of the Qur'an, performance of the daily prayers and other ritual duties, performance of acts of charity or supererogatory prayers and fasts done with pious intent. As Farah (2013; Chapter 4) explains, a person may choose to declare his or her intent of passing on the reward so earned (the concept of *ithal-i thawab*; Urdu *isal-i sawab*) to his or her dead parents or others s/he names specifically in personal supplication to God (*du'a*). South Asian Muslims, including Barelwis and Deobandis, have vigorously debated the merits of such practices in fatwas, pamphlets and other forms of print since the nineteenth century (Metcalf 1982; Sanyal 2010). At heart, the matter is simple: one performs meritorious deeds in order to thank God for blessings received and earn reward in the hereafter, whether for oneself or for loved ones who have passed away. Married women with families also often fast in fulfilment of a vow (*mannat*), thanking God for the return to health of a husband or child or for a range of other worldly challenges successfully overcome.[7]

Among South Asian Muslims voluntary fasting is largely a women's practice. Men observe a small number of voluntary fasts during the course of the year, whereas women do so much more frequently. This is a familiar pattern across religious traditions in South Asia. Hindu women also fast frequently during the course of the year (for Karva Chauth, in preparation for a major event such as a wedding and on many other occasions, as Kumar makes clear in Chapter 8), whereas Hindu men do so less frequently. Hindus also favour Mondays and Thursdays for the observance of voluntary fasts.

The etiquette (*adab*) of food consumption at the madrasa

For the students at the madrasa, fasting was of course an exceptional event. On regular school days, students ate simple healthy meals consisting of vegetables, lentils, rice or flat bread (rotis). Meals were prepared in-house in enormous cauldrons by a couple of cooks, though until 2014 fresh hot rotis were cooked daily in the boys' madrasa a few miles away and transported by van to the girls' madrasa. After the girls' madrasa was moved next door to the boys' madrasa in 2014, food arrangements became a lot simpler for the administration, as it became possible to use a common outdoor kitchen for all the students.

Occasionally students got meat curry. In 2013, I discovered to my surprise that nearly a third of the students would not eat meat other than chicken.[8] They were served eggs as a substitute on days when other meat was being served. This chance discovery reflected at the local level an internal distinction between Muslims who will only eat chicken and mutton and others who enjoy eating beef as well.[9] Since the early 2000s, cow protection has been a hot button political issue in north India, with a number of publicly reported murders of Muslims accused of killing cows or eating beef at home, though in every case the accusations were fed by rumour.[10]

One of the things the madrasa takes seriously is the task of socializing students into religiously and socially approved modes of behaviour. This applies to all spheres of everyday life, from the correct way to address others, particularly authority figures, to appropriate modes of dress and comportment, to the etiquette of handling books, particularly the Qur'an but also other books. Teachers told me that many of the students come to the madrasa without any prior literacy and very poor social skills. The etiquette (*adab*) of how one should eat and drink and how guests should be served is taught as part of the madrasa's broader educational goal of socialization and is addressed in both the *Sunni Bihishti Zewar* and the *Jannati Zewar*.

The religious authority for such rules of etiquette is of course the Qur'an, but more especially the practice (sunna) of the Prophet. How he ate, drank, welcomed guests and so on are recorded in the hadith literature and taught to students in fiqh and hadith classes. Madrasa students start to learn about these matters in the *Jannati Zewar* and *Sunni Bihishti Zewar* (both in Urdu), going on in successive years to complex Arabic texts which analyse the prophetic sunna in ever greater detail. Simple lessons of etiquette in the *Sunni Bihishti Zewar* include saying the *basmallah* out loud before the start of the meal and eating with the right hand and not the left: 'in fact, according to the shari'a many tasks should be started from the right side, hadiths tell us that the right hand should be used to eat and drink because Satan uses the left hand to accomplish these tasks. Nature has also inclined humans in this direction' (*SBZ* 2011: 375–80). Ibn-i Majah is cited as the authority for this. Food should be eaten in small morsels, water should also be sipped rather than gulped, food should be eaten in the company of other people rather than alone (here a hadith is cited in which the Prophet tells a group of believers that the reason they don't feel full at the end of their meal is that they are not eating together), good conversation should accompany the meal and so on. There are also words of advice on how guests and host should behave with one another with respect to meals.

On a day-to-day basis, food at the madrasa was a means of enacting social relations. Relations between teachers and students were close, as many of the teachers were former students of the madrasa who knew the students well and had long-standing ties of friendship with them. Thus, students remembered that when their teachers received something special at mealtimes which was not served to the students, some teachers would save a portion for them as a special treat (Farah interviews, 2015, in Sanyal and Farah 2019).

Food was also the medium through which students enjoyed special events, not only through its consumption but more importantly through its preparation, an activity not normally allowed to them. Although they were in the midst of end-of-year exams during the summer of 2012, they nevertheless celebrated a local festival called Koonde (see also Chapter 4 in this volume),[11] when people cook sweet puris (puffed deep fried dough), which is associated with this festival. The students spent several hours that night cooking puris for everyone in the madrasa, to be eaten at breakfast the next day. It was a night to stay up late and forget about exams for a while, as the girls displayed their culinary skills and prepared a simple feast for all to share the next day.

Student perspectives on the madrasa's impact on their lives

In interviews with a handful of former students of the madrasa in 2015, Sumbul Farah, my research partner for part of this project, got the students' perspective on their madrasa experience (Farah interviews, 2015, in Sanyal and Farah 2019). Most of the students agreed that the meals at the madrasa were not particularly good but some acknowledged that it was impossible to prepare flavourful food for such a large number of people. Many students expressed their surprise at the size of the cooking pots in the madrasa kitchen. Used to cooking for their households at home, they marvelled at the large number of onions that had to be sliced, potatoes that had to be peeled and the quantity of rice and vegetables prepared twice every day at the madrasa. The students were not involved in any of these tasks. Indeed, cooking was forbidden to them, and they relished the occasional special event when they were allowed to cook.

Indirectly, food preparation and domesticity in general played a role in whether the girls could attend the madrasa at all. Because daughters play a vital role in helping their mothers with everyday household chores, their absence from the home for months at a time causes their mothers great hardship, particularly when there are several young children at home. Ghazala had three brothers and a sister, none of whom were educated. She was the only one of her siblings who was educated and was also pursuing further studies while waiting for her parents to arrange her marriage. She credited her mother for her education because had her mother not supported her by taking over the household tasks that she, Ghazala, should have been doing, there was no way she could have completed her studies (Farah interviews, 2015, in Sanyal and Farah 2019). Hajira, Ghazala's cousin and neighbour, was not so lucky. She had also joined Jami'a Nur but was forced to quit partly because she was her parents' oldest child and had seven younger brothers, the youngest of them being six. Her mother could not afford to forgo her help at home as there was too much work to be done around the house. Hajira eventually had to drop out of the madrasa (Farah interviews, 2015, in Sanyal and Farah 2019).

In light of these considerations, it is not surprising that many of the students who answered my questions expressed their enthusiasm for being at the madrasa. They were aware that their presence there represented a hardship to their parents not only in monetary terms but more importantly, in terms of the extra effort their mothers had to make every single day to compensate for the loss of their household help. Some were aware as well of their parents' defence of their right to an education when members of the extended family objected to their leaving home to go to the madrasa (for similar findings in the context of a secular Muslim girls' school, see Gupta (2015)). The students spoke at length of their personal dedication to the madrasa's goals of living a pious (*dindar*) and ethical lifestyle in light of the teachings of the Qur'an and hadith as interpreted by the Barelwi school of thought, and their heartfelt desire to honour their parents, especially their mothers. They used words such as 'desire' (*shawq*) and 'to want, crave' (*chahna*) that expressed their personal desire for learning, a life lived in *pardah* regulated by the daily cycle of prayers, performed with mindfulness and attention to detail. Perhaps, as Lester (2005) suggests with regard to the Mexican novitiates seeking to become ordained nuns, their choice of words was dictated in part by their desire to prove to those at home who questioned their choice of vocation that they were 'good' girls who had chosen to leave home for the best of reasons, not for dishonourable ones (see also Gupta 2015). The students at the madrasa were also enthusiastic about passing on their knowledge to members of their families and maybe even starting a madrasa of their own one day. They told me:

> My older sister had a heartfelt desire to become an Islamic scholar (*'alima*). So when my father sent my older sister here, I came too … After I leave here I want to teach. I want others to benefit by the knowledge I have gained. I want the duties of God and his prophet to reach others. I want to encourage others to do good deeds. They should observe *namaz* and the fast, treat others well, and treat their parents well … Had I not come here the purpose of my life would not have been fulfilled. (Student #1, June 2012)

> After completing my studies here, I want to teach at a madrasa. I want to teach others what I have learned. And I want to serve my parents … I will teach my brothers and sister about the *shari'at*, and I will make them observe *namaz*, and I will keep them from bad things such as lies, backbiting, and bad company. (Student #8, June 2012)

Reflecting the close connection between everyday domesticity and madrasa education in the lives of students, Ghazala, whose mother had been so instrumental in permitting her to continue her studies, reflected on the importance of teaching by using a cooking analogy. In an interview with Farah in 2015, she said:

> Education finds its fulfillment in teaching. When I was a student, I did not realize the importance of all that I was learning. In fact, even after I had completed the course I could not gauge its true significance. It was only when I started teaching that I began to 'understand' all that I had learned. As I began teaching, I became like a blackened cooking pot being scoured clean with a scouring pad (*main bartan ki tarah manjhti chali gayi*).

As Farah notes, Ghazala's analogy was particularly evocative because it referred to an everyday household activity in north India. An open earthenware cooking stove (*chulha*) is often used in South Asia and was a popular cooking medium in north India before the introduction of modern-day gas burners. Farah remarks that when metal pots are mounted on the *chulha*, the bottom becomes black with soot. *Manjhna*, scrubbing, refers to the process of removing this soot and grime from the pot by scrubbing it vigorously with a metallic scouring pad. This is the process to which Ghazala likened her own increased understanding of the Islamic intellectual tradition. She was like the soot-blackened cooking pot being cleaned through constant scrubbing. Merely finishing her studies was not sufficient. It was important to be able to explain and teach what she had learned to others, in order to truly understand. She began to gain clarity of thought through the process of teaching others (Farah interviews, 2015, in Sanyal and Farah 2019).

Graduates of the madrasa, recalling their memories of madrasa life in a series of interviews with Farah, told her with hilarity and relish about an especially memorable occasion one year when some boys in the boys' madrasa next door to them played a prank during Muharram. This was the time of year when a special dish, *khichra*, was prepared (see also Chapter 4 in this volume). *Khichra* is a spiced meat, rice and lentil dish, considered a delicacy because preparing it is time consuming and labour intensive. It is associated with Muharram. The boys asked for a second helping, but the cook refused their request as the rest of the food was meant for the girls' madrasa. In retaliation, the boys added a laxative to the *khichra* when the cook wasn't looking. The remainder of the story unfolded as one might imagine: a number of girls had to be taken to the doctor the next day when they complained of being sick as a result of the food they had eaten. Nayla and Khushboo, recalling this event in conversation with Farah, were in splits of laughter as they told her about it. Normally, when somebody at the madrasa falls sick, she is taken to the doctor under supervision (as the warden had done after the students' voluntary fast in 2012, as related at the start of this chapter), but on this occasion the doctor was called to the madrasa to examine the girls because *everybody* had taken ill. Nayla laughed and said there was not much the doctor could do because every girl he examined had exactly the same 'problem'. When the culprits were found they were severely punished for what was, among other things, a flagrant violation of the rules of *adab* (Farah interviews, 2015, in Sanyal and Farah 2019).

To conclude these anecdotes from fieldwork, let me share with you, the reader, two personal experiences, both related to food-gifting. In June 2012, prior to leaving the madrasa I decided to treat the students (then numbering approximately 250) to a small gift of a cold soda, which seemed like a good idea given the heat we had experienced together. Alas, the administration was unable to chill the bottles as the madrasa had no refrigeration, and staff were unable to organize the purchase of large slabs of ice either. The students had to make do with warm soda, which they nonetheless enjoyed, as bottled soda is a luxury. In December 2014, at the end of another visit which had taken place amid record cold weather, the teachers treated *me* to a goodbye gift of food, this one a lot more successful. They pooled together enough money to pay for a live chicken, had it slaughtered and then cooked it in the staff room over the small bucket-sized clay oven (*chulha*) normally used to boil tea leaves, milk and sugar for hot tea. The staff room being an all-purpose room that also doubled up as a dormitory for the teachers at night, all of us enjoyed watching the meal being cooked over several hours and ate heartily at the end of the evening. The teachers evidently relished the opportunity to cook, my presence being the excuse for a small party on a miserably cold day.

Conclusion: food and agency

Studying everyday life at Jami'a Nur through the lens of food practices, as I have done in this chapter, gives me a new kind of window into students' lives. Although food plays a tangential role in the overall purpose of the madrasa, examining its role in the lives of students allows me to shed light on questions of agency in a different way. Agency in this case does not imply resistance to authority. Saba Mahmood (2001, 2005) cautions scholars against imposing their own liberal secular biases on Muslim societies when, for instance, they read Muslim women's practices as a form of resistance to male authority. Thus, 'agency, in this form of analysis, is understood as the capacity to realize one's own interests against the weight of custom, tradition, transcendental will or other obstacles (whether individual or collective)' (Mahmood 2001: 206). But such a reading may be contrary to the intentions and aspirations of the women being observed. We in the scholarly academy tend to assume that women universally desire 'to be free from relations of subordination … from structures of male domination'. However, positing such a universal desire, Mahmood argues, 'is a product of feminism's dual character as both an *analytical* and a *politically prescriptive* project' (206; emphasis in the original). In the case of the women's piety movement Mahmood studied, she observed women working on – disciplining – their own bodies to reflect the changes they were trying to bring about internally: 'The mosque participants – no matter how pious they were – exercised great vigilance in scrutinizing themselves how well (or poorly) their outward performance matched or reflected their inward dispositions' (216).

Madrasa students do not have much freedom to exercise choice over how they spend the school day. From the time they get up at dawn for the first of the daily prayers until they have prayed the last night prayer, every part of the day is tightly structured: the mornings are busy with morning assembly, followed by a succession of classes from about 8 a.m. to 1.30 p.m. The noontime prayer, lunch, a short afternoon nap and the afternoon prayer are interwoven into the academic schedule in predictable fashion. In the second half of the day, study sessions in peer groups are the dominant activity, taking up between three and four hours. Evening prayer, an hour of recreation, dinner and the last night prayer mark the end of the day.

This highly structured daily schedule is not, in principle, that different from the lives of students in other institutional settings, including that of Catholic nuns (Lester 2005). For madrasa students, the most acceptable means of expressing individuality is through the pursuit of excellence in terms of pious behaviour, this being the goal of the curriculum as well as the overall 'cosmology' of the madrasa, which Moosa (2015: 64–5) defines as the 'true picture of reality consisting of fundamental means *and* feelings that provide a sense of fullness to all other meanings' (emphasis in the original). The student learns that she must discipline her mind and body, and do this *by* herself *on* herself. Her reward for such behaviour will come from God in the afterlife, but also bears the promise of immediate reward in the respect it wins from her peers and superiors (though it must not be done for this purpose).

Fasting, or abstaining from food and water for a length of time, usually from sun up to sun down, is agentive behaviour not only in the sense that is a 'doing' but also in that it is a 'becoming'. It is, thus, transformative. By doing something repeatedly, by acquiring a pious habitus, one gradually *becomes* a pious person (see Mahmood 2005). This process occurs over time, and when successful, is carried over after the student graduates, into her home and the married life that will follow. And thereafter the student, now a wife and mother, will become a role model for her children and for society as a whole, which in turn will benefit from her piety and dedication to shari'a norms.

The Jami'a Nur madrasa seems to have been remarkably successful in the brief period of its existence. Students acquire the respect of others around them and gain self-confidence through the weekly opportunities for public speaking on Thursday evenings at madrasa events (the *anjuman*) in which each of them is required to participate. The experience of leaving home and living in a 'pious community' also enlarges their worldview and gives them a new sense of purpose. Like their young teachers, they have a high sense of morale and motivation to become agents of change in their home environments, whether through teaching (which many said they wanted to do after they had graduated) or simply by becoming role models in their families. Of course, the picture I have painted in this chapter is coloured by the idealism of the young teenage students I observed at the madrasa. When a student cried at the prospect of returning home to her parents because she was ill after having fasted the previous day in extremely hot weather conditions, I gained an inkling of the students' emotional attachment to the madrasa. While some might interpret the madrasa space and the ideology it inculcates as 'oppressive' and authoritarian in a Foucauldian sense, the atmosphere the madrasa sought to inculcate – and to a large degree, was successful in inculcating, in my view – was that of a family in which familial patterns of authority were superimposed on administrative and academic authority figures. Indeed, as Farah and I have explored elsewhere (Sanyal and Farah 2019), the ideological space of the madrasa is constructed around the model of the patriarchal family. The madrasa is successful in its mission of not only teaching scriptural texts but more importantly, of transforming a student's self-image into that of a pious practitioner and role model for others in her family, neighbourhood or village *because* it is modelled on the structure of the family.

But as Darakhshan Khan (2016; Chapter 10 in this volume), among others, makes clear, South Asian family structure itself has been in a process of transformation since the late nineteenth century. How the madrasa and the family interact and what degree of authority the madrasa student will be able to exercise in her marital family in the years that follow are at this point unknown. However that may be, the larger significance of this madrasa and others like it is related to community identity. Pernau (2003), writing about the practice of piety by Catholic women in nineteenth-century Germany and Muslim women in India, argues that in both cases women's piety was a means of creating community in the context of being a religious minority in Germany and India, respectively. In South Asia, it was also a means of achieving upward mobility and gaining social respectability (142, 158). In the nineteenth century, to the extent that Muslim women entered the public sphere in India, they did so by supporting the private efforts of Muslim men to educate future leaders of the community. Today they are taking the first steps towards becoming religious scholars and assuming leadership roles in their own right, within the nurturing atmosphere of their communities.

Notes

I would like to thank Barbara Metcalf, Margrit Pernau, Sumbul Farah, Laurel Steele and Pnina Werbner for their comments on earlier drafts of this chapter, which helped me enormously in thinking about how women's food practices relate to questions of piety, agency and social identity.

1 I speak from personal experience, as I was once a student in a Catholic boarding school in India. All the girls brought 'tuck' from home at the beginning of the school year; it was kept under lock and key outside the dining hall and shared with one's classmates at teatime. Students were intensely interested in what kinds of food each class had and how long into the school year it lasted.

2 The *Sunni Bihishti Zewar* begins by saying:

> For prayer to be valid, ritual purification (*taharat*) is such a necessity that without it there is no prayer. In fact, the ulama have said that if someone deliberately offers namaz without first ritually purifying him/herself, the person is committing [religious] infidelity (*kufr*). The Prophet, on whom be peace, says ritual prayer is the key to heaven, and the key to prayer is ritual purification. (Muhammad Khalil Khan Qadiri Barkati 2011: 19)

3 Whether one is required to do *kaza* or the more difficult *kaffara* (penitence for a sin, by fasting on sixty consecutive days, or failing that, feeding sixty poor people two meals on any given day or giving them the equivalent in grain or cash) depends on the circumstances that caused one to miss the fast. *Kaffara* is triggered by a major transgression of the shari'a, such as, for example, an improper divorce or a married couple engaging in sexual activity during the Ramadan fasting period, that is, during the daytime. See Muhammad Khalil Khan Qadiri Barkati (2011: 176). For more on *kaffara*, see Lange (2011: 138–43).

4 Faiza Hussain is a PhD candidate at the University of Erfurt, Erfurt, Germany.

5 According to Ibn Hanbal, *Musnad*, 'fasting on the day of 'Ashura makes amends for all sins of the preceding year'. Cited in Lange (2011: 141).

6 The *Sunni Bihishti Zewar* advises that the 9th of Muharram also be added, perhaps so that the person is not mistaken for a Shi'i Muslim. This is not explicitly stated in the text. Rather, it mentions that fasting on the 10th of Muharram was a Jewish practice in pre-Islamic days (*SBZ* 2011: 178–80).

7 A married woman must obtain her husband's permission to perform a voluntary (*nafli*) fast, though not so for an obligatory one such as the Ramadan fast. I do not know whether the madrasa students at Jami'a Nur have to get the permission of a superior before doing so.

There are striking similarities between the above-mentioned motives for undertaking a voluntary fast and those for hosting a *khatm-i qur'an*, as discussed by Werbner in Chapter 5 of this volume.

8 I did not ask whether they ate mutton (goat meat) as well.

9 A recent work of fiction throws light on this issue. In a section in his novel *Patna Blues*, Abdullah Khan (2018: 63–4) writes:

> 'What have you packed for lunch?' Arif asked Farzana.
>
> 'Paratha, fried potatoes and roasted kulma,' Farzana said in a mellow voice. She took out three tiffin boxes kept in the back of the bullock cart.
>
> As she opened the box of kulma, the idea of eating six-month-old sun-dried, spiced minced beef didn't appeal to him. Beef was never cooked in his house at Patna. His father had banned it from the kitchen the year before Arif was born.
>
> 'Many Hindu friends come to our house. We must respect their sensibilities. Anyway, we have the option of eating mutton or chicken,' Abba would say.
>
> When Farzana handed him a plate to pass to Yaqoob, the smell of the roasted kulma almost made him throw up. Arif cleared his throat and spat on the ground and then turning to Farzana, said, 'Please give me the fried potatoes only. I don't eat kulma.'
>
> Yaqoob began chewing his paratha and kulma contentedly.

10 There is an extensive academic literature on the cow protection issue in India. For some history, see, for example, Jaffrelot (1996). Vigilante attacks on Muslims in the early twenty-first century have been frequently reported in the Indian and international press.

11 See Farah, in Chapter 4 in this volume, on the foods associated with different months of the Islamic calendar.

References

A'zami, 'Allama 'Abdul Mustafa. 1995. *Jannati Zewar*. Delhi: Anjum Book Depot.

Borker, Hem. 2018. *Madrasas and the Making of Islamic Womanhood*. Delhi: Oxford University Press.

Farah, Sumbul. 2013. 'Piety and Politics in Local Level Islam: A Case Study of Barelwi Khanqahs.' PhD dissertation, University of Delhi.

Farah, Sumbul. 2015. Interviews with Jami'a Nur madrasa graduates. Unpublished. Bareilly.

Gupta, Latika. 2015. *Education, Poverty and Gender: Schooling Muslim Girls in India*. New Delhi: Routledge.

Jaffrelot, Christophe. 1996. *The Hindu Nationalist Movement in India*. New York: Columbia University Press.

Jeffery, Patricia, Roger Jeffery and Craig Jeffrey. 2004. 'Islamization, Gentrification and Domestication: "A Girls' Islamic Course" and Rural Muslims in Western Uttar Pradesh.' *Modern Asian Studies* 38(1): 1–53.

Jeffery, Patricia, Roger Jeffery and Craig Jeffrey. 2008. 'Aisha, the Madrasa Teacher'. In Mukulika Banerjee (ed.), *Muslim Portraits: Everyday Lives in India*. New Delhi: Yoda Press, 56–68.

Khan, Abdullah. 2018. *Patna Blues*. Delhi: Juggernaut Books.

Khan, Darakhshan H. 2016. 'Fashioning the Pious Self: Middle Class Religiosity in Colonial India'. PhD dissertation, University of Pennsylvania.

Khan, Darakhshan H. 2018. 'In Good Company: Reformist Piety and Women's Da'wat in the Tablighi Jama't'. *American Journal of Islamic Social Sciences* 35(3): 1–25.

Lange, Christian. 2011. 'Expiation'. In *Encyclopaedia of Islam (EI) Three*, vol. 2011–2, 138–43.

Lester, Rebecca J. 2005. *Jesus in Our Wombs: Embodying Modernity in a Mexican Convent*. Berkeley: University of California Press.

Mahmood, Saba. 2001. 'Feminist Theory, Embodiment, and the Docile Agent: Some Reflections on the Egyptian Islamic Revival'. *Cultural Anthropology* 16(2): 202–36.

Mahmood, Saba. 2005. *Politics of Piety: The Islamic Revival and the Feminist Subject*. Princeton, NJ: Princeton University Press.

Metcalf, Barbara Daly. 1982. *Islamic Revival in British India: Deoband, 1860–1900*. Princeton, NJ: Princeton University Press.

Metcalf, Barbara Daly. 1990. *Perfecting Women: Mawlana Ashraf 'Ali Thanawi's Bihishti Zewar, a Partial Translation with Commentary*. Berkeley: University of California Press.

Moosa, Ibrahim. 2015. *What Is a Madrasa?* Chapel Hill: University of North Carolina Press.

Muhammad Ehsan Miyan, Sayyid. 2003. *Islami Aadaab*. Shahjahanpur: no publisher.

Muhammad Khalil Khan Qadiri Barkati, Maulana. 2011. *Sunni Bihishti Zewar*. Delhi: New Khwaja Book Depot.

Nasr, Seyyed Vali Reza. 1994. *The Vanguard of the Islamic Revolution: The Jama't-i Islami of Pakistan*. Berkeley: University of California Press.

Pernau, Margrit. 2003. 'Motherhood and Female Identity: Religious Advice Literature for Women in German Catholicism and Indian Islam'. In Margrit Pernau, Imtiaz Ahmad and Helmut Reifeld (eds), *Family and Gender: Changing Values in Germany and India*. Delhi: Sage Publications, 140–61.

Sachar Committee Report. 2006. 'Social, Economic, and Educational Status of the Muslim Community in India. A Report'. By Justice Rajinder Sachar and six members (Saiyid Hamid, Dr. T. K. Oomen, M. A. Basith, Dr. Rakesh Basant, Dr. Akhtar Majeed and Dr. Abualeh Shariff), November. Available at: http://minorityaffairs.gove.in/sachar.

Sanyal, Usha. 2010. *Devotional Islam and Politics in British India: Ahmad Riza Khan Barelwi and His Movement, 1870–1920*. Delhi: Yoda Press.

Sanyal, Usha. 2013. 'Changing Concepts of the Person in Two Ahl-i Sunnat/Barelwi Texts for Women: The *Sunni Bihishti Zewar* and the *Jannati Zewar*'. In Usha Sanyal,

David Gilmartin and Sandria B. Freitag (eds), *Muslim Voices: Community and the Self in South Asia*. Delhi: Yoda Press.

Sanyal, Usha. 2020. *Scholars of Faith: South Asian Muslim Women and the Embodiment of Religious Learning*. Delhi: Oxford University Press.

Sanyal, Usha, and Sumbul Farah. 2019. 'Discipline and Nurture: Living in a Girls' Madrasa, Living in Community'. *Modern Asian Studies* 53(2): 411–50.

Winkelmann, Mareike Jule. 2005. *'From Behind the Curtain': A Study of a Girls' Madrasa in India*. Amsterdam: ISIM Press.

10

Praying in the kitchen: The Tablighi Jama'at and female piety

Darakhshan Khan

As a doctoral candidate, I was in Delhi in 2012–13 to research the impact of women's participation in the Tablighi Jama'at, a lay Islamic reform movement that focuses on austerity and personal piety. It was founded as a proselytizing movement in the 1920s by Maulana Ilyas Kandhlewi (d. 1944) to reform the 'nominal Muslims' of Mewat, a region about forty kilometres southwest of Delhi.[1] The movement's spectacular success in Mewat gave it a reach and longevity that would have pleasantly surprised its early members. At the beginning the Jama'at recruited only men. The assumption was that the tenets of Islam would trickle down to the women if the men were taught well. However, within a few decades women were participating in the segregated Jama'at meetings that were held in the homes of the members.

Any estimation about the number of members in the Jama'at is only speculation because the movement does not register its affiliates. The estimates fluctuate wildly from a few thousand to millions of Muslims around the world.[2] It is, however, clear that a fairly large number of women participate in its daily and weekly meetings and in the proselytizing tours.[3] Since I was interested in understanding the role and scope of women's participation in the movement, a conversation with the female descendants of Maulana Ilyas seemed like a good place to begin. So I landed at the *markaz* (the main centre of the Tablighi Jama'at) in Delhi's Nizamuddin area. A long-standing feud over leadership between two branches of the family has resulted in the partition of the domestic quarters. I first approached the family of Maulana Sa'ad, the great-grandson of Maulana Ilyas, whose followers claim that the movement's leadership rightfully belongs to him. After a brusque interview in the alleyway, the guard pointed me to the women's quarter. As I parted the thick, dark curtains I found myself in a brightly lit living room whose floor was covered in cushions and a thick carpet. Maulana Sa'ad's wife, his mother and a few other women were sitting in a circle, reading from the *Tablighi Nisaab*,[4] the seminal text of the movement. The readings were followed by supplications led by Maulana Sa'ad's wife, following which the group dispersed. I stayed back and introduced myself as a researcher. It immediately became clear that neither the wife of Maulana Sa'ad nor his mother was interested in talking to me. Our terse conversation quickly came to an end when they abruptly left the room to pray. I was alone and contemplating leaving when an old lady walked in with a large tray of snacks and tea. She placed the tray in front of me and poured me a cup of tea. She watched me silently as I nibbled on a biscuit. After a brief conversation about her many years of service to the family, I left.

A few days later I visited the home of Maulana Zubair, the son of Maulana Inam ul-Hasan (d. 1995), the third leader (*emir*) of the Jama'at. Once again, I walked through thick curtains into a different living room to find Maulana Zubair's wife and her daughters-in-law reading from the *Nisaab* to a larger group. After the reading and the late-afternoon prayer, a large tablecloth was spread out for the evening tea and snacks. Nearly all the women who had come for the reading stayed back for tea. The wife of Maulana Zubair personally served tea to everybody. It was clear that this was a weekly ritual for most women partaking of the meal.

My purpose in recounting the two anecdotes is not to compare the hospitality of one branch of the family with the apparent lack of it of the other. Instead, it is to highlight the commonality between them: despite the stark difference in the manner in which I was received, the content of my conversation on both occasions was nearly identical. The wives of Maulana Zubair and Maulana Sa'ad skilfully dodged my questions about women's participation in the Jama'at by bringing the conversation back to 'what the books say'. 'Everything you want to know about the family is printed in the books. We do not like to talk about ourselves,' Maulana Sa'ad's wife said.[5] Maulana Zubair's wife was less categorical in her refusal to talk to me, but my regular attendance at her tea parties for two months did not bring me any closer to getting her to talk to me about the women of her family.

I faced similar roadblocks in Bombay, where I conducted most of my fieldwork. In a pattern that mirrored the response of the women of Maulana Zubair's household, I was welcomed warmly in the Jama'at homes and community centres, and the women were eager to educate me about the good work the movement was doing. They were, however, reluctant to talk about their personal journeys with the Jama'at.[6] 'If I start talking about myself I am in danger of becoming vain and forgetting that the work of *dawat*[7] is bigger than all of us. The problem with talking about individuals is that it creates a culture of *shakshiyat parasti* (personality cult),' said Naeema,[8] a young girl in her mid-20s who had just started her career as a sermonizer.[9]

How does one conduct an inquiry into the practices and discourses of a movement whose members engage in circular conversations that keep critical questions out? In this chapter I suggest that non-scripted social moments, even if fleeting, present the rare occasions when the standardized discourses so typical of proselytizing movements break down, providing room for critical analysis. Using this strategy, I draw on my ethnographic fieldwork about the rhythms of cooking and eating during the month of Ramzan to analyse how the Jama'at's ideals of spiritual equality and patriarchal authority shape women's strategies of piety.

Tafrigh-e waqt among Jama'at women

The Tablighi Jama'at's emphasis on austerity can turn into a zealous elimination of anything that distracts a Muslim from the ritual worship of Allah. This distraction can take the form of material possessions, household chores, professional careers or intellectual pursuits. The trimming of worldly clutter from one's life, however, is different from the self-effacing withdrawal from the world practiced by the early Sufis, most notably by the eighth-century female mystic Rabea Basri (d. 801).[10] Instead, the Jama'at's focus on austerity dovetails with its principle of *tafrigh-e waqt*, the sparing of one's time for Allah.[11]

The movement's manifesto, *Che Baatein* (six points), lists *tafrigh-e waqt* as the last of the six qualities that a Muslim must cultivate in order to perfect her faith. *Che Baatein* is written in the form of a tract and claims to be a handy list of the attributes possessed by the Companions of Prophet Muhammad: the profession of the article of faith (*kalima*), the daily performance of the five ritual prayers (namaz), knowledge about religious duties and the remembrance of Allah (*ilm o zikr*), respecting fellow Muslims (*ikram-e Muslim*), sincerity of intentions (*ekhlas-e niyat*) and *tafrigh-e waqt*.

The principle of *tafrigh-e waqt* animates the Jama'at's unique proselytizing initiative called the *khurj* (from the Arabic root *kh-ra-ja*, which means to exit). It is a preaching tour undertaken by a small group of men and, often, women. While members cannot choose the destination of the tour, they can decide whether they will travel for three days, forty days or four months. It must be noted that men are required to make provisions for their families before signing up for a tour, though reports of failure on the part of many men to do so are common. A woman can undertake a *khurj* as long as she is accompanied by her husband, son, brother or father.

Khurj is the highest form of participation in the Jama'at. It requires Jama'at members to extricate themselves from their everyday lives and trains them in walking the fine line between staying in the world and withdrawing from it at once, such that members spend their time only in pursuits that bring everlasting spiritual rewards. For the men in the movement, this means pursuing occupations that will allow them the flexibility to proselytize. It is, in fact, telling that the Jama'at has made impressive inroads into the merchant and trading communities of Bombay and Gujarat because, as members reminded me frequently, a shopkeeper can shut down his enterprise to answer the call for prayer but an office employee is answerable to his boss. Men and women belonging to the service class find it difficult to keep up with the demands made on their time by *khurj*, and it is no coincidence that the vast majority of women at my field sites in Delhi and Bombay hailed from the merchant class. In fact, several of the stories about personal transformation that women narrated to me involved their husbands or brothers resigning from their white-collar jobs to start a business venture in order to fully participate in the Jama'at.

When addressing women, the command of *tafrigh-e waqt* takes a gendered form, constantly chiding them for spending too much time in the kitchen. 'The minute you complete a chore, the devil (*shaitan*) will create another one to keep you busy. It is important to make a break and focus on what is important,' said Nabila Apa,[12] who was helping me contact women who had laid down the early network for the Jama'at in central Bombay.[13] We were having this conversation in the house of Sabera Apa, a senior member who died in the early 2000s. Her daughter Maimoona welcomed us into her living room, narrating anecdotes about her childhood when her mother would lock her and her little brother up in the house with some food and leave for Jama'at meetings. 'My mother did not fuss about food. For that matter, neither did my father. She did not want to be encumbered by cooking and cleaning. She gave away all her large cooking ware to our neighbours,' said Maimoona, reclining on a narrow hospital bed set up in the corner of the modestly furnished apartment in south Bombay. Maimoona was bedridden and was being looked after by a caregiver. She compared her living arrangements with the time when her mother was on her deathbed. 'We were inundated with requests from women who wanted to help. The house would be packed with women who took turns caring for my mother. Women I did not know would phone me and tell me stories about how she had changed their lives,' she said with palpable pride.[14]

Maimoona's reference to her mother's indifferent approach to food and cooking is important because it points to a conscious decision on the part of Sabera Apa to reject the conventional division of labour that would have required her to manage the kitchen. It is clear from Maimoona's narrative that her mother's participation in the Jama'at was made possible by her decision to walk out of the house and away from the kitchen in the path of Allah (*Allah ki raah mein*). However, her explicit rejection of the sumptuous consumption of food has another genealogy, one that can be traced to the Jama'at's insistence on austerity. To pay more than minimal attention to worldly preoccupations, whether about food, clothes, one's physical appearance or housekeeping, is seen as a moral lapse, a surrender to one's base, bodily desires (*nafs*). The sermonizers at the women's meetings I attended in Bombay and Delhi never failed to point out that women spent too much time in the kitchen. 'All of you work so very hard to appease your taste buds. You stir the pots all afternoon so you can break the fast with delicious food. Even in the holy month of Ramzan you have succumbed to the fire of your bellies. Who will save you from the flames of hell?' asked a male scholar over a loudspeaker, addressing a massive crowd of women who filled two floors of a community centre in central Bombay.[15] The women nodded and appeared bashful as the speaker listed their weaknesses, one after another. I had walked to the community centre to listen to the 'big *bayan*' (sermon) with four other women, who were *bayan*-hopping that afternoon because there were no chores holding them back at home. 'This is one of the many blessings (*barakat*) of Ramzan. Our mornings are less busy because the kitchen is closed. But the minute Ramzan ends, we are back to dousing the fire of the belly,' said Amina, a married woman in her early thirties.[16] The comparison of the human stomach with hellfire – captured by the Urdu phrase *pet ki aag* – came up frequently in our conversations and in the sermons. The comparison acquired particular urgency during Ramzan when the Islamic injunction to fast from dawn to dusk and the Jama'at's emphasis on austerity combined to create a discourse about hunger and eating in which food was imagined as fuel for hellfire. A committed Jama'at member cultivated an indifferent, though never an ungrateful, approach to food so that she could escape the fire of the belly as well as the flames of hell.

Rehmat Apa, a woman in her late sixties and a member of the Jama'at for more than three decades, embodies the Jama'at's principle of austerity. Even when she travels on four-month tours, she packs only two sets of clothes and a large, thick shawl. 'I use the shawl to cover myself during the journey. It becomes my prayer mat during the day and at night it works as a blanket. It allows me to travel light and to worry about fewer things,' she said when I met her in Nizamuddin.[17] I have been following Rehmat Apa's work with the Jama'at for more than a decade and have been impressed by her gradual disentanglement from the world. She commands immense respect for her piety, humility and oratory. The younger women who attend her sermons told me that Rehmat Apa is among the handful of women who truly follow Prophet Muhammad's *sunnat* about food consumption, especially during Ramzan.[18] 'We are supposed to break the fast with dates and eat a light dinner. That is the correct Islamic practice that has come down to us from the Prophet. But we waste time in preparing lavish feasts for *iftar* (the sunset meal that breaks the fast). We have no control over our *nafs*. Rehmat Apa is the only person I know who breaks her fast with dates and maybe an apple,' said Parveen, a mother of two who is among the scores of younger women who gravitate to Rehmat Apa for guidance in an organization that does not believe in formal hierarchies.

The discourse against spending too much time in the kitchen reached a fever pitch in the second half of Ramzan. Muslims have traditionally used this period to start preparing for the feast of Eid that marks the end of Ramzan and the beginning of the next month on the Islamic calendar. This is when the focus shifts from fasting to feasting as families shop for clothes and gifts. An important component of Eid shopping is the buying of ingredients for delicacies, such as dry fruits for the sweet vermicelli (*sewai*) and spices and rice for the main course comprising some combination of meat and rice. The ingredients, especially the almonds and pistachios for *sewai*, have to be sliced and sun-dried days before Eid, and it is the women, rather than the men, who spend substantial time in the last leg of Ramzan preparing for the feast.

Sermonizers questioned this focus on Eid with fifteen days of fasting still remaining. 'This is the month of spiritual lottery. Allah's generosity knows no bounds in this month. Every good deed you do now brings a reward of seventy deeds. Why then do you spend your mornings peeling almonds?' asked Rehmat Apa passionately in a Thursday morning sermon about eight days before the end of Ramzan.[19] The most effective argument made by the Jama'at in favour of scaling down the Eid preparations is that the celebrations are not Islamic. 'The citizens of Medina did not cook *sewai* on Eid. The Qur'an does not command you to make biryani.[20] You think the pious women of Medina wasted time in these pointless pursuits? No, my sisters. They were the true followers of our

Prophet. They led simple lives. We, on the other hand, are led by the devil into the kitchen,' Rehmat Apa added.[21]

A pious Eid party

While the end of Ramzan marks the beginning of the three-day Eid celebrations, for Jama'at members it is an occasion filled with sadness. 'I do not understand the Muslims who celebrate the end of the holiest month. I do not know if I will live to see the next Ramzan. I want to make the most of this one. It could be my last,' said Safia, a 38-year-old doctor who is working hard to give her children an Islamic education by supplementing their convent school curriculum with evening courses at a madrasa.[22]

What would an Eid celebration that did not involve cooking *sewai* and biryani look like? On the Jama'at's reimagined Eid morning, women would wake up three hours before dawn to perform the non-obligatory prayers of the night (*tahajjud*), followed by the recitation of the Qur'an. Since they would not have to stir multiple pots in the kitchen, they would bathe and wear new clothes in time for the first mandatory prayer (the *fajr namaz*) of the day.[23] This would be followed by a light breakfast, and then the men would leave for the mosque to perform the special Eid prayers and the women would do the same at home. Traditionally, women in South Asia do not offer the Eid prayer, which is a *wajib* ritual that has to be performed in congregation. Islamic law divides every human action into one of five categories: (1) *farz/wajib* (obligatory/necessary); (2) *mustahib/sunnat* (recommended); (3) *mubah* (neither recommended nor prohibited); (4) *makrooh* (disliked); and (5) *haram* (sinful). The Hanafi school of law, which is the dominant school in South Asia, makes a distinction between a *farz* action that is obligatory and one that is necessary but not obligatory, calling the latter *wajib*.[24] The legal and moral ambiguity between the status of *farz* and *wajib* actions has ensured that generations of Muslim women have spent their Eid morning in the kitchen without having the chance to shower or pray but ensuring that the food for the feast is ready before the guests start trickling in. While this is not seen as a dereliction of religious duty by Hanafi jurists, from the Jama'at's perspective a celebration regime that keeps half the population away from an act of worship misunderstands the very purpose of life. 'Allah did not send us here to attend parties and strut around in expensive clothes. What good is the celebration if I have to miss the Eid prayer? Why should men alone get the chance to perform pious acts?' asks Safia.

Safia's critique of the traditional division of labour on the morning of Eid – one in which men participate in congregational prayer while women prepare for the feast – is a rejection of the traditional understanding of piety in South Asia. Both academic and lay discourses assume that a greater number of women than men are likely to be religious. It is also assumed that women's piety often takes the form of personal devotion and complicated rituals at the expense of scripturally mandated rituals.[25] Numerous edited volumes on piety as well as popular culture productions point to the overwhelming presence of women at Sufi shrines.[26] The argument that women relate to religion at an emotional level and require an interlocutor in the form of a living or dead saint (pir) is as old as the reform movements in South Asia. Male reformers as early as the eighteenth century had declared saint veneration by women as lying outside the pale of authentic Islam. In contrast, contemporary ethnographers find the evidence of thick Islam in the maze of women's practices at a saint's shrine. Both positions, nonetheless, posit Muslim women's religious universe as distinctly different and, in fact, in opposition to that of men.

Informed by the Jama'at's anti-shrine rhetoric, women like Safia have rejected the model of complementary spirituality that sends men to the mosque and women to a saint's shrine. Safia, and the many women I interviewed in Bombay and Delhi, were deeply invested in improving their prospects in the afterlife. In line with the Jama'at's teachings, they believed that staying close to the *sunnat* of austerity and piety embodied by the Prophet would lead them to eternal bliss. In this lifetime, it meant abandoning some traditional duties expected from a woman in order to make room for the performance of acts of piety that had previously been considered the purview of men alone.

The reconfiguration of household duties to make more time for worship is in line with the Jama'at's call for spiritual equality between men and women. Since every Muslim woman will be accountable for her good and bad deeds in this world, she alone is responsible for living a pious life. However, the push for spiritual equality has consequences, often unintended and unwanted, on household dynamics, especially because Jama'at sermons also maintain that the man is the economic provider for his family. In the relations between spouses, while both men and women have rights over each, particularly sexual rights, in the final analysis the man is the guardian of the woman. His superior status is justified by Qur'anic verses, prophetic *sunnat* and the writings of Islamic scholars such as Maulana Ashraf Ali Thanvi (d. 1943).

Maulana Thanvi is the author of many tracts and handbooks that explore the role of the woman in a reformed household. One such text, *A Gift to the Husband*

and Wife, claims to explain the rights and responsibilities of spouses. But many of its sections are dedicated to proving the social, legal and spiritual superiority of the husband. The message of the text is simple: while a husband cannot stop his wife from performing the mandatory rituals (the *faraiz*), his permission is required before she undertakes any non-obligatory religious rituals, especially if they come in the way of serving him.[27] The full extent of what constitutes 'serving him' remains undefined, though the text makes it clear that fulfilling the sexual needs of her husband is the duty of a wife. So is keeping his house and income safe, and while she is not required by Islamic law to cook for him, a good wife would be wise to take charge of the kitchen, according to Maulana Thanvi. Among the many examples of careless wives that he lists are the women who leave all the cooking to the domestic help.[28]

Maulana Thanvi is among the most influential colonial-era South Asian ulema. His scholarly and lay works continue to be in circulation in South Asia. He had close spiritual, intellectual and emotional ties with the family of Maulana Ilyas. His *Bihishti Zewar* (*Heavenly Ornaments*), a handbook for women, is the only text that the Jama'at recommends for women, apart from the *Tablighi Nisaab* and the hagiographies of its founders. Maulana Thanvi's influence on the Jama'at's understanding of spousal relations is evident in its patriarchal ethos. For women like Safia, who have embraced the movement's message of spiritual equality, everyday piety is about finding ways to restructure their domestic responsibilities without impinging on the exalted status of their husband. It means finding ways to entertain guests on Eid without foregoing the important but non-obligatory late night and early morning prayers. 'Last year we tried to order biryani and curry from a local caterer. It was a disaster. The food arrived late because the caterer was overbooked. My husband's parents and brothers left without eating. This year I am planning to serve simpler food. Maybe kebabs,' Safia said, when I asked her about Eid plans. 'Will your guests be happy with that?' I questioned further. 'Maybe his [her husband's] family will not like that. We have always had them over for lunch on Eid. So they will be expecting a proper sit-down meal. One option is to invite them the next day. I have to check with them if that is alright,' she wondered. Naeema, who was walking with us, joined in. 'Maybe you can start cooking ahead of time. That is what I am planning to do this year.' As Naeema and Safia discussed their menu and strategies, I asked if it could ever be done. 'Is it possible to spend the last night of Ramzan on the prayer mat and still host guests the next morning? How does Rehmat Apa manage?' They laughed at my last question. 'She does not have to cook. Neither do the other women in her house. Every member of her family is in this line [is part of the Jama'at]. They do not fuss about parties,' Naeema said.[29]

As our conversation turned to the pros and cons of cancelling the Eid lunch altogether, certain things became clear about the possibilities of piety for women in the Jamaʿat. The social conservatism of the movement, especially its position on the role of women in the household, is deeply steeped in patriarchal assumptions. While it is true that the movement attracts a large number of women, it is equally true that it lays down extremely rigorous terms for their participation, especially with regard to purdah and seclusion. Women in the Jamaʿat wear gloves and socks, apart from a burqa that covers the face, in the heat of Bombay and Delhi. They are discouraged from pursuing careers, and several families I met during my fieldwork did not send their daughters to school. It can, of course, be argued that the movement places similar limits on men. They too have dress codes that recommend an 'Islamic garb' such as a loose shirt and trousers that end above the ankle. They grow long beards. The boys are educated in madrasas and are expected to run their own commercial enterprises because the Prophet earned his livelihood through trade. However, the sartorial and behavioural recommendations for men never take the form of mandatory injunctions as in the case of women. Also, in addition to the restrictions it imposes on men and women, the Jamaʿat places women under the guardianship of their husbands, brothers and fathers.

Scholars have highlighted the internal contradiction between the Jamaʿat's message of spiritual equality and its patriarchal outlook, and the many ways in which women have explored this inconsistency to mark their presence in the public sphere.[30] Women like Rehmat Apa and Sabera Apa are indeed examples of the liberatory potential of the ideology of austere piety. However, the success of a handful of women in breaking away from normative expectations only serves to highlight the many inequities that hold women like Safia and Naeema back. Nowhere is this more apparent than in the women's discussions about food – its preparation, serving and consumption – as they catch up with each other before and after the sermons. Stepping out of the mould of scripted conversations, they talk about 'returning home to the *chullah-chakki*' (the gas stove and grind mill), revealing the tightrope they walk between accumulating spiritual merit for the afterlife and fulfilling their duties as good wives in this one.

Like any social movement of global proportions, the Tablighi Jamaʿat attracts followers from diverse socio-economic and ideological backgrounds. It draws women like Sabera Apa, whose husband encouraged her to join him in *khurj*. The movement is an excellent platform for women like Rehmat Apa, whose piety convinced her brothers and nephews to join the Jamaʿat. However, it is also made up of women like Safia and Naeema who struggle to keep up with the rigorous prayer routine. They admire the narrative of Sabera Apa's early struggles but find themselves unable to follow her out of the kitchen. 'The tongue (*zubaan*) is our enemy. It demands taste (*lazzat*). It demands variety on the dinner table. We need to teach it to recite the names of Allah. Once we do that it will not matter whether we are standing in the kitchen or kneeling on the prayer mat. We will always be in prayer,' Naeema said in her final Ramzan sermon, as she urged her audience to reorganize, albeit in small measure, the world around them. Her message was distinctly different from Rehmat Apa's, and in its divergence it revealed the unequal access to piety the Jama'at offers to its women.

Conclusion

The founders of the Tablighi Jama'at embarked on their first proselytizing mission in the 1920s, a period in the history of colonial South Asia that spawned a variety of reform movements across religious and caste denominations. The ideology of moral reform was deeply intertwined with the goals and concerns of the emerging middle class that imagined the reformed household as the site of a heterosexual union in which the educated man and his pious wife would shoulder complementary responsibilities. While the reformist thrust on personal piety and individual responsibility empowered women as independent moral agents, its patriarchal underpinnings had the effect of reaffirming the role of men – as fathers, brothers, husbands and sons – as the guardians and providers of the women. The religious and domestic literature from this period emphasizes moral parity between men and women. The same literature also insists that the spiritual equality between men and women should not be mistaken for social and legal equality. The underlying assumption that the stark disparities in the material world do not have any impact on how men and women conceive of and conduct their religious affairs is flawed and has only a dim understanding of the routines and rhythms of the everyday lives of women, the intellectual and spiritual resources at their disposal and the complex web of hierarchies and demands they have to negotiate.

In pre-colonial South Asia, persons of exceptional piety sought to remove themselves from society through acts of asceticism and non-conformity to expected norms. But reformist discourses of the twentieth century treated the figure of the wandering saint, the fakir or the *qalandar*, with disdain and suspicion. Their mode of religiosity was considered inauthentic, their rituals were declared syncretic and their morality was deemed lax. Reformist piety valued moderation, conformism and a strict adherence to scripture. Instead of fabulous displays of physical and spiritual rigour, it relied on the correct and constant performance of scripture-sanctioned piety: the obligatory and non-obligatory namaz, fasting during Ramzan and on other holy days in the Islamic calendar, frequent trips to Mecca for the pilgrimage and the giving of charity. While exceptional piety was the calling of a few mavericks in pre-reform societies, the ideology of reform, based on the fundamental belief that every adult woman and man is accountable for her or his actions, argued that every Muslim was capable of cultivating piety. It is in this context that the reformist move to turn the mundane into the pious, to transform domestic responsibilities into religious duties – as long as the intent animating the household chores is to please Allah (*Allah ki raza ke liye*) – throws a lifeline to the women. It enables them to transform their everyday lives into a meaningful religious experience and gives them the tools to shape their spiritual universe. Nonetheless, in merging the Islamic ritual cycle with the rhythms of daily household chores, reformist movements like the Tablighi Jama'at end up limiting the scope of women's piety. It makes women like Sabera Apa and Rehmat Apa, whose peculiar personal circumstances relieved them of household responsibilities at an early age, the exception rather than the rule.

Notes

1 The sociopolitical context for the formation of the Tablighi Jama'at is the launch of the *shuddhi* campaign in north India in the early twentieth century by Lala Munshi Ram (Swami Shraddhanand). The term *shuddhi* or purification refers to the return of Muslims to the fold of Hinduism. The *shuddhi* campaigners argued that the Muslims of South Asia were lapsed Hindus who had to revert to their original faith and thereby become pure again. This argument did not apply to the upper-caste Muslims who traced their lineage to Central Asia, Persia, the Hijaz and so on. While the *shuddhi* movement and its Islamic response, the Tablighi Jama'at, claimed that communities like the Meos from Mewat were either lapsed Hindus or nominal Muslims, neither group was sympathetic towards the communities it wanted to reform and rarely thought of them as equals. For further readings on the subject, refer to the works of Mayaram (1997), Sikand (1998), Jaffrelot (1999) and Gupta (2011).

2 In the absence of official records, it is impossible to offer even a ballpark figure for the number of Jama'at members around the world. However, the annual meetings (*ijtima*) of the Jama'at in Raiwind (Pakistan), Bhopal (India) and Tongi (Bangladesh) attract more than a million men and women over a period of three

days. Researchers who have worked on the Jama'at in the context of nation-states peg the number of members from fifteen thousand in a country like Gambia to fifty thousand in the United States of America. For more information on the Jama'at's reach and presence in various countries, see Masud (2000).

3 At any given time in the year, the women's assembly hall in the *markaz*, situated behind the main mosque and the men's area, is occupied by about two hundred women, most of whom are either training to go on a proselytizing tour or have just returned from one and are preparing to go home. There are also some local women who spend the day in the assembly hall, praying and listening to sermons, though they have to leave the premises before sunset. Finally, there is a small group of women, about ten to fifteen, who stay in the *markaz* for a month. Their job is to assist the women and maintain order in the hall. They serve food, clean the kitchen and give sermons. Every woman who stays at the *markaz* overnight has to be accompanied by a male relative who stays in the men's area.

4 *Tablighi Nisaab* is a two-volume collection of hadith narratives (entitled *Fazail-e Amal*) compiled by Maulana Zakariyya Kandhlewi (d. 1982), the nephew of Maulana Ilyas. Volume I focuses on the topics of *tabligh*, Ramzan and sending salutations to Muhammad. Volume II narrates hadiths about the hajj pilgrimage and about charity (*zakat*). For further reading, see Metcalf's (1993) article on the canons and practices of the Jama'at.

5 Notes from fieldwork, 9 April 2013.

6 I met some of the women interviewed in this chapter in the late 1990s when they visited my neighbourhood in south Bombay to give sermons. I contacted them again in the summer of 2011 when I was in Bombay to conduct preliminary research for my dissertation, spending most of my afternoons at the Jama'at's community centre in central Bombay, which became my primary field site. My continued engagement with the women created opportunities for longer, meandering conversations that were less formulaic.

7 The term '*dawat*' is a gerund form, derived from the Arabic root *da-aa-wa*. It means calling or inviting somebody. In this context, it refers to calling a person to Islam. A person who performs the work of *dawat* is called a *dai*.

8 The names of all the women have been changed to protect their identities. The dates and locations of the interviews and sermons have been retained, except in cases where the disclosure of that information can lead to identification of the women.

9 Notes from fieldwork, interview in south Bombay, 9 August 2012.

10 Attar (1966).

11 In some versions of the publication, the sixth principle is listed as *dawat o tabligh*, which translates as 'inviting or calling people' to religion.

12 Jama'at members use the Urdu honorific *apa* (elder sister) to address a senior member who gives weekly sermons (*bayan*) and leads the didactic *taleem* sessions.

Few of the female sermonizers I met in Bombay and Delhi were trained in a formal madrasa, though some of them had attended Islamic schools. The process of becoming an *apa* in a Jama'at involves regular attendance at the weekly meetings, familiarity with the *Tablighi Nisaab* and a willingness to commute in the local neighbourhood to give lectures.

13 Notes from fieldwork, interview with Maimoona Apa, south Bombay, 19 July 2012.

14 Notes from fieldwork, interview with Maimoona Apa, south Bombay, 19 July 2012.

15 Notes from fieldwork, south-central Bombay, 2 August 2012.

16 Notes from fieldwork, south-central Bombay, 2 August 2012.

17 Notes from fieldwork, interview with Rehmat Apa, Nizamuddin, Delhi, 26 March 2013.

18 The Prophet Muhammad is seen as the most perfect creation of Allah. Emulating him is considered the most straightforward path to perfect piety. To this end, Jama'at members comb through approved hadith compilations for Muhammad's *sunnat* – what he did, said or tacitly approved in various contexts – and hope that reliving his actions will bring them closer to the golden period of Islam. Unlike the fulfilment of Islam's binding obligations (the *faraiz*), the performance of *sunnat* is praiseworthy but ultimately non-obligatory. However, it is the *sunnat* that heavily informs the Jama'at's guidelines on everyday minutiae. The studied emulation of Muhammad's lifestyle as a strategy to perfect piety lends a sacred aura to even non-religious chores such as eating, getting dressed and responding to involuntary body reflexes such as sneezing and coughing. The correct performance of these actions becomes an essential component, even evidence, of one's commitment to the movement and ultimately, to the Prophet and his religion.

19 Notes from fieldwork, south-central Bombay, 9 August 2012.

20 A very different view of biryani is expressed by the Jama'at members of Malaysia, an important Tablighi hub in Southeast Asia. Commenting on the spiritual superiority of South Asia over the Middle East, a Malaysian Jama'at member said, 'India is the place that is most ideally suited for our work, which is the struggle for truth (*haq*); for there the food is balanced and moderate in quantity. If it's *briani* (rice), then it's only *briani* that you will eat; if it's *salen*, then it's just *salen* with one type of vegetable; if it's *dhal*, then it will only be *dhal* with bread. That is so different from the Arab countries where wealth has overcome them.' See Noor (2012: 105). I would like to thank Professor Farish Noor for bringing this passage to my attention.

21 Notes from fieldwork, south-central Bombay, 9 August 2012.

22 Notes from fieldwork, central Bombay, 5 August 2012.

23 Bathing and wearing new clothes on the morning of Eid is the Prophet's *sunnat*, and is, therefore, highly recommended by the Jama'at.

24 See the essay by Kevin Reinhart (2002) on the early Islamic debates about the difference between *farz* and *wajib* commands in Weiss (2002).

25 See Sikand (2003); Bellamy (2011); Obeng (2014); and Boivin and Remy (2015).

26 This does not take into account the fact that unlike men who pray in mosques, women pray at home, away from the eyes of the researcher. It is extremely likely that a woman who visits a shrine for wish fulfilment every Thursday returns home in time to pray. Many women also offer their ritual prayers at the shrines.

27 Thanvi (1999: 47–9).

28 Thanvi (1999: 75–80).

29 Notes from fieldwork, south-central Bombay, 9 August 2012.

30 See Schröter (2013). For women's presence in the Jama'at in Bangladesh, see Siddiqi (2012).

References

Attar, Fariduddin. 1966. 'Rabe'a al-Adawiya'. In *Muslim Saints and Mystics: Episodes from the Tadhkirat Al-Auliya*, translated by A. J. Arberry. Chicago: University of Chicago Press, 39–51.

Bellamy, Carla. 2011. *The Powerful Ephemeral: Everyday Healing in an Ambiguously Islamic Place*. Berkeley: University of California Press.

Boivin, Michel, and Rémy Delage (eds). 2015. *Devotional Islam in Contemporary South Asia: Shrines, Journeys and Wanderers*, vol. 107. London: Routledge.

Gupta, Charu. 2011. 'Anxious Hindu Masculinities in Colonial North India: Shuddhi and Sangathan Movements'. *Cross Currents* 61(4): 441–54.

Jaffrelot, Christophe. 1999. 'Militant Hindus and the Conversion Issue (1885–1990): From Shuddhi to Dharm Parivartan: The Politicization and Diffusion of an "Invention of Tradition"'. *The Resources of History: Tradition and Narration in South Asia*, 127–52.

Masud, Muhammad Khalid (ed.). 2000. *Travellers in Faith: Studies of the Tablīghī Jamā'at as a Transnational Islamic Movement for Faith Renewal*, vol. 69. Leiden: Brill.

Mayaram, Shail. 1997. *Resisting Regimes: Myth, Memory and the Shaping of a Muslim Identity*. New Delhi: Oxford University Press.

Metcalf, Barbara D. 1993. 'Living Hadith in the Tablighi Jama'at'. *Journal of Asian Studies* 52(3): 584–608.

Noor, Farish A. 2012. *Islam on the Move: The Tablighi Jama'at in Southeast Asia*. Amsterdam: Amsterdam University Press.

Obeng, Pashington. 2014. *Rural Women's Power in South Asia: Understanding Shakti*. London: Springer.

Reinhart, Kevin A. 2002. 'Like the Difference between Heaven and Earth: Hanifi and Shafi'i Discussions of Fard and Wajib in Theology and Usul', In Bernard G. Weiss (ed.), *Studies in Islamic Legal Theory*, vol. 15 Leiden: Brill.

Schröter, Susanne (ed.). 2013. *Gender and Islam in Southeast Asia: Women's Rights Movements, Religious Resurgence and Local Traditions*. Boston: Brill.

Siddiqi, Bulbul. 2012. 'Reconfiguring the Gender Relation: The Case of the Tablighi Jamaat in Bangladesh'. *Culture and Religion* 13(2): 177–92.

Sikand, Yoginder. 2003. *Sacred Spaces: Exploring Traditions of Shared Faith in India.* New Delhi: Penguin Books India.

Sikand, Yoginder Singh. 1998. 'The Origins and Development of the Tablighi Jama'at (1920s–1990s): A Cross-Country Comparative Study'. PhD dissertation, Royal Holloway, University of London.

Thanvi, Ashraf Ali, Maulana. 1999. *A Gift to the Husband and Wife.* Mumbai: Bilal Books.

Weiss, Bernard (ed.). 2002. *Studies in Islamic Legal Theory*, vol. 15. Leiden: Brill.

Index

www.ingramcontent.com/pod-product-compliance
Lightning Source LLC
Chambersburg PA
CBHW050430280326
41932CB00013BA/2061
* 9 7 8 1 3 5 0 2 7 8 0 3 5 *